Successfully Achieving Strategy Through Effective Portfolio Management

Successfully Achieving Strategy Through Effective Portfolio Management

Frank R. Parth, MS, MSSM, MBA, PMP

BEP

BUSINESS EXPERT PRESS

Leader in applied, concise business books

Successfully Achieving Strategy Through Effective Portfolio Management

First published in 2021 by
Business Expert Press, LLC
222 East 46th Street, New York, NY 10017
www.businessexpertpress.com

ISBN-13: 978-1-63742-084-3 (paperback)
ISBN-13: 978-1-63742-085-0 (e-book)

Business Expert Press Portfolio and Project Management Collection

Collection ISSN: 2156-8189 (print)
Collection ISSN: 2156-8200 (electronic)

First edition: 2021

10 9 8 7 6 5 4 3 2 1

Description

Organizations are successful based on their ability to achieve strategic goals.

Why didn't you achieve your strategy? Too many organizations waste time and money on developing strategy but don't achieve their goals. What goes wrong? Poor predictions about the future; internal politics that impact the projects selected; biases in the decision-making process, and other stumbling blocks.

This book provides the approach that *significantly increases* an organization's ability to achieve its strategy. This is not a book about developing strategy. This is a book that will help you actually *achieve* the strategy the organization's leadership has developed.

Strategy is necessary but it is a complete waste of time unless it is effectively turned into *real results*. If you want to see where an organization will be in 5 years, don't look at its strategic goals. Look at where management spends the money.

Keywords

strategy; project management; OCM; organizational change management; scheduling; decision-making; benefits management; organizational challenges; priorities; project budgeting; risk management; project selection; requirements; requirements management; strategic changes; asset classes; project portfolios; financial calculations; stakeholders; project scope management; task estimating; project organization; roles and responsibilities; software implementation; EPMS; enterprise portfolio management system

Contents

Preface

Strategy without tactics is the slowest route to victory. Tactics without strategy is the noise before defeat.

—Sun Tzu

Organizations have had a love/hate relationship with strategic planning. Large organizations spend huge amounts of time and effort on determining their "strategy." Well-known authors in strategy such as Michael Porter and many others have written hundreds of books and articles on what strategy is and how an organization can best define their strategy. New names, such as "Blue Ocean Strategy," are being given to approaches that were first documented decades ago. Yet, 85 percent of strategic goals are changed before they are met. Why spend the time of the executives and hire expensive strategy consultants when the reality is that nobody is very good at predicting the future? Organizations need a goal to aim for. Without a goal, organizations quickly wither and die because they waste their money on products and services that do not support long-term growth.

This is not a book about strategy. There are more than enough of those. This is a book about (drum roll please …) *implementing* strategy.

Strategy is necessary, but a complete waste of time unless it is effectively implemented into real results. If you want to see where an organization will be in 3 to 5 years, do not look at its strategic goals. Look at where management spends the money.

Project Portfolio Management (PPM), or Enterprise Portfolio Management (EPM), is the most recent wave of improving how businesses accomplish their strategic goals. The first wave occurred when businesses realized that developing a product or service was better accomplished using project management techniques than operational management approaches. The first wave of project management in modern private industry began during the Second World War when businesses realized that developing a product or service was better accomplished by focusing on projects rather than using operational management approaches. Some industries, such as engineering/construction, aerospace, shipbuilding, and others, have been doing projects since the beginnings of the industry. Most industry segments started to see the benefits of projects very late. They concentrated on optimizing daily operations worshipping at the altar of efficiency, not on developing projects. Virtually, all books on management are dedicated to becoming operationally more efficient.

In this book, we discuss both projects and programs. To be more efficient, we will use the term project to refer to both projects and programs.

The second wave occurred when organizations realized they had a lot of projects and programs in work, but little coordination among them. This led to the growth of Project or Program Management Offices.* This wave really developed during the years just prior to the Year 2000 computer rollover (Y2K) environment, when organizations began multiple projects to assess their Y2K risks without any coordination among the projects.

The third wave is still in very early stages and is the forerunner in how organizations will select the right projects to do—the ones that will provide the greatest strategic benefit at an acceptable level of risk. This is what we will try and achieve in this book—showing you how your company can become a world leading organization in supporting strategic goals by selecting the right projects to achieve them. This is the realm of portfolio management.

Another way to look at this is as an approach to benefits management. As Svejvig[1] stated in mid-2020: *There is substantial and growing interest in benefits management ... with discussions about how to carry out benefits*

---

* Unfortunately, there is no standardized terminology in use. Different industries call the same thing different names. Strictly speaking, a Program Management Office is the senior organization managing a single large program. But, some organizations call their PMO a Program Management Office instead of a Portfolio Management Office overseeing multiple, unrelated projects. Some organizations are using the term PPMO for Project/Portfolio Management Office. In this book, we will distinguish carefully between offices that manage multiple projects, and offices which manage single, large programs. We will use the term Enterprise Portfolio Management (EPM) and Enterprise Portfolio Management Office (EPMO).

management and how to reach high maturity levels in benefits management. It is reported that "organizations that report high benefits realization maturity also report better project outcomes"

Why manage your projects benefits better? From an executive viewpoint, it increases the value of the business.[2] This provides financial benefits such as cost savings, increased profits, money for growth, and new product development. Improving business value is the goal of the executive level and is how they are measured. This is done through the use of projects, and the more efficiently the business can manage projects the more effectively it can produce benefits.

Enterprise Portfolio Management is the most efficient way to achieve that.

Is This Really Important?

In March 2013, the Economist Intelligence Unit[3] did an in-depth survey of 587 senior executives globally as well as academics specializing in organizational strategy. The survey revealed that developing strategy and implementing it are distinctly different practices. C-level executives considered developing strategy their domain, while implementation should be done at the operational level. However, a more effective approach would be to consider strategy development and implementation as a continuum rather than two discrete functions.

In an article on stakeholder share repurchases, Michael Mauboussin[4] states: *"The purpose of a company is to maximize long-term value. As such, the prime responsibility of a management team is to invest financial, physical and human capital at a rate in excess of the opportunity cost of capital. Operationally, this means identifying and executing strategies that deliver excess returns."*

The ability to execute strategy is an organizational differentiator between more successful organizations and less successful organizations. 61 percent of corporate leaders admit their firms struggle to bridge the gap between strategy formulation and implementation. On average, only 56 percent of strategic initiatives have been successfully implemented in the past three years. Companies fail or fall short of their potential not because of bad strategies, but because of their failure to implement good ones.

> *Strategy is only as good as the execution behind it*
> —Bill Padda, COO of the LEGO Group.

On the academic side, well-known strategist Michael Porter believes creating strategy is an activity that is deliberate and comes prior to implementation. Equally well known in strategic circles is Henry Mintzberg, who believes changing external conditions and experience gained during implementation can modify an organization's original intentions. Thus, the optimal strategy is reveled over time as necessary adjustments are incorporated.

The primary driver in implementing strategy successfully is leadership buy-in and support. However, only 50 percent of respondents say that strategy implementation has appropriate C-suite attention.[5]

The second biggest source of strategic success is skilled implementation. Necessary skills include project management skills and organizational change management skills.

> *Commonly people put strategy together from a theoretical perspective. They haven't factored in practical matters such as operational complexity and budget constraints.*
> —Michael Astrue, former U.S. Commissioner for Social Security

Only 18 percent of organizations see hiring people with the necessary business or leadership talent to drive strategy implementation as a high priority. Only 11 percent of organizations say developing those skills in-house is a high priority. Organizations that make it a high priority outperform those who do not.

Lack of formal processes are a weakness. Specifically processes for:

- Project management
- Learning and feedback
- Change management
- Reporting requirements

Those organizations that have the best implementation results are twice as likely to consider processes for strategy implementation a high priority.

Strategy *is* important. Without strategy, you are sailing in the ocean with no firm direction or goal, totally subject to the vagaries of the current economic environment and totally reactive to your competition. Bad strategy is almost worse. Heading in the wrong direction can quickly kill the organization. No matter how well you implement bad strategy, the organization will fail. Perhaps, we should call that implementation office the OEPD—the Office that Executes Poor Decisions.

Strategy is implemented through projects. That is the most effective way to make the changes required. But, why is it so difficult to select projects? One reason is internal politics. Each senior manager wants the projects that create the greatest improvement in their area. But, there is another significant reason. The Spring 2020 edition of the *Harvard Business Review*[6] discusses this from the viewpoint of decision making and clearly points out that executives are averse to selecting risky projects. They are much more comfortable selecting "safe" projects even if the return is not as great.

Why would you go through the trouble, frustration, and expense of developing your own EPMS when there are many commercial products available that will do everything you want and can be deployed quickly? (If you don't believe that, just ask one of their salespeople.) The answer is that no tool will give you 100 percent of what you want. The software salespeople will tell you that their "EPMS in a Box" will do everything you want, but they are selling a generic tool that covers multiple industries and multiple size companies.

You can spend $100,000 on a Bosendorfer or a Yamaha piano, but that will not get you onto the stage at Carnegie Hall as a soloist with the New York Philharmonic. You have to understand what you are doing before you can take advantage of a commercial tool. If you have already been told to purchase a commercial product, then the most useful section of the book is Chapter 2. This is where we will get into determining exactly what management wants, and configuring the tool to provide it. There are three things that executives need to know in order to approve, or not, projects: how much will it cost, how much benefit will we gain by doing it, how likely is it to be successful (how risky is it).

Research by McKinsey[7] showed that organizations that refreshed their portfolio between 10 and 30 percent a year significantly outperformed companies that did not. Organizations that had effective PMOs significantly outperformed organizations that did not have strong PMOs.[8]

Outline of the Book

This book is divided into the steps you need to take to successfully implement portfolio management into your organization. Read it from the viewpoint that you are in charge of the effort to develop the EPMS. You are in charge. This is a project, so it will require a project plan and a team to implement the plan. If you are successful, you will make a significant change in how the organization implements its strategy. Change is hard, and implementing significant change is orders of magnitude more difficult than implementing a new software tool or changing a minor business process. There will be resistance from parts of the organization that see their operations threatened. You should expect that part of your job as the project manager is to identify those people and be able to compromise. Extensive use of real-life examples is done in this book to show how other organizations are implementing portfolio management systems.

Extensive use is made of a fictional company, MegaNews International, with a well-defined strategy and a selection of projects. These projects are followed through the various financial filters and risk analysis to illustrate how the process works.

The project management approach described here is not technically an agile approach, although agile approaches can be used as part of the development project as appropriate. Agile methodologies are highly useful in a situation where the requirements are not understood or keep changing. The approach used in this book is the approach that should be used for significant infrastructure development—identify the requirements before any significant design is done, get them approved and lock them down. Locked requirements make the rest of the project much simpler with a much higher probability of meeting both cost and schedule goals.

Step 1: Prepare the Organization

In this step, you will start identifying exactly why management in your organization decided that the solution to their strategic implements is by implementing an EPMS and what their needs and expectations are. What are their pain points in achieving strategic goals? How will an EPMS help improve accomplishing their strategy?

You will also identify who is going to be supportive of the effort and who is going to be subversive (You don't believe there are subversive people out there? Just because you don't believe it doesn't mean they're not there. Trust me, they will be there once you start). You will also learn how to use the techniques of Organizational Change Management (OCM) to prepare the organization for this large change that's coming.

Step 2: Design Considerations for the Portfolio Management System

In this step, we will discuss exactly what goes into the design of the system:

- Different asset classes that the EPMS should include, the various types of projects that we deal with, and developing the business case for a proposed project. We will also discuss alignment to organizational strategy and dealing with strategic changes.
- Nothing is done in an organization without costing money. We'll discuss various financial justifications for projects so that we approve the projects that have the greatest benefit to the organization.
- We will also discuss how to write a business case for the projects that will be proposed, how to identify the risks, and how to ensure that resources are available once the projects are approved.
- We know that the projects that give us the greatest benefits are also the most risky ones. How can we do a risk assessment of a project we haven't started yet? We'll learn how to do that here so that we can balance out risk and benefits in our portfolio.

While it would be convenient to assess projects totally using financial numbers, those are only part of the considerations. We also have to assess the probability of success before we even begin the project and identify whether we have the resources to do the work.

Step 3: Planning and Executing the EPMS

Here's where you will learn how to implement the new system. Implementation is a project by itself and needs a project plan, resources, and everything else needed to install a new system into an organization.

Step 2 discussed the design requirements. In Chapter 3, we'll learn how to do the detailed design of the system so that it meets management's needs. We'll also learn how to plan out the implementation.

"Other Areas"

Throughout the book, you will find items titled "Law of Project Management." These are nuggets of wisdom that are passed from one project manager to another and reflect the reality of what we deal with in practicing our profession.

Throughout the book, you will find stories that amplify on the point being made in the text. For the most part, these are actual events that happened either to the author, to other project managers who have shared their experiences (both good stories and horror stories), or stories that are well known in the field. A couple of them have already been published in articles. These have been properly attributed, and permission has been received to include them in this book.

Final Closure on the Preface

Having said all that, we must honestly admit that selecting a project based solely on the EPMS filters can fail when the project is a potential breakthrough project. Anyone who has ever taken a marketing course can describe the horror of the Ford Edsel—complete failure despite the significant amount of customer surveys done. Contrarily, Steve Jobs of Apple fame was noted as saying when it comes to customer surveys *"People don't know what they want until I show them.* "If the iPhone had been subject to the same filters, it is unlikely to have been selected because:

- Financial value—inconclusive. Very high project costs and unpredictable revenues.
- Technical risk—very high. New and innovative technologies need to be employed with no guarantee they will work in a high-production environment. Touch screens had been tried before and failed.
- Market risk—very high. Will consumers be willing to pay $600 for a phone that can access the Internet, have a built-in camera, and replace the iPod?
- Competitive advantage—unknown. There is a lot of competition in the market from companies that have been building successful phones for years.
- Time-to-market—unpredictable due to the severe technical challenges.

Was it successful when launched in 2007? Despite Microsoft's Steve Ballmer famously stating that he's not worried about it because it will fail, the iPhone alone provided more income to Apple in 2012 than Microsoft earned with all of its products.

A final word: One way to view an enterprise-level portfolio management system is as an air traffic control (ATC) system. Just as the ATC adjusts and guides thousands of airplanes to enable to them fly safely, the EPMS guides the projects within the portfolio to obtain the greatest benefits to the organization. By eliminating unneeded work and by focusing the efforts on the most beneficial projects, the EPMS guides the organization into the most effective pathway to achieving strategic goals.

STEP 1

Prepare the Organization

Step 1 Introduction

Nothing worthwhile in business was ever accomplished, unless it was done by a monomaniac on a mission.

—Peter F. Drucker

Let's begin at the beginning with a definition. The Project Management Institute defines portfolio management as: "the centralized management of one or more portfolios which includes identifying, prioritizing, authorizing, managing and controlling projects, programs and other related work, to achieve strategic objectives."

In order to be successful in delivering an EPMS that will significantly benefit the organization, you must understand that you are going to make a significant change to how the organization operates, and any significant change can expect to encounter resistance. You need to understand the organization's current problems and priorities, define the solution, and be prepared to overcome resistance. You must truly believe you are going to make a difference and to dedicate your efforts to making it successful. As the change leader, everyone is looking to you to make this work.

What we're going to talk about in these next sections will help you see the strong benefits of enterprise portfolio management, help you convince others of those benefits, and become the leader in implementing the effort. How much improvement should you expect? The following graphic from PMI's Pulse of the Profession[1] should help your management understand:

For a more detailed analysis of how to prepare the organization, see Chapter 5 of *Project Portfolio Management Strategies for Effective Organizational Operations.*[2]

Historically, organizational strategy* has always been challenging to accomplish. Most strategic goals are changed before they are ever met in response to rapidly changing market conditions. Quoting Mark Cotteleer

---

* Strategy can be defined as: "the direction and scope of an organization over the long-term: which achieves advantage for the organization through its configuration of resources within a challenging environment, to meet the needs of markets and to fulfill stakeholders expectations" (Johnson, Scholes and Whittington)

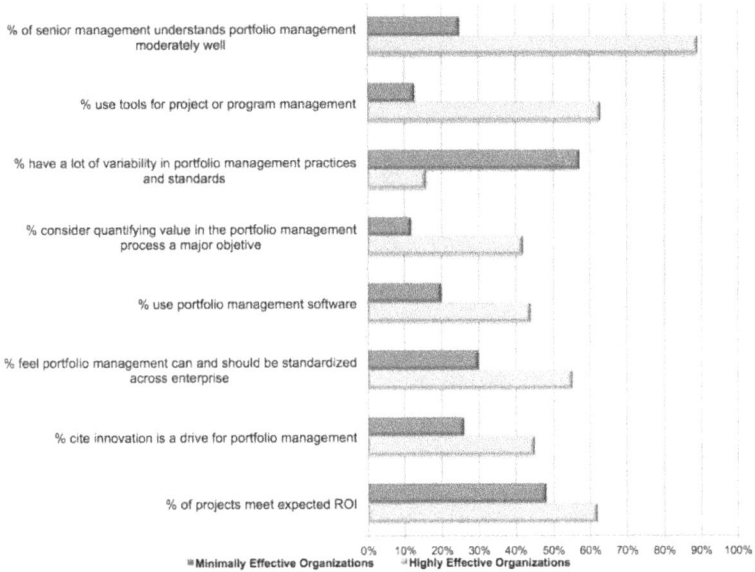

Figure 1.1 Improvements resulting from enterprise portfolio management

of Cutter Consortium *"Saying something is a strategic investment is about as productive as saying, 'This is something cool that we want to do.'"* Yet if we select the right projects, we can be more successful. If a project does not support the organization's strategic direction, why are you doing it? *"If you want to find out where your company is going to be three to five years from now, don't look at your stated strategy. Instead, look at your Project Portfolio. That's where you're making your investments, and it's those investments that determine your firm's direction".*[3]

In 2012, the international bank PNB Paribus discovered it was spending 70 percent of its project money on compliance projects and only 2 percent on new products. This led the executive director to state that *"We will be a very compliant bank with no customers."*

As Intuit's founder Scott Cook put it, most decisions are based on *"politics, persuasion, and PowerPoint"*. According to Bivins,[4] the traditional way of determining which projects to do is called BOGGSAT:

BOGGSAT is an acronym for "bunch of old guys/gals sitting around talking". This is a common method that produces decisions that are often painfully slow, unproductive, and of poor quality. Although it is the most common decision approach in use today, BOGGSAT is not appropriate for complex decisions such as project portfolio selection and determining benefits. A major reason BOGGSAT fails as a decision technique is that, as psychologists have found, the average human brain can discriminate among only seven elements, plus or minus two, and can hold in short-term memory only seven objects, plus or minus two. That is, we humans have cognitive limitations that prevent us from mentally processing the complexity that exists in PPM selection decisions.

There is a better way, and that's what this book is about.

The concept of managing multiple independent projects within an organization was first proposed by McFarlan[5] in 1981 as a more efficient way to deal with the risks in IT projects. According to Payne,[6] up to 90 percent of all projects within an organization by value occur in a multiproject environment.

Most of the literature definitions of portfolio management revolve around selecting and managing project in support of the organization's strategic goals. This is a good way to approach the topic. However, looking at the reality of what projects organizations are doing, we see that a great many projects, especially in the IT group, have little relation to long-term strategic goals but are done to fix existing problems or to make short-term improvements. We'll discuss how we can combine *all* the project work whether strategic or operational.

Even in the mid-2000s, a portfolio management approach was oriented only toward selecting the "best" projects for an organization to implement strategic goals. More and more portfolio management is taking on the roles traditionally done by a project management office (PMO) and getting involved in how projects are being managed (governance) and in benefits realization. The lines between the two areas are getting blurry as organizations attempt to find the most effective and efficient approaches to achieving their strategy. Research done jointly by the Project Management Institute and Forrester Research (Forrester[7]) shows that Project Management Offices are increasingly getting involved in portfolio management and governance as shown here.

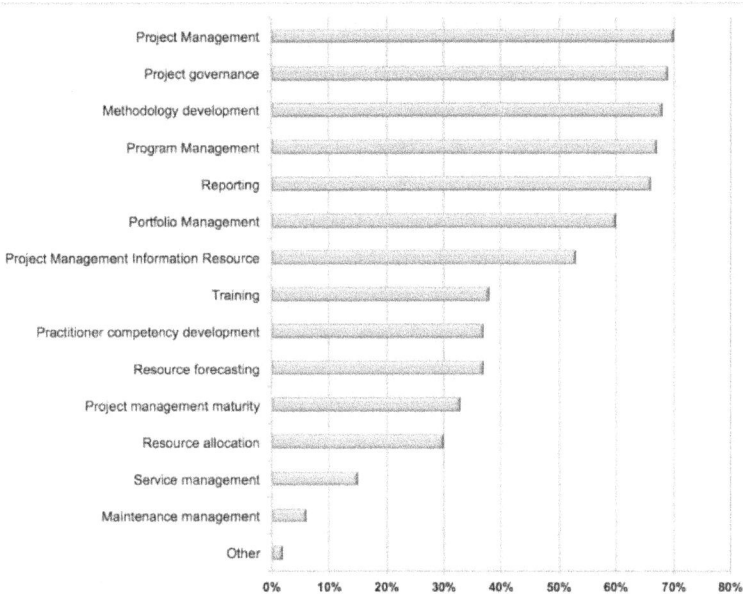

Figure 1.2 PMO involvement

You can select the best projects for the organization, but if they're badly managed, the money will be largely wasted. Organizations with good, mature project management processes can do projects less expensively and more quickly than organizations with a low project management maturity level. We'll discuss this later in the book.

While portfolio management has reached widespread use in IT, there are significant advantages to expanding it enterprise-wide. In the construction industry, for example, a significant issue is to allocate personnel and equipment across multiple construction projects. Portfolio management includes processes for identifying how best to spread resources around and can alleviate that problem. There is no profit-making organization in the world that has unlimited resources. Making the most efficient use of those resources is only part of what an enterprise portfolio management system (EPMS) can provide.

Most enterprise portfolio management systems (EPMS) in real organizations are managed by an enterprise-level Portfolio Management Office (EPMO). This is not a mandatory requirement, just a convenient way to work. The detailed division of roles and responsibilities between the EPMO and the EPMS must be defined clearly within your organization.

Does the EPMS monitor and track existing projects or is that done elsewhere in the EPMO? Who can recommend projects be killed? The EPMS or the EPMO? These and other items need to be clearly defined before the EPMS is created.

One caution before you start: It is the tendency of every project manager to want to design the most sophisticated and "best" product possible. But the reality of how useful an EMPS is depends on the data fed into it by people who want to get their projects selected. As Cooper[8] said *"… saw this time and again: portfolio task forces designing and trying to implement very exotic portfolio methods, only to be thwarted by the very poor quality of the data inputs"*. The goal is to create and deliver a system that will benefit the organization and that people will find it easy to use.

There are three basic approaches to developing an EPMS. The first is to design the system and the processes, develop it yourself, and host it on your IT infrastructure or in your cloud service. This gives you the greatest flexibility, the greatest privacy, and the most control over your portfolio. Hosting it internally generally provides greater security so long as your IT department provides good security firewalls and processes.

The second is to identify your new processes and buy a software package that supports your needs. Since no commercial package will provide exactly what you need, you will have to customize it and adapt it to your specific requirements. There's usually an annual fee for a complex package such as this. You can host it yourself or pay the vendor to host it.

The third approach is to buy an EPMS as a SaaS (Software as a Service) product or a cloud based product and have the software vendor host your system. In this approach, you can implement much more quickly because the configuration has already been done by the vendor. You are basically just leasing the software from them. Why would you not use this approach?

- You can't configure the system in a way that's best for your organization;
- There are on-going maintenance costs that continue as long as the vendor hosts the system; and
- You are giving your internal and proprietary information to an outside party for hosting your data.

Since most portfolio management vendors that offer SaaS charge by the seat, the costs can easily run into tens of thousands of dollars per year whereas rolling your own EPMS is a one-time expense (plus on-going internal software maintenance costs and occasional updates).

Step 1.1 The Decision-Making Process

1.1.1 The Decision-Making Process

Man is not a rational animal, he is a rationalizing animal.
—Robert Heinlein in the short story Gulf, 1955

The goal of portfolio management is to facilitate the decision-making processes involved in selecting the projects that best move the organization toward its strategic goals. These processes provide management the information they need, and only the information they need, to decide which projects to select. One of the major difficulties in designing the system is to understand what information management really needs and setting up the filters and priorities to improve the project selection decisions.

A properly designed system takes into account its own limitations, primarily the inability of an algorithm-based system to make perfect selections on which projects should be prioritized and funded. Corporate strategies change, technologies change, the economic environment changes. The human brain is much better adapted to filtering all the parameters of a continually changing environment than any software based system. The downside of the human brain is that it is biased. Think about it. Haven't you run into people who look at the data you are presenting and just refuse to change their mind despite the data? We have all dealt with people like that.

There are always more ideas for new projects then there is time and money to do them, and the ideas come from all parts and all levels of the organization. Everyone has an opinion on how to improve, so we will design our system to accept inputs from anyone in the organization without filtering. The system will filter the inputs based on criteria determined by upper management and then present a list of possible projects with recommended priorities taking into account resource and budget constraints. Management will have the opportunity to select the best projects

based on the information. They are not constrained with blindly following the list presented but have the option of selecting projects that rank
closely together in the prioritized list.

Decision making is not an end in itself, it is a means to an end. The
goal is not to make a decision, but to solve a problem or to make a change,
such as selecting the "best" projects to approve, and then take action to
implement the decision. To ensure we make rational, unbiased decisions
that produce the results we want, critical decision making requires you to:

- Obtain complete and accurate data
- Examine your logic and your biases
- Examine your premises
- Be aware of your motivations
- Think through both short-term and long-term impacts
- Know your "flight" envelope—what can you do efficiently
  and what will be a large stretch in your capabilities
- Check with others
- Be comfortable with uncertainty

A decision requires several things:

- An event that drives a need for a decision
- A timeframe within which to make the decision
- Facts and information that need to be taken into account
- A desired positive outcome

A decision also requires assumptions about:

- Things we don't know—what can we safely assume?
- The facts themselves—are they accurate and unbiased?
- The outcomes of the decision—can we predict the future
  accurately enough to select the best long-term solution?
- Our own objectivity and the objectivity of people giving us
  information
- The acceptability of the decision—will everyone involved fully
  support our decision?

Most of us consider ourselves competent decision makers based on our own history of making reasonable decisions in the past. Yet there is a great deal of recent neurological research that indicates our brains really are not normally logical, in fact, most decisions are made by the most lazy portion of our brains and only later justified, if questioned, by the rational portion of our brains, the cerebral cortex. Once a person has made a normal, non-critical decision, they search for data to support that decision rather than the other way around. Managers do this all the time because they very often have to make decisions with minimal data and are forced to rely on their experience. They make a decision, and look to justify it.

Because decisions are heavily influenced by how the information is presented to us, a better approach is to have a gatekeeper in charge of collecting the data and presenting it in a complete and unbiased format to the decision makers. This is what a well-designed portfolio management system does.

1.1.2 The Decision Environment

At the working levels of the organization, it seems obvious which projects should be done—the projects that provide the greatest benefits. The assumption here is that the projects selected should have the greatest benefits to "our" part of the organization. The lower in the hierarchy, the more narrow the viewpoint and the shorter the time outlook.

The decision on the best project is not as obvious as you go higher in the organization. The upper management team and the executive level have multiple groups and divisions they are responsible for, if not the entire organization. They must decide which parts of the organization to allocate the money to for the projects. Priorities in multiple parts of the organization must be balanced against each other based on assumptions about the future. Not just the near-term future, but how to position the organization five years from now. Unlike Warren Buffett, who once famously said *"My idea of a group decision is to look in a mirror"*,[9] these decisions require the focused and committed agreement among multiple high-level stakeholders each of whom has a different priority and vision.

The decision environment takes into account not only the organization, its resources, and its strategic goals but also the external environment.

Every organization, whether government, privately owned, publicly owned, or nonprofit exists in the overall environment and is heavily influenced by that environment. The environment consists not only of the economic environment and physical environment, but for privately-owned and publicly-owned organizations, also the competitive environment. What our competitors are doing now has a direct influence on what we will be doing in the future.

The future is unknowable. (If it were, psychics would not sell their services but would be playing the stock market. Any store-front fortune-teller is a phony.) Accurately predicting it requires developing organizational capabilities that may not pay off immediately. For the long term, projects should be selected not just for their short-term financial benefits but to develop future new markets and knowledge growth. These are termed exploration projects and often go un-selected because their ROI is unpredictable, but they will build the capabilities for the company's future growth and profitability.[10] The CFO should never be the final decision maker because they are always focused on the short term and tend to be very risk averse.

These exploration projects are potentially the most beneficial ones because the products they produce will be the organization's future. Sony changed the whole music world with the Sony Walkman in 1979, Apple changed it again with the iPod in 2001. In between the two, Sony improved its original Walkman, but with only one major change— to create a CD-based portable player. There were no other substantial, ground-breaking changes. When the iPod was released, it completely overtook Sony's bread and butter income stream in portable music players.

The history of modern-day management is rife with stories of poor decision making at the highest levels of the organization. Xerox famously sold a young Apple Computer the rights to develop the GUI interface because the executives at Xerox headquarters on the East Coast did not believe the Xerox West Coast scientists had anything useful to offer. Kodak invented the first digital camera in 1975 but their income stream was from selling film and management shot down any project that threatened that income. IBM invented the first really usable PC but was unable to get any priority on it because the decision makers viewed the company as a mainframe company and wanted nothing to threaten that. These are the kinds of decisions that can either make or break a company in a changing external environment. Our job is to make the best case for these exploration projects so show the future benefits are greater than the high risks involved in doing them.

Project decisions are based on the best analysis of the environment. But no decision maker is perfect. As Davies[11] states:

> *CEOs are naturally wary of some investments. Large capital projects in politically unstable countries, common among companies in the mining and oil and gas sectors; speculative R&D projects in high tech and pharmaceuticals; and acquisitions of unproven technologies or businesses in a wide range of industries all carry what many see as an above-average degree of risk. The potential returns are alluring, but what if the projects fail?*
>
> *Weighing the pros and cons of such deals, executives delve into the usual cash-flow projections, where they often make one seemingly small adjustment: forgetting what many of them learned in business school, they bump up the assumed discount rates in their cost-of-capital calculations to reflect the uncertainty of the project. In doing so, they often unwittingly set these rates at levels that even substantial underlying risks would not justify—and end up rejecting good investment opportunities as a result. What many don't realize is that assumptions of discount rates that are only three to five percentage points higher than the cost of capital can significantly reduce estimates of expected value. Adding just three percentage points to an 8 percent cost of capital for an acquisition, for example, can reduce its present value by 30 to 40 percent (depending on its long-term growth rate).*

1.1.3 Where Does the PMO Fit?

Understanding how successful PMOs fit in the organization helps us understand the level of decision making that we're dealing with. According to Forrester[12] research, successful PMOs have the following attributes:

- *They have a seat at the executive table.* Strategic results require strategic positioning. PMOs that are highly effective in driving business growth report to varying levels of executive management, ranging from senior vice president to the C-level, and are regarded as members of executive management. Champions are strategically positioned, too. The majority of the leaders interviewed have highly visible sponsorship at the C-level.

• *They are a vital part of the strategic planning team.* Since portfolio management is a core competency, PMOs actively participate in strategic planning and help shape strategy by providing feedback to executives about performance, labor costs, and customer feedback.

• *They embrace core competencies.* Excellence in project management remains a critical capability for PMOs. The most successful organizations recognize the specific role of the project manager and build significant learning and development programs to mature project management skills.

• *They use consistent objectives across industry and regions.* Customer-facing or business-facing, strategic PMOs share the same objectives: Drive success through alignment with business stakeholders and operational excellence. Meeting these objectives is differentiated by such factors as orientation, region, and culture.

Step 1.2 Challenges in Today's Organizational Environment

1.2.1 Background to Organizations

An organization of any type is a living entity. It grows and expands when environmental conditions are right. It contracts, often painfully, when conditions are poor. All parts of the organization work together, more or less efficiently, toward the goals of the organization. The environmental conditions for a small not-for-profit are vastly different than they are for an international, for-profit organization or for a government organization. Yet each organization responds to its specific environment.

In an organization, nothing is done in isolation. All company activities are done in an environment created by all the other company activities as well as by the organization's competitors and outside environment.

PREPARE THE ORGANIZATION 13

Whether or not a project gets approved and funded depends on how that project benefits the organization in comparison to the other projects being considered in the existing environment.

This internal environment includes the culture of the organization, its financial capabilities, its geographic location(s), the legal and regulatory framework it operates in, how well established its internal processes are, its technology infrastructure, internal competitiveness between and among the divisions, and all other internal influences. Some organizations, such as General Motors before its bankruptcy, are intensely competitive internally to the point of becoming dysfunctional. For an interesting read, look up the history of GM's Fremont, California, factory. The labor/management relations were extremely poor, resulting in the worst quality record in the industry and a high percentage of absenteeism among the workers. GM fired all the workers and sold the plant to Toyota. Toyota rehired the majority of the workers, changed the relationship with them, and produced high quality cars much more efficiently with the same workers.

Story

The author had some personal experience with this approach to decision-making while leading the requirements development team for a major infrastructure improvement. When TRW Information Systems changed their name to Experian in November 1996, they did so to create a unique name that showcased their advanced credit processing system. This new system had spent two years in development with the programmers writing about 5 million lines of new code to change from the flat file data base they had been using to a fully-relation data base (IBM DB2). This effort took an extensive amount of overtime during the development process to meet deadlines. The company was sold to the investment firm Bain who turned around and sold it to Great Universal Stores in Great Britain. When the sale was announced to the employees at an all-hands meeting (which had to be held outside because there was no room big enough in the office buildings), the executives were completely enthused about the sale. It was reported the next day in the Wall Street Journal that the executives were paid a significant amount of cash for the sale. A month later, a memo came down from the executive layer to the software engineers who made the sale possible that they would not receive their annual bonuses. Bonuses were tied to market share and because the developers were completely engaged in the new system, there were no new products released, market share had gone down, so the developers would not receive any bonus. The author headed up the systems engineering group that developed the requirements for the new system and was extensively involved in the development effort. Needless to say, by the middle of January, a significant percentage of the experienced development staff had mailed out resumes and were job hunting.

Other organizations are internally highly cooperative, and some organizations are so big that they are internally competitive, such as Hewlett-Packard before its 2010 reorganization, that they do not even realize that divisions are competing with each other because of poor internal communications among upper management. An organization where the directors and executives are highly competitive with each other only creates an environment that discourages communications.

Think about the organization that you will be implementing the EPMS into. The culture will dictate the details of the approach you will plan out.

While project managers don't like to deal with constraints, the reality is that project management exists within the physical, cultural, and economic environment of every company. Your ability to manage projects is constrained by many factors outside project management itself. These limitations extend to the EPM system itself and, in fact, are major inputs to the filtering criteria used to analyze and approve projects.

While we would love to believe that organizations are well-planned entities that are focused on their long-term goals, have well-designed internal processes, and provide a highly-rewarding experience for their employees as well as many benefits to their external stakeholders, this is not the reality of life today and probably has never been the reality.

Many organizations are poorly planned to start with and deteriorate from there. They start out small and develop internal processes that are sufficient to help them operate in their existing environment. The emphasis is on survival and growth and not on efficiency. The rapid growth, and even more rapid death, of most dot-coms is a good example.

As organizations grow, their internal processes grow with them until it becomes obvious that the processes no longer work. Processes are created as needed and rarely documented. At some stage of growth, the organization is large enough that this ad hoc management style no longer works and professional management is brought in. Processes are re-designed, maybe documented or maybe not, and for a while, the organization continues its growth in a more planned fashion.

As growth continues, these re-designed processes are also overcome and become less efficient. Redesigning them is not a high priority so the inefficiencies are lived with until it becomes obvious to upper management that there are serious internal problems (the employees saw these problems long before management did). Further, in an expanding business environment, a lot of growth occurs through mergers and acquisitions (M&As). When two companies merge, their existing processes are rarely merged effectively and the resulting entity becomes less efficient as employees struggle to figure out how to do their jobs. When the employees are treated poorly by upper management, they are not likely to support any change.

1.2.2 Challenges in Today's Project Management Environment

The parts of the organization that are impacted the greatest by changes are the layers at which, sorry to say, much of the project management work is done. In today's rapidly changing, internationally-competitive environment, management is under a lot of pressure to reduce costs and to become more profitable. The normal approach is to reduce headcount, either by laying off staff, by attrition, or by outsourcing to the current low-cost provider somewhere else in the world. The result of this approach is to put more work on fewer people.

This means that a very typical project environment involves both the project manager and the team working on several projects instead of being focused on one. Everyone is multitasking, with well-researched and documented reductions in productivity.[13] When you're working on five different things, you can't be as effective or as efficient as when you're concentrating on just one or two. This was researched thoroughly[14] with results shown in the following figure:

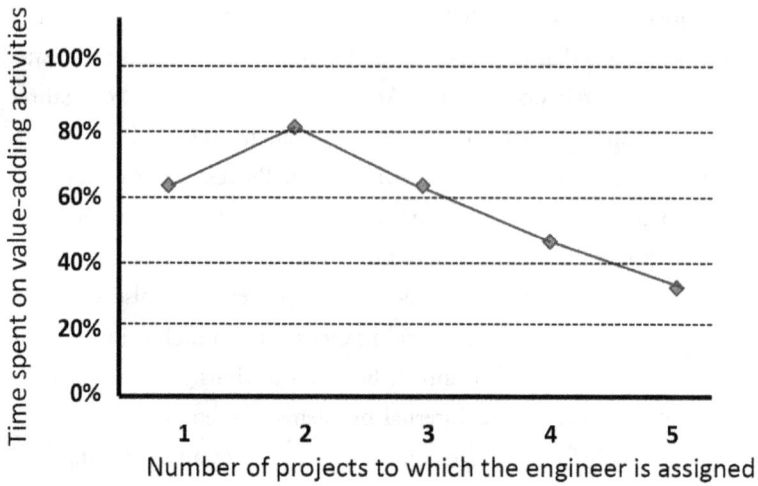

Figure 1.2-1 Impact of multitasking

In the IT department, the situation is even worse, the staff there not only works on projects, they are usually working on daily operations and at the same time: bug fixes, application upgrades and implementations, system maintenance, security patches, and so on. All of which distract them from project work. Recent research on multitasking shows that doing multiple things at the same time is equivalent to an IQ drop of 10 to 15 points, the same IQ drop as smoking a joint of marijuana.

In addition to the reduced productivity, more mistakes are made leading to more work having to be checked and redone. Rework, which is always unplanned, has ripple effects because it takes people away from what the planned work was, further impacting projects in work. There is a large body of research on the negative impacts of multitasking. See, for example, Bannister and Remenyi.[15]

Law of Project Management
There's never time to do it right.   *There's always time to do it over.*

Many, perhaps most, mature organizations share the same problems and internal situations.

Story

At one company, while the author was implementing a PMO for them, an IT project started based on a request by a senior executive. The project was to implement a product web site. It was approved and given to IT to implement. After six months, IT told the executive that the project was in work. Six months later, they told him it was in work. Again six months later, and six months after that. After two years of hearing that the project "was in work," the executive asked to see the results to date. At that point, IT had to admit it had started the project, but actually hadn't done any work in the past 18 months because there were other priorities that had come up. At this point, the project was canceled as being too late to be useful.

Let's face it, managing a project in the typical organization is highly challenging. We are often using a central pool of personnel that are working on multiple projects. Our "teams" often do operational work outside of projects. Management's typical response to this situation is sometimes derogatorily referred to as "Peanut Butter Resource Management"—we just spread the people around over more and more work.

Too many factors that impact projects are outside the project manager's control. Worse, in many organizations, there is no common agreement on what a project manager should be doing. Functional managers do things the way they have always done them and consider the project managers to be schedule keepers. This is very frustrating to the project managers.

Strong inter-dependencies among multiple projects compounds the problems. These dependencies can be created by sharing personnel, equipment, facilities, or by competing for limited funding. A problem on one project quickly spreads to others (think of the cascading reaction in a nuclear bomb). For example, scheduling uncertainty on one project means we don't know exactly when tasks will happen. When one task on that project runs late, there's an impact on other projects that need those resources. This makes scheduling projects in a multiproject environment very challenging and is a major source of projects running late. It is also a strong driver to implement an EPMS and to install an enterprise-capable project management tool.

Creating accurate schedules is subject to a wide variety of influences as shown here:

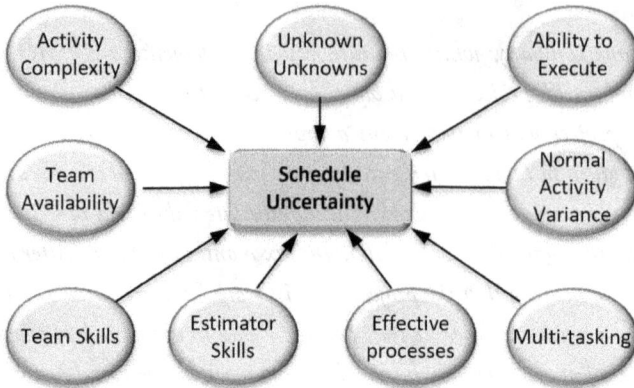

Figure 1.2-2 Inputs to schedule uncertainty

All of which lead to uncertainty in the schedule. In a multiproject environment where resources are shared, as we have just seen, there is an additional, and very strong, cascading effect from other projects that are scheduled to use the same resources as we are. Any slippage in one project impacts the other projects that have scheduled that resource.

In the manufacturing industry, there is a well-known constraint called Little's Law. It says that cycle time equals the work in progress divided by the throughput:

$$CT = WIP/TP$$

In order to improve how quickly projects get done, reduce the number of projects you're doing. By recognizing that "things will happen" to disrupt the plan, leave people the ability to recover from unplanned changes instead of forcing them to work continual overtime.

We can view a multiproject environment as a complex system. There are interdependencies among the various components of the system (as shown by the previous example of shared resources). The field of systems analysis teaches us that one characteristic of a complex system is that responses are nonlinear. You don't always get the same response from the same input. A response to a particular demand for a resource is not a repeatable event, it is dependent on the time in which the demand is made. We would likely offer the resource to another project next week but we can't offer it today because we need that resource. Same request, different response.

Other typical impacts we commonly see are that adding resources to one project usually means removing them from other planned work, often another project. Increasing overtime means lowering productivity. Adding more projects reduces the ability to finish any of them on schedule.[16] These are common situations that are often not taken into account before a change is made to the portfolio.

Because there's a time delay between making a change and seeing the effects, complex systems are inherently unstable. The danger is to try and overmanage the full collection of projects. You cannot manage ten separate projects the same way you manage a single project. In this environment, flexibility is more important than rigid adherence to plans. Why spend weeks planning out a project schedule in detail when there's a 90 percent chance the schedule will be impacted by other things?

Another area that is impacted by adding more projects to the portfolio without analysis is quality. The more overworked people are, the lower the resulting quality in the project, in the product, and in the decision-making process. Quality in a physical product can be measured and there are many quality systems that are in commercial use. Quality in processes and in decision making is much more difficult to quantify and to measure. Mistakes are made more often but they are rarely traced back to the fact that people are seriously overworked, tired, and making bad decisions.

An interesting experiment in quality improvement[17] led to the following conclusion: "When the quantity goal is easy to achieve, setting a difficult quality goal results in increased quality. When a difficult quantity goal is set, setting a difficult quality goal does not result in increased quality." In other words, when your people are not overworked, quality improves.

In a complex environment there are many of these impacts and inter-dependencies that are not knowable in advance. No one in the organization understands the entire set of projects in work or their inter-dependencies. A functional manager that needs a resource from a project may not realize that obtaining that resource impacts not just one project, but several projects that had scheduled that resource.

This is where an EPMS can be most beneficial. A common solution is to use a PMO to provide the infrastructure within which the EPM system can exist. The PMO provides a central location for all information related to projects in work. It presents the information in a way that allows management to understand what's going on in all projects.

In order to overcome the objections that will be raised by the managers and division heads that don't want an EPMS because it reduces their control, the person implementing the new system must understand all of these constraints, problems, dependencies, and impacts and prepare to counter the arguments that will be raised.

1.2.3 Projects, Programs, and Portfolios

We talk about projects, programs, and portfolios. How do they all fit together? Sometimes it can get confusing. Both programs and portfolios include multiple projects. Often when we talk about a program, we call it a project. What are the distinctions? Using definitions published by the Project Management Institute,[18] we can define them as follows:

Project: A temporary endeavor undertaking to create unique products or services.

Program: A group of related projects managed in a coordinated way so as to obtain benefits not available by managing them individually. Programs may include related work outside of the scope of the discrete projects within the program.

Portfolio: A collection of projects or programs and other work that are grouped together to facilitate effective management of that work to achieve strategic business objectives. The projects or programs of the portfolio may not necessarily be interdependent or directly related.

A good way to look at it is that a project is a specific effort to produce a deliverable, whether a new product, a service, a business process, or any other beneficial output. A program is so large and complex that it includes multiple projects to produce the outcome, such as a construction program, an engineering program, new aircraft development, and so on.

A portfolio is a collection of both projects and programs. A large portfolio, such as an enterprisewide portfolio, may include lower-level portfolios within it. This hierarchy is shown in PMI's documents as:

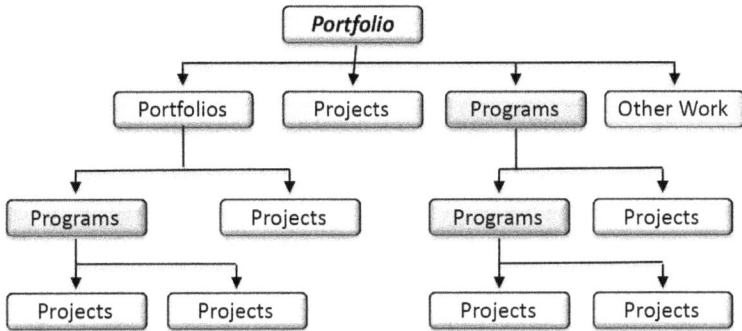

Figure 1.2-3 Portfolio hierarchy

Since both programs and portfolios have multiple projects within them, what's the difference? One way to look at it is that if a project within a program fails, the entire program fails. If a project within a portfolio fails, it doesn't affect the other projects within the portfolio. Indeed, sometimes an IT portfolio is better off when a project fails because it frees up resources to work on other projects.

1.2.4 PMO Versus EPMS

There is confusion, particularly among commercial software vendors, about the differences between a program management office and a portfolio management system. In order to sell their products, the vendors frequently combine both of these functions into a single package, most often by buying existing independent platforms and somehow slapping them together into a single package (Oracle Corp. is notorious for doing this badly). As a general rule, these large software packages are clumsy and awkward and rarely deliver on the sales promises.

There is a clear distinction between a PMO and an EPMS. A PMO focuses on project management—providing templates and tools, assigning resources, keeping central databases for risks, offering support, and other project-management-specific items.

An EPMS is designed to select and prioritize projects. Nothing else. It is oriented toward supporting organizational strategic goals, not supporting operational items. In order to optimize resources, an EPMS may organizationally be part of an Enterprise PMO, but it does not have to be.

Step 1.3 Who's in Charge?

An EPMS should only be implemented for the long-term benefits of the organization. It has few benefits in the short term, and in fact the implementation process will be disruptive and confusing to many people in the organization unless they are properly prepared. Until people get comfortable with the EPMS and familiar with the changed processes, productivity is likely to temporarily decrease.

Long-term growth and improvement is the province of upper management. Ultimately the results belong to executive level under the overall guidance of the board of directors (in theory, anyway. In real life, the executives make the decisions and the Board often just approves the decisions that have already been made, rarely offering effective strategic guidance different than what executives recommend). Under various levels of presidents, executive vice-presidents, senior vice-presidents, and just plain vice-presidents comes the lower level of directors, and under them, multiple layers of managers. Further down, we have supervisors in those organizations that have a large level of working-level employees. At each level, the managers are working toward the growth of the organization in their particular area.

The higher up the management level, the more the person is charged with the long term improvement of the organization. These are the people who have to (a) buy into the benefits of enterprisewide portfolio management, (b) approve the funding and the resources for it, and (c) who will be members of the Governance Committee and the lower-level Steering Committees who will make the decisions on which projects to approve and to fund.

In a large organization you may have separate companies, divisions, or groups. Their relationship to the top of the organization will vary from completely autonomous, to semiautonomous, to completely controlled by the central organization. At each level, there are responsibilities commensurate with that level.

At the top level of every large organization, we have an executive Governance Committee or something equivalent. The members of this structure will make the highest-level decisions on where the organization's money will be put in the next year's expenditures. Below them, depending on how large the organization is, we have Steering Committees that make the same decisions for individual business units, divisions, or groups.

Ideally, the executive level sets the strategy and the portfolio manager takes this direction and drives it forward. In reality, conflicting priorities or day-to-day activities can often interfere. *"To prevent this, the portfolio manager needs the executive support,"* said Dr. Wanda Curlee, PMP, PgMP, PfMP, Director Portfolio and Program at Hewlett-Packard. *The role of the CEO is to articulate clearly what a company's future is in one-year, three-year, and five-year timeframes. The portfolio manager's role is to evaluate the portfolio to ensure it meets the strategic goals, continually reviewing the company's landscape for newer projects and programs that may need to be a part of the portfolio.*[19]

A very simple organization chart for an international company might look something like this:

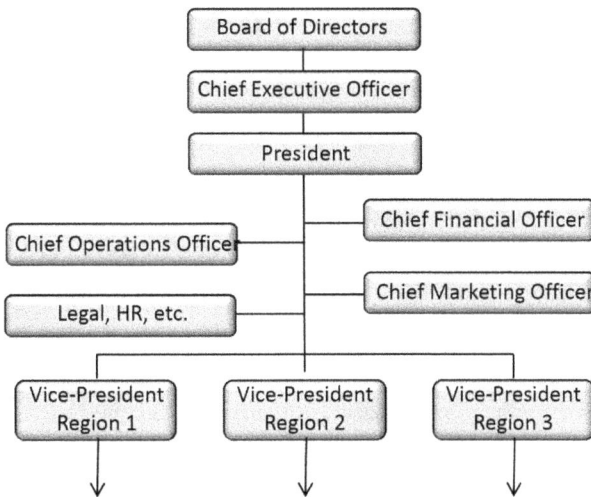

Figure 1.3-1 Organizational hierarchy option 1

Not all international companies are organized around geographic regions. Some are organized around product lines as illustrated in the following chart:

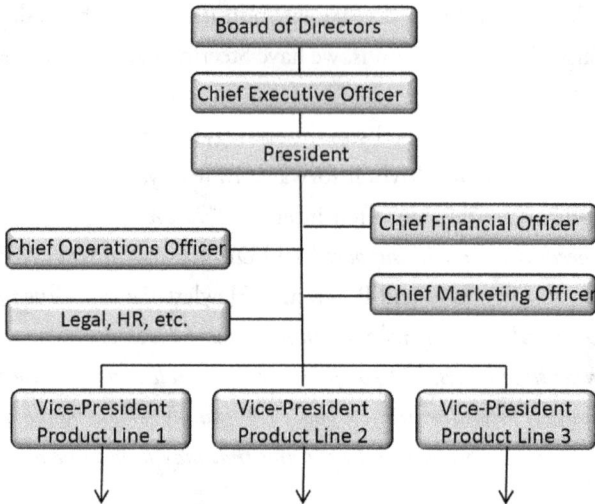

Figure 1.3-2 Organizational Hierarchy Option 2

Either way, enterprises organize in the way that makes sense to them. The exact organizational structure is important because it has an impact on how the EPMS is designed. Depending on the level of the organization that is doing portfolio management, an EPMS that is designed for one division or business unit of a medium-size consumer products company would have a very different structure than one designed for an international corporation that sells products worldwide.

With all these layers of people, who should make the decisions on which projects to fund? The primary criterion for who should be on the committee is that group of executives or managers who have budgetary control over that part of the organization. The ultimate responsibility for allocating the annual budget of the organization belongs to the executive level. As the budget is detailed down into different parts of the organization, there will be lower-level governance committees that make the decisions appropriate to that level.

If internal coordination and communications is good (usually not the case but let's pretend for the sake of discussion), then the various levels have a good understanding of the strategic goals of the organization and how their area supports those goals. They then make rational decisions on the most effective way to achieve those goals.

As will be shown later on, there are various categories of the budget that are dependent on the strategic goals of the organization. The specific categories will depend on the level of the organization that is making the project decisions. For example, at the division or group level, there will generally be a specific budget for IT projects. How this money is allocated will depend on what the IT goals are. (Again, in a perfect world, IT goals are obtained from the business and reflect how IT can best support the business goals.)

The aforementioned discussion is a very academic and simplistic description of the governance structure in most organizations. It ignores one of the critical aspects of selecting projects—dealing with the internal politics.

While it is true that everyone in a management role cares about the long-term growth of the organization, in the short term, they care more about advancing their own small part of the organization, and in fact they get rewarded and promoted for doing so. Their emphasis is on their group (whatever the size) growing and advancing. In turn, this will lead to more responsibilities and greater advancement for themselves.

Why is this important to us? Because this structure often pits one manager or one group against another in competition for financial resources and projects. While most managers would acknowledge that all parts of the organization are important, each manager also feels that his or her part of the organization is more critical to the overall organization than other groups.

Story

In one California utility the author has dealt with, upper management realized rather late that the workforce in one Business Unit was entering retirement age (Note: for a normal organization, this is predictable years in advance. The executives simply didn't think far enough ahead, so it came as a surprise to them that their workforce was getting older).

The executives decided to implement two solutions in parallel—the first was to install an ERP system (SAP) and the second was to perform an enterprise-wide business process integration (BPI) effort.

While everyone applauded the BPI effort, once it began, it pro-
gressed very, very slowly. While the business unit managers and general
managers appreciated the need to improve processes, each process had
a process owner whose ownership and power was threatened by the
BPI effort. These process owners, all high-level managers, publicly sup-
ported the effort but privately did not cooperate at the level needed for
success. They didn't see the benefit to themselves, and in fact they were
very protective of the business processes that they were in charge of.

From this inherent situation will come most of the resistance to implementing the EPMS and most of the difficulty in managing it. By taking
away the ability of managers to make individual decisions on which projects to fund, the EPMS will take away some of their power and authority.
Unless managers are sold on the benefits of the EPMS to themselves individually, they see no benefits to it, only downsides.

In this hierarchy from the bottom of the organization to the very top,
where does portfolio management fit in?

Looking from strategy, to portfolio, to program, to project, and finally
to operations, we can compare the focus of each of these, the alignment,
the stakeholders, and the indicators as Abdollahyan[20] has done:

Table 1.1 Focus of different stakeholders

	Strategy	**Portfolio**	**Program**	**Project**	**Operations**
Focus	Mission, vision, and objectives	Strategy delivery	Outcomes, "benefits"	Outputs, "deliverables"	Sustained business
Buzzword	Strategy	Strategic alignment	Benefits realization	Product and capability delivery	Business-as-usual
Stakeholder	Owners, shareholders, market	C-level and middle management	Sponsors, beneficiaries, and other stakeholders	Sponsors, clients, users, and other stakeholders	Management, clients, users, and other stakeholders
Indicators	Enterprise value indicators	Portfolio value indicators	Benefits and project performance indicators	Project performance indicators	Operational excellence indicators

Abdollahyan's use of the term buzzword may be understood as alignment.

This matrix shows how portfolio management fits into the overall framework of implementing strategy within the organization so that the day-to-day operations of the company support the long-term goals.

Step 1.4 Managements Goals and Expectations

Our ultimate goal is not to deliver an EPMS. That's just the mechanism. Our goal is to deliver the information that management needs to decide on the best projects to deliver strategy. Our tool is to develop an EPMS that does that, to deliver a system that satisfies what management needs and that the participants will want to use. Does the last sentence sound like two different goals? They are not. They are in fact the same goal, but inexperienced project managers may lose sight of the distinction. You're not just delivering technology and a new business process, you're delivering a way for the entire organization to become more efficient and more effective. You are making a significant improvement in how the organization works. How much of an improvement? We will give you some numbers later, but you can tell your executive sponsor that a paper on effective portfolio management systems published by IDC[21] shows that for the companies surveyed:

- Number of projects managed increased 35 percent
- Cost per project was reduced 37 percent
- Redundant projects dropped 78 percent
- IT staff productivity increased by 14 percent
- Project failure rate dropped 59 percent
- The total annual benefit per 100 users is $83,500
- Payback occurred in 7.4 months
- Return on investment was $5.57 for every $1 spent on portfolio management

PMI's annual Pulse of the Profession (op cit.) showed the following drivers for portfolio management:

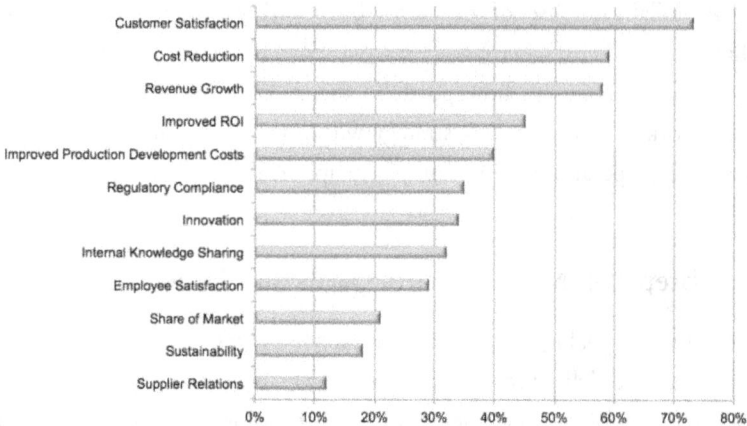

Figure 1.4-1 Portfolio drivers

Determining goals and expectations is the process of gathering the business needs for the EPM system. What is it that management expects from it? Why did they decide to do it? Are their expectations realistic? Did someone read a one-page article in a management journal on the benefits of portfolio management and decide this is what we need?

Story (Remember Windows 8?)

A survey of over 1200 people by TechRepublic[22] showed that 74 percent of organizations have no plans to implement Windows 8. Considering the many millions of dollars Microsoft spent on developing the new OS and that much of their income derives from selling the OS, that's a potentially huge hit to their future income.

Some selected quotes from the interviewees were:

"Nightmare waiting to happen in the corporate world. [The] UI will be difficult to train people [on]."

"Win 8 is not suited for an enterprise due to the metro interface and pathetic dual screen support."

"Windows 8 offers our laptop and desktop environment no compelling features. Pandering to tablets with [their] UI did not go over well at [all]."

"The user interface is just too much of a change...I did a test demo [and the users] all hated it."

"A reduction in productivity due to bad GUI design."

What happened? How could such an expensive project return such poor early reviews?

Determining management's expectations, both stated and unstated, is a major part of starting the effort. This part of the project is too often either forgotten entirely or done poorly. Too many nonproject managers think that spending time determining in detail what they need, determining the requirements, doesn't seem like "real work"—you're not planning the schedule, you're not coding, you're not meeting with vendors, you're not testing. But, and let me emphasize this, *everything else you do and the success of the project will depend on how thoroughly you understand what people need, want, and expect.* Literally, everything else on the project is based on that. How well your requirements are determined and approved will dictate your project management approach

How do we measure whether we have been successful or not? The EPMS itself will use financial criteria as part of the decision criteria for approving a project, and a common financial filter is Return on Investment (ROI). ROI measures the financial returns from the money your company is spending on the project. It is a straightforward and very simple calculation, but every financial filter has limitations. A more sophisticated EPMS will compare ROI, Internal Rate of Return (IRR), and Net Present Value (NPV) to select the projects that provide the greatest benefits.

But not all projects are susceptible to purely financial filters. Think about the traditional public works project—a new highway, a dam, or a bridge. How do you calculate the financial return on those? For these types of projects, the Benefit/Cost Analysis is typically used. While fruitful, the BCA is subject to a lot of assumptions and is highly inaccurate. Research by Flyvbjerg,[23] for example, has shown that public works such as roads has a typical cost overrun of 20 percent and an overestimate of the benefits of almost 10 percent.

For projects such as the EPMS itself, sometimes a better calculations is Return on Expectations (ROE). This should answer the question whether the EPMS delivered what was expected.

Story

Let's look at one success story in Portfolio Management—Chevron Oil Company (This material is based on a presentation given on

4 March, 2009, by Janinne Franke of Chevron's IT department and is used with permission). They are developing advanced capabilities in IT portfolio management by having a thorough understanding of how it can benefit the business and centralizing portfolio management in a PMO (Portfolio Management Office) for each business unit. This is a journey that they're still working on. It will take some years to achieve their goals.

In 2009, Chevron was the 6th largest company in the world by revenues with over 65,000 employees worldwide. Their IT group had over 6,900 people located in 64 locations around the world. Before they began a transformation of IT, the department was focused on their customer's, the business unit's, immediate needs. While this is normal for IT departments, it is a very tactical approach, not a strategic one. The end result is generally a patchwork of non-integrated systems, numerous incompatible applications, and no long term planning. Chevron's goal was to transform the IT organization to focus on the best way to achieve long-term business strategies.

IT had five key focus areas:

1. *Run and support Chevron's IT assets securely, safely, reliably, and efficiently*
2. *Improve reliability, the transparency of IT spend, and our overall project planning, prioritization, and execution capabilities*
3. *Deliver the critical few IT Investment Strategy initiatives with excellence*
4. *Sustain the value of these investments through effective support and an improved ability to extract the intended value*
5. *Shape the 10-year vision and strategy, and set priorities for Information Technology at Chevron*

The emphasis of the PMO was on the second focus area—improve reliability, the transparency of IT spend, and the overall project planning, prioritization, and execution capabilities. Although in addition, the third focus area involves identifying the critical few IT investment strategy initiatives is also a valid goal of portfolio management.

How were they going to achieve this? Their stated objective was to develop processes, tools, and analytics to enable, measure, and advise on the following areas:

- *Balanced Portfolio: Balance projects according to the organization's strategy and other parameters in order to achieve a desired return. Maximize the value of the Portfolio via key metrics while keeping an acceptable level of risk.*
- *Optimized Resources: Allocate resources to the highest value projects and ensure that resources are being appropriately utilized. Manage the "peaks and valleys" of resource use.*
- *High Value Work: Ensure that the Project Portfolio reflects the business strategy and that the breakdown of spending aligns with business priorities.*

In order to achieve their ultimate goal of being a great business partner, beginning in 2005 they created processes for becoming first a great service provider, then a good business partner, then a great business partner. Each of these goals had a series of lower-level goals to accomplish. One of the ways to becoming a great service provider, their steps include understanding the business needs first, then achieving operational excellence, then managing their IT costs.

On their way to becoming a good business partner, the steps involved first understanding the business strategies, translating those strategies to clear credibility gaps, then finally aligning IT strategy, portfolio, and the enterprise architecture. It was in these steps that the portfolio management process was created and implemented.

Once this is achieved, they can use their portfolio management process to develop an IT strategy that's integrated with and supports the business strategy. (This process puts the ownership of IT strategy on the business, where it properly belongs. It's the business who should be driving IT's strategy and let IT determine how best to achieve that strategy.)

As we will see later, a normal project selection process under a portfolio management system selects the projects that are most beneficial (usually using financial criteria) at an acceptable level of risk. For

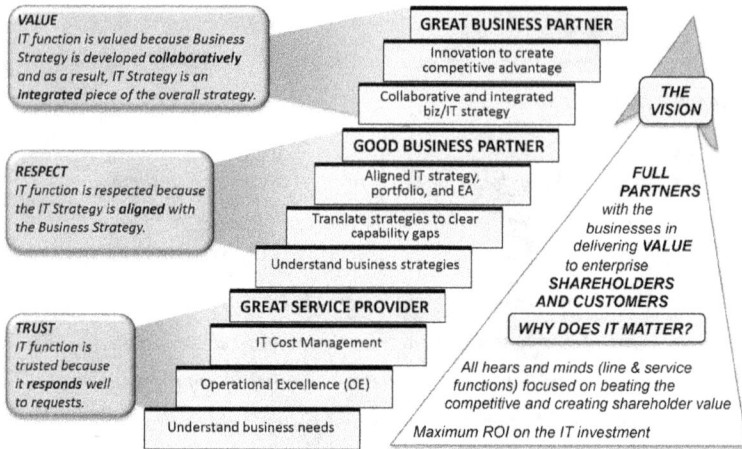

Figure 1.4-2 Chevron's IT goals

Chevron, their system includes financial calculations and risk assessments, but in addition, they filter projects for strategic fit:

- *Enterprise Strategic Fit—Support of strategy with emphasis on an enterprise-level view*
- *Business Unit Strategic Fit—Support to specific Business Unit level strategies*

Because the oil/gas industry sector is highly-regulated, Chevron's first filtering criteria is related to whether this is a compliance project or not. (Any regulated industry must use this filter as a first one before any other filters are utilized. We will look later at Toyota USA's project selection criteria and see that they have the same one.)

There is no progress without measurement. You have to know where you are to understand whether you have improved or not. Chevron developed a 5-tier maturity model similar to that developed by the Software Engineering Institute's Capability Maturity Model (CMM). They defined four areas of competency (Strategy, Process, Tools/Technology, and Organizational Capability) and measure these across five levels of maturity:

- *Level 1: Informal*
- *Level 2: Defined*

- *Level 3: Managed*
- *Level 4: Measured*
- *Level 5: Optimized*

as shown here:

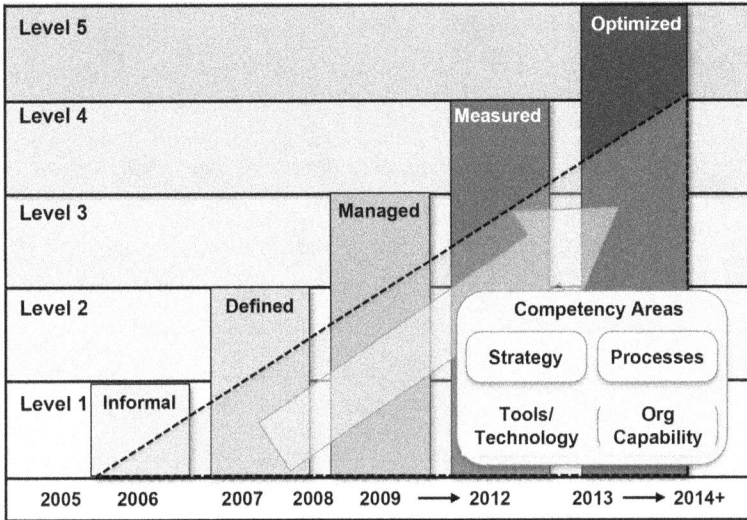

Figure 1.4-3 5-Level hierarchy of maturity

Not all of Chevron's business units aspired to be at level five on all competency levels. Some are happy to stop at level three (shown by the sun between levels 2 and 3), which would be the minimum rating of an impactful Portfolio Management Office. Any level lower than that would move the PMO to a project management office.

The end result of an effective PMO is enhancing business values in:

Planning

- *Enhanced partnership between Business and IT enables business strategy*
- *Objective project selection and prioritization based on business drivers*
- *Balanced Project Portfolio mix to maximize return*

- *Comprehensive data enables improved decision making around resource allocation and portfolio investment*
- *Relationship visibility between all projects, programs and portfolios and alignment to business strategy*
- *Reduction of disparate Portfolio Management tools*
- *Reduce number of projects by understanding cross-functional synergies/overlaps/redundancies*

Execution

- *Greater agility to respond to changes in business conditions decreases time-to-market*
- *Improved On Time On Budget performance through enhanced project planning capability*
- *Reduced cycle times through improved and standardized Portfolio Management processes*
- *Productivity gains through increased automation and process refinement*
- *Cost avoidance and reduction of project delays by more proactive resource planning and optimization*
- *Maximize the efficient use of resources and assets with an emphasis on safety and reliability*

Realization

- *Centralized Project and Program data enables improved decision quality through portfolio analytics*
- *Ability to monitor progress through measured attributes and KPIs (Key Performance Indicators) against business objectives*
- *Application of industry performance benchmarks*
- *More control for continuous improvement*

While other approaches are possible, the one Chevron is using is very well thought out and well planned. Did they achieve their goals? By 2014, they had achieved Level 4 and were part of the way into Level 5. According to stock analysts Chevron is one of the best managed major oil companies.

The stepped development process is highly recommended for implementing a major change such as implementing an EPMS. The Mayo Clinic[24] used exactly the same incremental approach to delivering benefits as shown in the following figure:

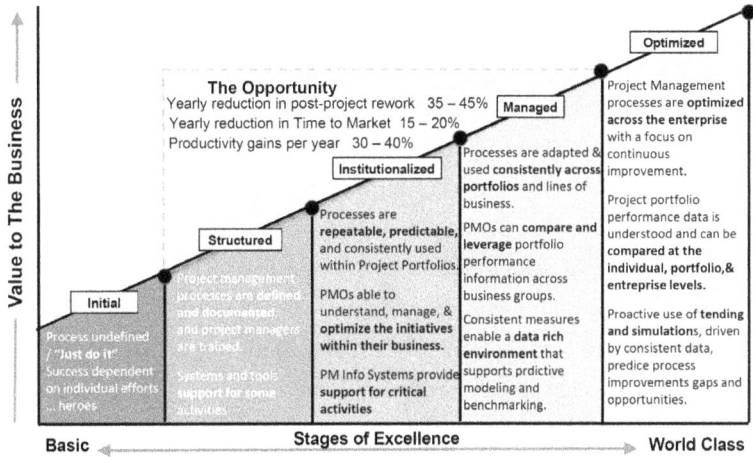

Figure 1.4-4 Mayo clinic's hierarchy of benefits delivery

We will talk in some detail later about supporting the strategic goals of the organization, but do you know what they are? Sometimes they're described in the Vision and Mission statements that are commonly published in the organization's annual SEC filing of their annual report (for publicly held companies) or in some other high-level document. But any large organization can have multiple strategies.

Let's look at one well-known worldwide organization, Pepsi Cola. They have a product strategy, a marketing strategy, an advertising strategy, an environmental strategy, and other strategies. And these are not only for the overall corporate organization, these also exist for each company in the Pepsi family. There are multiple drinks, "convenience" foods, cereals, cookies, and other product companies within the family, all having their own strategic goals and plans, which are subsidiary to the top-level organizations. So strategic goals really mean the specific long-term goals at the level of the organization you are developing the EPMS for.

Sometimes the long-term goals can be very tactical instead of strategic. For example, look at the car industry during the recent economic downturns. Instead of planning for 5 to 7 years of growth and advancement, the major U.S. car manufacturers were planning for survival and cost savings. General Motors,[25] as an example, was looking in 2009 at:

- Cut its North American nameplate lineup from 48 down to 36 by 2012. Hummer, Saab, and Saturn will account for most of those cuts.
- Reduce workforce by 47,000 globally, including 10,000 white collar (3,400 U.S. white collar)
- Close 14 North American factories by 2012, five more than in the December 2 plan
- Reduce U.S. dealers from 6,200 currently to 4,700 in 2012 and 4,100 in 2014
- Seek to convert bondholder debt and funding to autoworkers' retirement health care funds into GM stock

Each one of these efforts is a project, a big one, and will consume a lot of time, effort, and resources. You can very easily build an EPMS at the corporate level of GM just to handle these types of projects.

1.5 The Business Case

After you have done the initial work to research the benefits of an EPMS and have sold the idea to the upper echelons of the organization, you have to get their formal approval for the effort. It's time to write the business case and get blessing by the upper levels of the organization to start the project. This has to be done prior to interviewing the decision makers on exactly what they want out of it, de-conflicting their needs, researching ways to properly prepare the organization for the coming changes, and do all the other prep work, you still have to get formal approval to design, develop, and implement it.

What is a business case? It's a written justification that convinces upper management that this project should be done. Right now, it is how you will show the benefits (emphasizing the financial benefits) of the EPMS. In the future, it will be a major input to the project selection process.

It provides the benefits of the project to the organization, the costs of the project, and the risks associated with it. A major part of the business case is the financial justifications that we discussed in the previous section. Your business case is used to "sell" the project to the decision makers.

Competent high level decision makers don't make most major decisions based on their gut feelings. At the top of the organization, their primary interests lie in moving the entire organization toward its strategic goals. They need numbers that show the benefits, and the more you can justify the numbers, the more convincing your argument will be.

During periods of economic growth, executives are more willing to spend money to grow the company. There's a feeling of "we can do even more" and a desire to get bigger. During periods of economic downturn, it would seem rational that the executives would be more willing to authorize work that reduces costs or to improve productivity. Unfortunately, the opposite is usually what happens. They become more reluctant to spend money no matter how good the long-term payoff is and so the justification needs to be even better. Hint: Get someone from the marketing department to help you gather the information needed here and to help you write it. Marketing people are, as a rule, better at communicating these areas than technical people are. They've been doing it a lot longer.

Executives need hard numbers. The kind you find in a business case justification. So what goes into the business case? There are many different templates for business cases depending on the type of project. Exactly what goes into the document depends on the type of project and in what your management wants to see. A business template for an IT project would be very different than that from a pharmaceutical development project or for a new factory. The organizations that have the most detailed business case templates are government organizations because of the heavy oversight of government projects and the probability of an audit if the project runs into trouble. So, there is strong emphasis placed on justifying the project. Some of the best templates available are freely downloadable from government websites.

A business case is designed to provide financial justification of the proposed spending initiative (which in our case is a project to implement an EPMS) as well as its risks. While most organizations have its own internal template for one as we have just seen, normal sections include the sections necessary to "sell" the project to upper management:

- An Executive Summary
- A description of the current situation—the business need
- Project Benefits—how does the project fit into the strategic plan?
- Description of the Solution
- High-Level Objectives
- Competitive Position (not necessary for an internal project such as this)
- Impacts to the organization and on-going work
- Potential Risks
- Assumptions
- Alternatives
- Financial Costs and Benefits

Experienced project managers will recognize a lot of these sections. They are commonly documented in the project charter. The differences are the emphasis on the business benefits so we include some competitive analysis and ROI calculations. Sometimes the business case is appended to the project charter. Oftentimes the business case substitutes for the project charter. If you already have a business case, there is very little that needs to be added to it to make it a proper project charter. If you develop a separate project charter, at the very least, attach the success criteria and the financial justification from the business case.

1.5.1 Executive Summary

This is a short summarization of the rest of the document. It emphasizes the benefits, costs, and risks. Most of the executives will read the summary, make a decision, and browse the rest of the document to reinforce their decision. This should be the last section written but it must be the most well written. The project is highly likely to be approved or rejected on how well the executive summary sells it.

1.5.2 Current Situation

Why are we doing this? What's the problem, the pain, that's causing us to develop an EPMS? Or what's the benefit of doing so? If there's no real problem, why should we approve this?

This section must be written so that the decision makers see the problems that not having an EPMS causes. Typical problems that occur by not having an EPMS may include:

- Duplicated work and waste because there are multiple projects trying to do the same thing
- Time-to-profit for new products is poor because of the long timelines involved in developing new products
- Projects continue even though the reasons for them have disappeared, wasting time, and money
- Managers are approving projects that benefit their own part of the organization instead of the overall organization, leading to suboptimal use of scarce resources
- Et cetera, et cetera, et cetera ad nauseum

The more you can convince people there are significant problems the EPMS can solve, the more likely you are to get it approved. If you can put financial numbers around the preceding items showing how much productivity is lost or how much money is wasted, you will significantly improve your chances of getting approved even in a downsizing economy.

1.5.3 Product Overview

Here's where you describe what the EPMS will look like, and how it will operate, once it's implemented and integrated into the overall organization.

1.5.4 High-Level Objectives

High-level objectives for the EPMS should be the solution to the problems described in the section on the current situation and they should be quantifiable to the extent possible. For example:

- Increase productivity of the IT department by 10 percent by killing duplicate projects
- Reduce time-to-profit for new product development by 6 months
- Select more projects that support strategic rather than departmental objectives
- And so on

Remember our goal—to implement a system that will significantly improve how the organizations selects projects and moves toward its strategic goals. The more you can make that goal specific and measurable, the better your chances of getting the project approved. The PMO the author created at the car company mentioned earlier reduced the time required to approve new projects from 6 months to 3 weeks. That's the kind of benefit that convinces management this is a good thing to do.

1.5.5 Competitive Position

Typically not required for an internal business process change such as implementing an EPMS.

1.5.6 Impacts

This section describes the impacts to the on-going work in the organization. What are the impacts to operations? What are the impacts to existing projects? How many people will be pulled away from their normal daily work, and for how long?

Here's where your writing must phrase things very carefully. There will be negative impacts, especially in the short term. You will need to have people working on the project who are doing other work and will need to be pulled off it. You will likely be disrupting other projects in work. Mid-level managers will be reluctant to loan their best people to a project that is going to be disruptive.

Once the EMPS is implemented, it will look first at the existing projects in the organization and identify any overlapping projects, duplicate projects, and projects that need to be killed. Once project managers and team members hear you are going to do that, they will either stop working on projects that, in their minds, are likely to be cancelled or they will protest vigorously to protect their projects. So there will be impacts to doing the EMPS, but it must be emphasized in the business case that the negative impacts are short term and that the organization will be much better off in the long term.

1.5.7 Potential Risks

Every project has risks. This one is no exception.

What is a risk? A risk is anything that can happen in the future that will impact the success of your project.

In this section, you capture the risks you know about at this point. Have a tight schedule? That's a risk. Don't have dedicated resources to implement the EMPS? That's a risk. Because implementing a major organizational process change like you're doing impacts how people work? You will face a lot of organizational and political risks also. We'll cover risks more thoroughly in the next chapter.

1.5.8 Assumptions

An assumption is anything you expect to be true for planning purposes. If you think you'll have enough dedicated resources to do the work, that's an assumption. If you think this project will have interference from managers in other departments, that's an assumption. If you plan out the project expecting that software and hardware prices will not change in the future, that's an assumption.

Your entire plan—schedule, budget, deliverables, is based on assumptions. The more of these assumptions you can define and document, the better your planning processes will be. Determine what your assumptions are so that you can understand better the weak points in the plans. But for the business case, just write down the major, high-level assumptions that management can understand.

One statement that is always true in planning projects—any assumption becomes a risk if it turns out not to be true. There's an inverse relationship between risks and assumptions. If you assumed you would have a highly skilled data base analyst (DBA) to design your data base, and later find out there is none available, now you have a risk.

1.5.9 Alternatives

A section of alternative solutions to the stated problems is a common one in the business case. What other ways are there to solve the problems stated in the Current Situation? Are there simpler solutions? Is there something less costly or less disruptive that we can do instead? Because you have been thinking so much about the portfolio management solution that you have become focused on it; you should get inputs from other people to help write this who are less tied to a single solution.

Of course, one solution is always to do nothing. This is the default solution. If upper management isn't feeling enough pain from the problems or if you haven't convinced them of the benefits of this project, this is the solution they will often pick—to do nothing and to keep the status quo as it is. Even a bad status quo has more supporters than people willing to change.

We can avoid reality, but we cannot avoid the consequences of avoiding reality.

—Ayn Rand

1.5.10 Financial Costs and Benefits

This is the crux of the business case. Here is where you justify the benefits of implementing the EPMS. The emphasis of this part of the business case will be hard numbers, the more detailed the numbers, the better. Because this is your best guess, plus or minus 20 percent variation is normal.

For most projects, it is easier to identify the costs than it is the benefits. We can estimate the size of the project, the resources we'll need, and any expected expenditures and develop reasonable rough numbers for the costs.

It is much harder to come up with valid numbers for the benefits. There are always a lot of loose assumptions in defining the benefits of a project. Do we expect an increase in market share because of what this project will provide? How much? 5 percent market share increase? 10 percent?

2 percent? Do we expect to increase the productivity of the IT department by implementing an EPMS? If so, how much? A 2 percent increase in productivity for 250 people is a significant improvement. But where did you come up with that 2 percent number? It's an assumption on your part at this point unless you can show how you calculated that. Hubbard's book "How to Measure Anything" discusses the difficulties in detail.[26]

Total Costs of Ownership include any on-going licensing and maintenance fees for software and hardware and the operating costs once the EPMS is in use. Typically, these life-cycle costs would be calculated out for a period of 3 to 5 years. Your financial people will tell you what the planning horizon is for financial calculations. The greatest benefits from an EPMS come in the future. If you just calculate the cost of the EMPS implementation itself you will not have the opportunity to show the benefits.

Whatever numbers you come up with, be prepared to justify them and show that they are reasonable approximations. Management is used to reading a business case that has best-guess estimates in it, but you should have the backing for what you put down.

For the majority of projects, the benefits will be financial—Return on Investment, New Present Value, Internal Rate of Return, payback period, and so on. This is a valid justification because an organization is not going to spend money and resources on something that will not provide a positive payback.

As we will see later, some projects are mandatory. Regulatory-driven projects, required maintenance projects, and others. For these projects, the financial justifications are almost irrelevant. Management will approve these projects because they must, not because there is a financial benefit to doing them. So when we are using the EPMS to identify these projects, don't spend much time on the financial benefits, just capture the costs.

Because the EPMS itself will perform financial calculations once it's in place, we discuss how to do this in great detail in the next chapter.

Step 1.6 Organizational Change Management (OCM)

One hundred victories in one hundred battles is not the most skillful, subduing the other's military without battle is the most skillful.

—Sun Tzu

In implementing the EPMS, the most difficult part is obtaining acceptance for it from the rest of the organization. By acceptance we mean more than just acknowledging that it exists, we mean a willingness to use it because they see the benefits of it and it is user friendly. By comparison, everything else in your effort is straightforward and relatively easy.

It is easy to design and install an EPMS. It is far more difficult to implement it so that people will use it effectively and efficiently. This is no different than implementing any other significant process change in an organization. This is not necessarily a short-term effort. When the hardware retailer Lowe's implemented a portfolio management system in their IT department, they realized that it impacted the entire organization. They established a Business Solutions Group (BSG) of 85 employees who knew project management, the detailed business processes, and had an understanding of technology. They also set up an IT steering committee at the C-level of Lowe's. According to Waxer[27]:

> *For all the benefits of portfolio management, companies shouldn't expect to glean immediate results from it. In fact, experts suggest that it can take as long as five years to reach the highest level of business value. This is because one of the greatest challenges companies face is responding to employee resistance. To help drive adoption, Lowe's integrated portfolio management metrics into performance reviews for the company's IT project directors and vice presidents. Compiled both midyear and end-of-year, these reviews outline which projects were delivered on time and on budget and include detailed explanations for missed targets.*

Comparable enterprise-level IT and process changes include efforts such as implementing Enterprise Resource Planning (ERP) systems. These are complex packages that international organizations manage their operations with. The failure rate for ERP packages is extremely high. Poor implementations have literally driven companies into bankruptcy. Don't believe it? Problems with Hershey's ERP startup cost the company $150 million. FoxMeyer Corp.'s bungled ERP installation cost the company a $1 billion lawsuit and ended in bankruptcy for the company and it being sold to a competitor. Waste Management also spent $150 million before it abandoned its ERP implementation. For business process re-engineering projects, only 20 to 30 percent of them are successful.[28] We could equally cite many examples of business process improvement (BPI) initiatives that never deliver the benefits expected.

The problem is not with badly-designed technology, the software works very well. Nor with poor business process design. The problem is the people. Many business processes in an organization interact with people, and getting people to change how they do their job is the most difficult of all project management efforts.

Law of Project Management
The only human being who truly enjoys change is a wet baby.

People don't mind changing, they change all the time. They just resent having change forced on them. A survey of Fortune 500 executives said that the primary reason changes fail was because of internal resistance.[29] In a similar survey conducted by Deloitte Consulting at about the same time, 80 percent of the CIOs surveyed said that resistance was the main reason why IT projects failed.

Before you can even start the effort to implement the EPMS you must understand the comfort level of the organization to accept it. Just because upper management wants something doesn't mean lower level managers do or the employees do. Start by asking yourself six questions:

1. What's our history of implementing significant changes? How successful have we been in the past?
2. Does our organizational culture support changes and taking risks?
3. Do people trust each other from different departments and play nice together?
4. Can people handle more change?
5. Can they be convinced the change will benefit them?
6. How disruptive will this change be? (Because it will be disruptive until everyone accepts it.)

This last point is important. As we will see in the next section implementing an EPMS will be disruptive to work and that needs to be addressed during the process.

1.6.1 Resistance and Why It's Important

What is resistance? For our purposes, resistance is any behavior in an orga-nization that slows or stops change. There is nobody in the organization that has the title of "resistor" and who is just waiting to ruin our great EPMS implementation. People don't resist just to resist, they resist because they see the change as detrimental to everything they've worked for in the organization. They don't see what they are doing as impeding progress, they see it as survival. This attitude is worse in large, old organizations where people have worked for years. It is less of a problem in smaller, newer companies because change happens all the time in a small company.

It would be nice if you could get people supportive of this major change you're going to make by putting up motivational posters or by printing a slogan on a coffee cup, but experience shows it doesn't work that way. (For fun, see the website www.despair.com for examples of how people really think.) Managers who think motivational posters actually work are insulting the intelligence of the employees.

Story

Several years ago, my team and I did an audit of a Peoplesoft imple-mentation (an ERP system that was bought out by Oracle and later destroyed because it competed with their own internal product) being done by the CIO of a U.S. Federal government organization. The office of the CIO was putting in the human resource modules of Peoplesoft to enable better management of the 8000+ employees at the organization.

Before this change, the HR department of the organization was in full control of any changes to any employee. No one could hire a new employee, change a job description, move an employee to another department, give a raise or a promotion, or any one of 90+ other changes without filling out the HR paperwork, submitting it, and waiting for HR to process the changes. Needless to say any changes took months to work their way through the system. While most departments of the U.S. Federal government are not exactly models of high-tech, this 19th Century HR department was particularly slow. None of the work was done using computers. Everything was done by moving a blue piece of paper around. That blue piece of paper became a symbol for our audit team. It had been there for 25 years and the person who designed it was still there.

This Peoplesoft HR implementation would have completely changed that. It would have given full authority to the department heads to make any changes for their employees. The departments loved the change and set up all sorts of study and implementation groups to help the process. The HR department absolutely hated the change and refused to support it. There were posters all over the HR area showing that the change was coming. The HR employees got weekly e-mails talking about the change. And yet when we interviewed them during the audit we heard, universally, that they didn't know what was going on. Nobody communicated with them.

The communication was all around them, but they didn't want to hear it.

There is an old saying in change management, so old that there is no reliable reference for it, that in any significant organizational change, 20 percent of the people impacted will be supportive of the change, 20 percent will not change no matter what you do, and the middle 60 percent can be swayed if you implement the change correctly.

The people who are most willing to change are either new to the organization, are very accepting of change, or see the problems with how things are done now. The people who will never change have often been

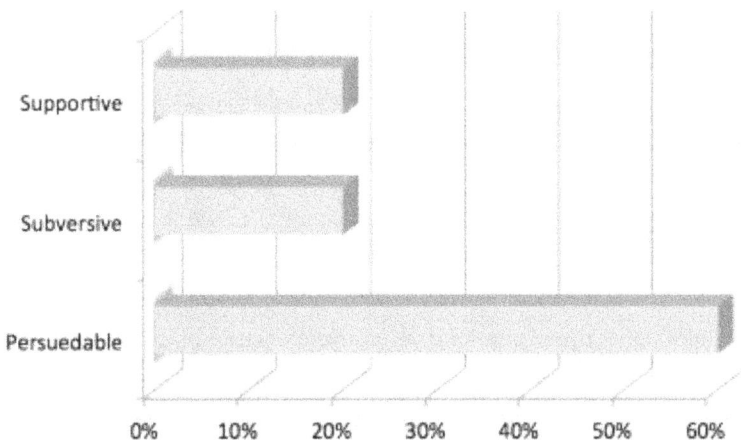

Figure 1.6-1 *Variations in supportability*

there the longest, see no reason for you to change how they work, or simply dislike change. You're aiming for the hearts and minds of that middle 60 percent. If you implement the change correctly, you can slowly win them over. If you have a failure early in the implementation process, you will move them into the "I'll never change" camp.

1.6.2 Categories and Types of Resistance

Ignoring, for a moment, the people who just dislike all changes, we can look at three different categories of resistance: rational resistance, emotional resistance, and personal resistance. Each category requires a different approach. You need to spend some time very early in your efforts to determine which resistance you're facing and by whom.

Rational resistance occurs because people honestly believe that your efforts are not the right approach. They have looked at the same problems the EPMS is trying to solve and have determined there's a better solution. This is the easiest type of resistance to deal with because it's defined by facts and logical arguments. Sharpen up your ROI calculations and prepare your PowerPoint presentations to overcome rational resistance. Unfortunately, too many managers think that *all* the resistance is rational resistance when in reality most of it is not.

While the processes involved in providing a prioritized list of possible projects is very rational and data-driven, the reality of decision making is that most people, even top-level managers, make decisions at a subconscious level, even an emotional level.[†,30]

Emotional resistance is what happens when people are concerned that your efforts are going to reduce their power, take staff away from them, change their working relationships, get them laid off, or do something else detrimental to the jobs they have worked so hard to protect. Once you start talking about making changes to work processes, people immediately start worrying about their jobs. This is called the FUD factor—Fear, Uncertainty, and Doubt. A lot of efforts of Organizational Change Management are designed to overcome the FUD factor by recognizing it, dealing with it, and reassuring people that their current jobs are safe or that they will be retrained for their new jobs. Any really major

---

† http://hbswk.hbs.edu/item/5952.html

change effort in an organization needs to spend a significant amount of effort in this area to be successful.

I'm afraid I must point out some bad news here. One of the major sources of resistance to EPMS will come from the existing project managers within the organization. While it would be nice to think that they are fully behind any improvements to project management, the reality is that they are the ones who are most impacted by implementing an EPMS. Currently, they are free to manage projects their own way and to report progress in the ways that make their projects look best. By implementing an EPMS you will be reducing their ability to look good by instituting a set of progress metrics that apply consistently to all the projects. Undoubtedly, some projects that looked good before will look much worse when the new metrics are put in place. They will lose the ability to paint a rosy picture and gloss over problems. They will also lose some freedom in managing projects the way they want.

Existing project managers will be a major source of resistance within the organization and they must be given special attention and their inputs considered carefully in the design and implementation process. Fortunately, they will also receive a great benefit from the new system. Research has shown that the organizations that take EPM seriously do fewer projects, so the workload of the PMs can be reduced and they can concentrate on doing a better quality job on fewer projects (if management decides that they can lay off project managers and keep a heavy workload on them, the EPM implementation has failed before it is done. This is not a viable option. Gently check with senior management before you start out and see if that's what they are thinking.)

Personal resistance is resistance to you personally or to the department or group that you represent. You should never take it personally. Well, almost never. The source of this category of resistance is based on history with you or with your department/division/group or even a poor history with your department head. In a large, mature organization, this is unfortunately not as rare as one would hope.

Story

In a major insurance company where the author built a PMO, the corporate CIO had created such bad personal relations with the CIOs of the seven separate companies within the organization that they had developed strong incentives to disagree with anything he said or proposed. Personal resistance can be overcome by having the EPMS sponsored and supported out of a group or a division that is well thought of by the rest of the organization or at least has a neutral reputation.

Many, perhaps most, of today's organizational leaders have Master's in Business Administration (MBA) degrees or the international equivalents. They are taught an analyze/think/change process in making changes to an organization. Information about a problem is collected and analyzed, logical solutions are presented in documents and PowerPoint presentations, and people will change based on the hard facts presented. This is a very rational approach. It is also completely unrealistic. Wishful thinking at its best.

Assumptions of this rational approach include:

- Managers have "perfect information"
- Objectives are known and agreed to
- Managers are rational, systematic, and logical
- Managers work in the best interests of their organizations
- Ethical decisions do not arise in the decision-making process
- The problem is clear and unambiguous
- The alternatives and their consequences are known or predictable
- Time and resources are not a consideration
- The decisions will be implemented willingly and supported by all stakeholders

The problem with this approach is simply that it is not how people think. People, at all levels of the organization only behave rationally when it is to their best interest to do so. The rest of the time they behave in a manner that protects and expands what they have. If they think your change is going to have a negative impact on them, they will immediately, and subconsciously, be suspicious of it and start to resist it. When you're dealing with Emotional or Personal Resistance, reacting with a rational argument will be completely ineffective. When someone is worried about losing their job after the change, giving them more data about how good the change will be for the organization is a waste of time. You must deal with them at the level they are reacting from. Distributing a monthly newsletter about the project will not communicate what they need to hear.

Not all types of resistance-motivated behavior are the same. There is active resistance (actively working against you) and passive resistance (slow responses to e-mails, not showing up for meetings, etc.). There is also overt resistance where people tell you straight out they are not going to support your effort, and there is covert resistance where they just are not going to cooperate with you, but they won't tell you that.

1.6.3 Steps in Organizational Change Management (OCM)

In the literature on OCM, there is a great deal of emphasis on getting the active involvement of the people who are going to end up living with the change. They *must* be involved from the earliest stages to the final implementation and operations. They have to buy into the change, not just intellectually but emotionally as well.

People truly must believe that the change is to their benefit. All motivational posters and all the great talks by management on the benefits to the organization will not convince people that the change is going to help them in their day to day jobs and their relationships with the people they interact with. As soon as management starts talking about change, the FUD factor comes into play as we mentioned earlier.

In classic OCM theory, there are four stages of involvement that are required:

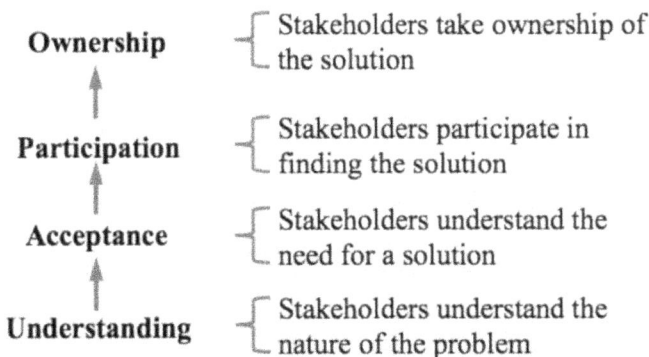

Ownership — Stakeholders take ownership of the solution

↑

Participation — Stakeholders participate in finding the solution

↑

Acceptance — Stakeholders understand the need for a solution

↑

Understanding — Stakeholders understand the nature of the problem

Figure 1.6-2 Levels of commitment

Understanding: At the initial level, the employees must understand the nature of the problem. This is where the memos and the presentations can be used. Don't tell them what the solution is except at a very high level, just get them to understand the issues. This is where you can tell them that EPMS can solve the problems that are being seen and what the benefits of the EPMS are. It is critical to make a compelling case for the EPMS at this stage because if the stakeholders are not completely convinced of the need for it, everything else you do after this will be like digging your way out of a hole. In Hammer and Champy's classic book *Re-engineering the Corporation*,[31] they talk about the "burning platform." Massive change is happening and if we don't change quickly we'll die.

In James Collins book *Good to Great*,[32] organizations that create a culture where people understand the business challenges seldom need to worry about getting alignment, motivation, or even managing change While there is more to success than just making a case, when people do "get it," less time is wasted getting ready for each new initiative.

Acceptance: Once the major stakeholders understand what the issues are and the benefits of EPM, have them define the challenges that they are currently facing by not having EPM: wasted efforts on duplicate projects, low-benefit projects being approved while high-benefit projects suffer from lack of resources, conflict, and so on.

During this stage, have them outline an EPM solution that would work within the culture of the organization. At this point, you have thought about the most effective EPMS more than anyone else, so you should provide guidance into their thinking process. Also, have them define the challenges that would be seen in implementing the EPM solution. Encourage different viewpoints but create a very clear vision and start developing the tactical approach to the implementation.

A significant number of your stakeholders are going to be the project managers currently in the organization as mentioned earlier. It is important that they accept the new EPMS because it provides them greater benefits than the pain they're suffering now with the problems of changing priorities, having a heavy workload, and having their resources taken away by higher priority projects.

Participation: The next stage of OCM is to have the stakeholders actively participate in defining the solution. You can provide the outline of the EPM approach but they must be involved in the details of how it works on a day-by-day basis. People are much more likely to be supportive if they have an input to the design. An additional benefit is that you don't need a whole team of expensive outside consultants to design and implement the new system. Internally-developed solutions are much more personal and acceptable.

Ownership: The final stage is to get the key stakeholders to own the solution by getting them involved in the design and implementation. They act as Subject Matter Experts (SMEs) and will guide the implementation in a way that gets the greatest percentage of that middle 60 percent to be supportive.

The ADKAR model for individual change management was developed by the research company Prosci[‡] with input from more than 1000 organizations from 59 countries. This model describes five required building blocks for change to be realized successfully on an individual level. The building blocks of the ADKAR Model include:

Awareness—of why the change is needed
Desire—to support and participate in the change
Knowledge—of how to change
Ability—to implement new skills and behaviors
Reinforcement—to sustain the change

General Guidelines

While identifying the impacts to a project that changes how people work, there are general guidelines that can be followed for any business process change:

- Identify the business processes that will be affected by the change

---

[‡] http://prosci.com

- List the processes that will be significantly changed
- List the processes that have an interaction with those processes
- List the processes that will not be changed
- Identify "how" people's work will be impacted by the change
- List the people who will remain in their current jobs after the change
- List the people who will need to be retrained after the change
- Identify any organizational cultural issues that may cause resistance
- List those cultural issues and why they may create resistance
- Identify possible resolutions to those issues
- Clearly communicate to the people affected
- Identify the managers that will be resistant to the change
- List the managers' concerns about the change by working with them
- Identify the positive impacts of the change—make the positive impacts as personal as possible for them
- Continue following up with those managers who still seem to be resistant
- Monitor other concerns as they arise during the course of the project

Step 1.7 Selling the Benefits of EPM

Even in the executive suite, there are disconnects between theory and reality. These are the smart guys, right? They are the ones who will make decisions that can grow, or kill, the organization. Yet even knowing how important portfolio management is to achieving strategy doesn't mean it will actually happen that way. According to the Economist Intelligence Unit[33]:

> ... only 10 percent of companies tightly align portfolio management with strategy implementation and only an additional 10 percent broadly align it. Far more common is no use of portfolio

management at all (19 percent) or an inconsistent application of it
to strategy implementation (34 percent). What Tanai Charinsarn,
a strategy consultant and member of the board of DCON Products,
a Thai concrete manufacturer, says of his experience in Asia-Pacific
applies more widely: Companies, especially large ones, may have "a
project management office, but its role is often just to make reports
to senior management. It is seen as doing something of low value."

How can the executives show they are supporting our efforts? They
have to demonstrate:

- Active support for change
- Communicating the importance to the organization
- Involvement in the critical few
- Allocating funds and resources based on strategic importance
- General oversight—not micro management
- Obtaining feedback so future projects learn from the past

And it is our job to ensure that happens.

There are many direct and indirect benefits to EPM. There are also
some downsides to implementing it. Fortunately, the downsides are temporary while the benefits are long term. Which benefits should be emphasized when you market EPM to your management will depend on what's
most important to them: long-term financial savings? A higher project
success rate? Fewer duplicated projects? Making better management decisions faster? Increased profitability? Less stress on the employees? All of
these are potential benefits of EPM. IBM's "Center of Excellence" PMO
has been around for almost 20 years and has reduced the number of
troubled projects by 25 percent since 2007 while supporting more than
26,000 project managers worldwide.[34]

During the implementation process, people will spend less time working and more time worrying about the new approach and talking about it
with their co-workers. In their executive training manuals a few years ago,
IBM showed the disruption using the following graphic:

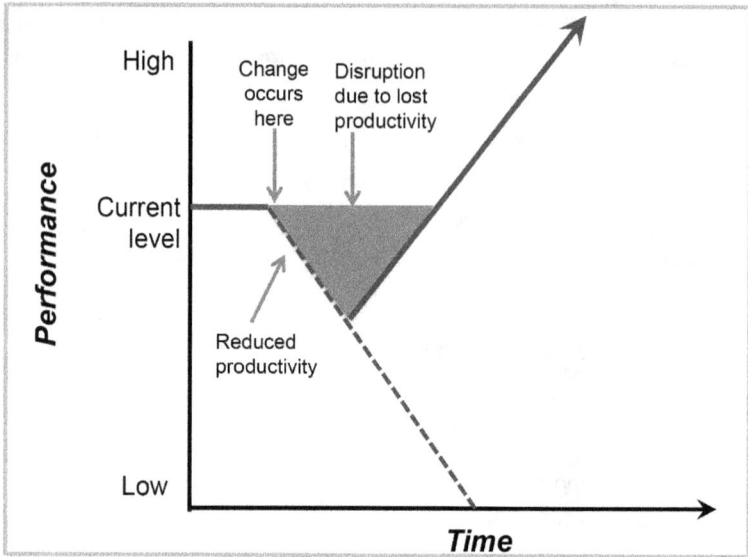

Figure 1.7-1 Productivity impacts of changes with OCM

Looks horrible. But there would be a much greater loss of productivity without using an Organizational Change Management Approach as shown here:

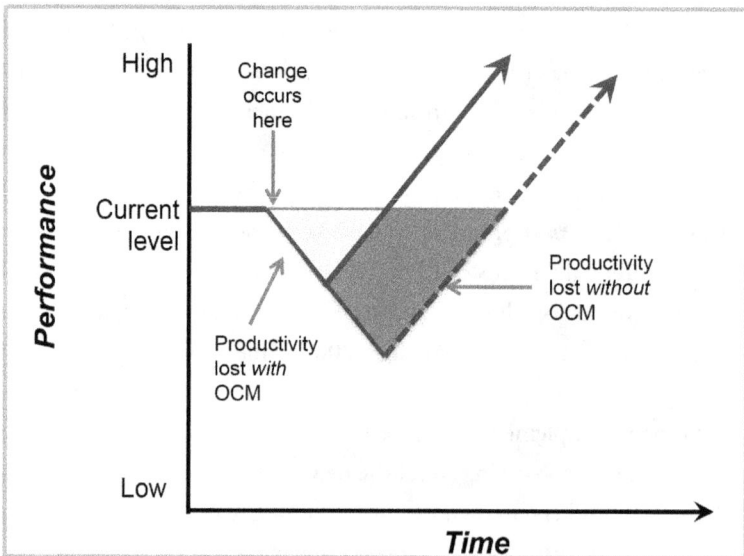

Figure 1.7-2 Productivity impacts of changes without OCM

Your efforts at this early stage should be directed toward understanding how accepting the stakeholders will be in receiving and using the EPMS.

People need time to adapt to significant change, and only if they believe it is truly in their best interests to change. Once employees believe the change will be beneficial, they begin to commit to it, and it's your job as the OCM lead to bring them to that point.

The OCM needs to include the executives, not only the lower-level employees. Even when the executives agree on developing an EPMS, there is still a large gap between what they actually do and what they know they should do. Of the many research articles on EPM, the results are consistent. If you do portfolio management well, you can expect to significantly improve the business as shown here[35] (we will give you additional justifications later):

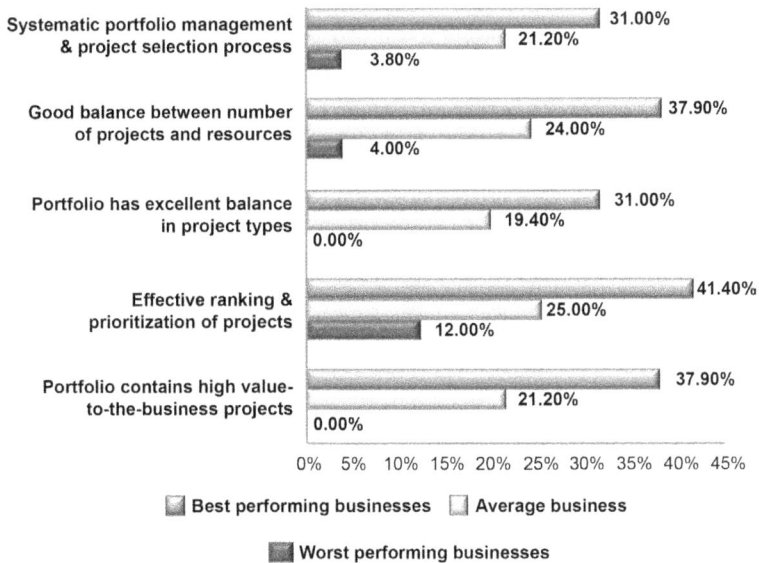

Figure 1.7-3 Comparing best performing vs worst performing

Story

In an article titled "How Lowe's Grows", author Cindy Waxer (op cit) describes how the US-based hardware chain Lowe's is "using EPM to make decisions that hold serious implications for the company's growth and survival. Take, for example, recently announced plans to open six to

10 stores in the Toronto market in 2007. 'Portfolio management and the concepts around portfolio management helped us in determining if it's right for us to look at a Canadian expansion,' says Steve Stone, CIO. ...

By providing a holistic view of the company's IT projects, Stone says Lowe's was able to measure an expansion's impact on available resources. After all, penetrating the northern border means dedicating personnel to the processing of multiple currencies, the introduction of new merchant programs, the deployment of back-office systems and cross-border merchandising projects. Because upgrading systems for multi-language and multicurrency functionality demands the assistance of internal subject matter experts, Lowe's ran various scenarios through its EPM system to determine a manageable growth rate for expansion. In the end, the EPM solution illustrated that internal experts would be a 'constrained resource' in the coming months—a revelation that Boerst (Steven Boerst, manager of Lowe's strategy and planning) says served as a valuable 'reference point' in planning Canadian store expansion."

1.7.1 What to Sell

Keeping in mind our discussion on OCR, which emphasized that benefits should be personal to the person you're selling to, some of the possible benefits of a strong EPMS that have been shown include:

- Closer alignment of the organization's strategies and long-term plans with the money spent
- Decreased Time to Market[36]
- Maximize value of project investments while minimizing risk
- Increased profitability[37] by reducing waste and improving efficiencies
- Improve communication and alignment between managers and executives
- Allow planners to schedule resources more efficiently
- Reduce the number of redundant projects and make it easier to kill projects
- Closer alignment of groups/divisions/business units with the overall enterprise: With an understandable, top-down view

of their entire project portfolio, executives and managers can more readily understand where dollars are being spent and which projects continue to be worthwhile. Whatever EPMS approach is implemented, it will provide a more consistent and accurate view of where the project money is being spent.

- Better governance: EPM helps managers monitor project progress in real time and measure each project to the same metrics
- Cost reductions and productivity increases: EPM helps managers identify redundant projects, inter-project dependencies, and poorly-allocated resources.
- Business-based decision making: Executives can make decisions based not only on projected costs and risks, but also on the expected returns in relation to other initiatives. Business managers can make decisions faster and with more confidence.[38]
- Improved productivity for individual employees: By better selection of projects and less wasted time on poor projects, the system will provide each employee less multitasking and overtime, making everyone's job a lot easier and less stressful.

When coordinating with upper management, remember the mantra "Numbers are Good." Just keep repeating that and you will learn what is important to the executives. What numbers? Generally, the benefits they will get for their investment of time and money in EPM. PMI and PMSolutions annually do surveys of portfolio management and PMOs. For 2012, PMI[1] showed the following benefits:

Table 1.2 Benefits of portfolio management

	Highly effective at portfolio management	Minimally effective at portfolio management	% Increase
Average Percentage of Projects			
Completed on time	68%	50%	36%
Completed on budget	64%	54%	19%
Met original goals & business intent	77%	65%	18%
Met/Exceeded forecasted ROI	62%	48%	29%

Results are fairly consistent from one year to the next. The report from the Economist Intelligence Unit quoted earlier shows the same results:

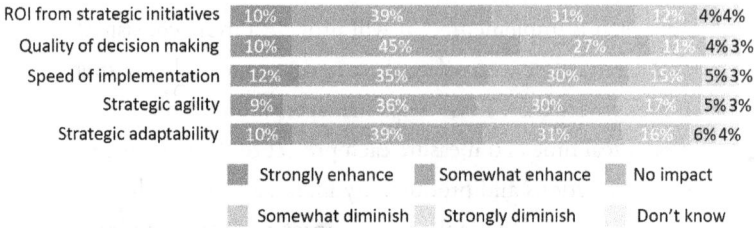

	Strongly enhance	Somewhat enhance	No impact	Somewhat diminish	Strongly diminish	Don't know
ROI from strategic initiatives	10%	39%	31%	12%	4%	4%
Quality of decision making	10%	45%	27%	11%	4%	3%
Speed of implementation	12%	35%	30%	15%	5%	3%
Strategic agility	9%	36%	30%	17%	5%	3%
Strategic adaptability	10%	39%	31%	16%	6%	4%

Figure 1.7-4 Benefits of portfolio management

This is exactly the type of numbers that will get the C-suite interesting in supporting the project. Their success is measured by how well the organization does and these are the types of numbers that will get their attention.

META Group research shows that organizations that evaluate IT projects by what their business impacts are and what their potential business values will be, implement projects that result in 25 percent more improvement to the bottom line. The Commonwealth Bank in Australia does about 300 projects annually at a cost of AU $500M to $1B. If they saved even 5 percent of their project costs by implementing EPM, that's a savings of AU $25 to $50 million. These are the sort of numbers that get management's attention and need to be emphasized during your presentations to upper management.

While a rational, numbers-based approach works for upper management, lower level managers will require convincing in other areas than financial. They will be interested in how this new major system will make their jobs easier and help them expand their areas. Project managers, for example, will be able to concentrate on actually managing their projects and not on data gathering and analysis. We will discuss this more later.

Many of the organizational benefits can be calculated from a financial perspective, and this is what we're going to concentrate on in this book. But keep in mind that there can be nonfinancial benefits to a EPMS solution also.

IT industry analyst Al Passori[39] finds that:

> ... CIOs who have already implemented one or more full cycles of [portfolio management] have significantly improved their organizations' return

on IT investment, with some enterprises able to reduce costs 30%+, while improving effectiveness with enterprise wide asset deployment and management. Line-of-business (LOB) executives state they now have information never seen previously, greatly enhancing their understanding of IT investment impacts and improving decision quality.

1.7.2 How to Sell an EPMS

So let's get down to it. How can we most effectively "sell" the concept of an EPMS. There are many, many books, articles, videos, and presentations on sales techniques. There is sufficiently free information on the Internet that finding good sales approaches is not difficult (it's equally easy to find bad sales approaches, so be careful). We are not going to replicate them. What we want to understand here is that we're selling an idea, an approach that will benefit the organization in the long term, but it will impact how some stakeholders will do their day to day job.

In executive-speak, we can communicate three goals of portfolio management[40]:

Goal 1: Value maximization: To allocate resources so as to maximize the value of the portfolio in terms of some business objectives such as profitability. The values of projects to the business are determined, and projects are ranked according to this value until there are no more resources. At that point, we stop adding additional projects to the mix.

Goal 2: Balance: To achieve a desired balance of projects in terms of a number of parameters: long-term projects versus short-term ones; high-risk versus sure bets; and across various markets, technologies, and project types.

Goal 3: Strategic direction: To ensure that the final portfolio of projects reflects the business' strategy, that the breakdown of spending across projects, areas, markets, and so on, mirrors the business' strategy, and that all projects are on strategy.

The typical EPMS implementation starts with upper management (the C-level, VPs, senior directors, etc.) learning that there are benefits to it.

They will authorize a study to see what the benefits can be to the organization. Once these benefits have been defined and upper management agrees, what usually happens is that the implementation project is approved.

BUT! As we have already stated, just because upper management agrees that something needs to be done doesn't mean that anyone else wants it. A solid EPMS impacts the ability of several lower levels of management (directors, senior managers, managers, including project managers) to decide where to spend their annual budget. It also impacts the freedom of project managers to manage projects the way they want to. They will be required to spend more time keeping the project schedule updated than they did before and gives them less time to do true management. This is where the last section's discussion of Organizational Change Management becomes so important. Those are the principles you utilize when you work with these people to understand their concerns and to get their inputs to design a system that will ultimately benefit them.

In a normal large organization, each business unit comes with a certain amount of autonomy in how that unit is managed. Upper management for that unit will be oriented toward projects that primarily benefit their unit and not necessarily toward projects that benefit the organization as a whole. Their choices may duplicate or actually conflict with other business unit projects. There was a period of time when Hewlett-Packard had multiple different business units all developing printers. Business unit leaders who do best as autonomous decision makers have a very hard time following a process that takes away their ability to optimize their organization regardless of the overall benefit to the larger organization.[41]

These two groups of stakeholders will look at the proposed EPMS project and immediately decide what the impact is to them, often even before you've given your presentations or briefings. In both cases, the short-term impact is not highly positive and you can expect resistance from both groups. Middle management won't like the fact that they are not free to select their pet projects and project managers won't like the constraints on their freedom to manage projects.

For both groups, the specific benefits need to be identified and communicated to them on a very personal basis as we have mentioned. How does it benefit them doing their job on a daily basis? This is truly a sales job—you need to:

1. Propose the idea and tell them that it's important to upper management because of the long-term benefits to the organization.
2. Listen carefully to their concerns and be honest about understanding the impacts to them.
3. State what the benefits are to them. This will require meeting with them to understand how an EPMS can most benefit them. That is, get their inputs as described in the last section.
4. Get them involved in designing and implementing the EPMS. This gives them a much greater understanding of the system and how it can benefit them. People will "buy into" something they have helped create much more readily than something that is imposed on them.

The best salespeople have a deep understanding of both the product they are selling and the people they are selling to. Your "customers" here are professional managers and skilled technical people. They are very intelligent and have usually spent many years both in education and in experience to get where they are. They expect to be dealt with seriously and to have their concerns listened to. Perkiness is not an asset here. You're not selling TV sets, you're selling a process that is going to impact their work life. Listen to them, take notes on what they tell you and respond to each concern. Repetition is important here. There is marketing research that clearly shows that a message is not effective the first time, the second time, or even the third time it's heard. People start to remember the message after they've heard it seven times. That's why you see the same television advertisements over and over again (assuming you're not watching a show you've recorded and are fast-forwarding through the commercials!)

The approach to getting the highest percentage of support for the EPMS implementation is to use what the goals and expectations are that you gathered by interviewing people earlier (remember the section titled Goals and Expectations). During this effort, you determined the fundamental problems that the organization was trying to address by implementing an EPM system and can target those expectations in selling the benefits throughout the organization.

Some departments in the company learned how to justify their efforts many years ago. Marketing departments know it's critically important to show the expected financial benefits of a marketing project before it gets approved. The fact that often these numbers are not achieved does not slow them down. IT departments, by contrast, are only just now learning how to build a solid business case to justify their investments. (The noted high failure rate of IT projects does not help their cases.)

Research[42] done in the area of new product development helps underline some reasons for doing portfolio management. According to the following figure, the primary reason to do portfolio management is to maintain a competitive position, following closely by making best use of scarce resources:

Category	Value
We are risk averse, must be careful	2.7
Strategy means spending money	3.5
Gives right balance of projects	3.8
Helps to yield focus	4.1
Links to business strategy	4.1
Resources are scarce	4.2
Maintains our competitive position	4.3

Figure 1.7-5 NPD advantages to portfolio management

where 1 is not a major reason and 5 is a critical reason.

It has long been said of marketing that 50 percent of a company's marketing dollars will be wasted. You just don't know which 50 percent. So guaranteed returns on the investment is not a necessity in building justification for a project. Upper management has learned through experience that nothing is certain. You make decisions based on the best information you have at the time. It's incumbent on you to give them accurate information on the costs and benefits of the EPMS effort in order to get them to approve it.

One very important consideration to keep in mind is that in any organization, especially a mature, established one, there will be internal politics. We reward the members of that organization for doing a good job in the area that they are in by promoting them. This establishes a personal emphasis on expanding and improving the area you work in. Good managers strongly believe that their areas are highly important and will fight to grow them. But in portfolio management, the emphasis is on the overall organization, not on any one individual area. This means that each manager has to compromise their area for the higher-level benefits, in contrast to what's been important to their career growth up until now. This is not normal behavior for them.

Be honest about the downsides of beginning such an extensive change process. There will be lost productivity during the process until the employees and managers become comfortable with the new system. As shown by the graphics at the beginning of this section, there is time lost due to disruption. IBM's research (IBM 1998) has shown that on a normal workday the employees spend 60 percent of their time in productive work, 21 percent of their time on personal matters, and 19 percent of their time socializing with other employees. During a period of disruption, productive work drops to 16 percent, socializing increases to 40 percent of their daily time (did you think people would stop their socializing instead?), personal time remains at 21 percent, and retraining takes up 23 percent of their time.

Now that we have determined what the organization is looking for, identified those who are supportive and those who are critical, just how do we go about the details of actually selling the EPMS? It is critical to identify who will be supportive of the project and who will be subversive.

Story

The author led a team to implement a Program Management Office at the U.S. headquarters of a major car manufacturer. After about six months' worth of work by the team, progress had just not been made as fast as it should have been, but there were no obvious signs of anything being done wrong.

In discussions with some of the functional managers, it was discovered that one functional manager was highly supportive of the PMO effort in public meetings, but after the meetings, she would go around to other functional managers and attack the effort.

In private discussions with her (never have this meeting in public!), I determined that her major concern was that the PMO would

take away her ability to use her resources as she needed. If not now,
then in the future. To some extent that was true, this is what upper
management wanted. We spent a lot of time with her to reassure her
that she would still have full control over her resources unless they had
been approved to work on a project, and she had a vote in that. We
were never able to make her 100 percent supportive of the PMO, but
she stopped being subversive and started expressing her concerns in our
weekly meetings.

Appendix 1.7 is a file titled: Stakeholder Planning Template. We will
start by identifying the stakeholders that:

- Are involved either directly with the project
- Whose interests will be affected by the project, both positively
  and negatively, and
- Who will be impacted by the end product of the project,
  either positively or negatively (if this is a large group of end
  users, then categorize them as well as you can)

Identify the stakeholders by name, by the part of the organization
they're in, their functional role in that part of the organization, their
active role in the project (if any), how they will be affected (good or bad)
by the project, their ability to influence the project, what support we need
from them, and if their support is not what we need, how can we get it.

The level they will be affected by the project can be numbered from
1 to 10, 1 being a low level of impact and 10 being a very high level of
impact. The level of impact should not be a guess by you, it needs to come
from them. Let them tell you how they think they will be impacted by
the project.

In a similar fashion, the level of support can also be numbered from
1 to 10, with 1 being a low level of support and 10 being a high level.

Their ability to influence the project is a critical item. If they are negatively impacted by the project AND their ability to influence it is high,
this will cause you problems because you will be fighting them during the
entire implementation effort (odds are they'll win). If they are negatively
impacted BUT their ability to influence it is very low, your action plan

should be to keep them informed of the project but put your efforts into other areas. Influence can be direct influence over your schedule, budget, and resources. Indirect influence is their ability to influence the people who do have direct influence over the project.

There are many seminars, books, and articles on how to give communications that will convince people. You should be familiar with some of the more common presentation design/delivery principles so that your stakeholders are not turned against the project by an unconvincing presentation.

Law of Project Management
If you don't truly believe the project will be 100% successful, *you'll never convince anyone else of it.*

Remember that as the project manager, you know more about this project than anyone else. You have to first of all truly believe yourself that this EPMS implementation will be successful. Second of all, presenting information in a winning style is a skill all by itself. Just knowing as much as you know about EPMS is not the same as being able to educate others, especially those who might not be fully supportive.

Managers at all levels deal with so much information that the more efficiently they can grasp the benefits the quicker you will receive acceptance and buy-in. Multiple articles and books in how to present information point out that graphics is a much more effective way to communicate ideas than text is. A simple graphic such as the following will convey a lot of positive information.

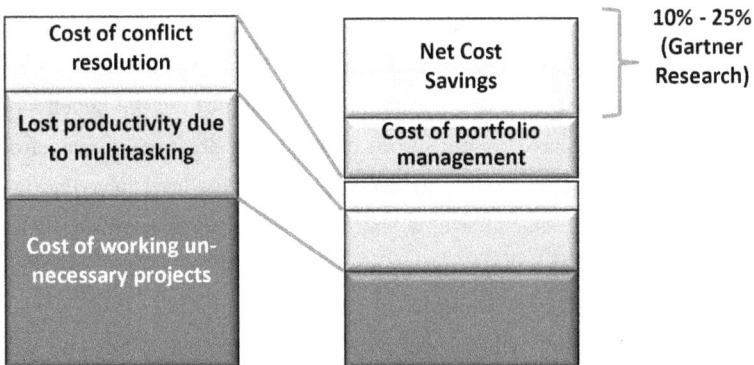

Figure 1.7-6 Example of good graphic design

1.7.3 The Political Dangers

According to a recent survey done by PMI, 67 percent of organizations surveyed have a Portfolio Management Office, and an additional 7 percent are considering one. Most of these PMOs are performing portfolio management, so the value of doing portfolio management is widely recognized by top management.

However, just because the executive level recognizes the value does not mean that this appreciation filters down through the rest of the management layers. Most projects are still selected based on what is best for the individual managers, not for the organization as a whole. Decision makers often try to go around the process to get their pet projects selected.

Story

Returning to the car manufacturer mentioned earlier, during the definition process we decided that any effort under 100 hours of work was not done as a project, but fell into daily operations. In one group, one particular manager showed up in the statistics as never having any projects, and yet we knew that that group was doing multiple projects. Upon examination we found out that this manager had multiple efforts small going on, all in the range of 90 hours or less.

He was going around the process by defining the work at a lower level than was necessary to fit into the portfolio process and so avoided losing control of his projects. Whatever rules you set up, be aware that managers will try and go around them to keep control.

Commitment across all levels of the organization are crucial to success of the effort. Part of your job is to determine if the organization is just "going through the motions" to make the Board of Directors happy or are they really trying to improve. Do managers really not see the benefits or have they just not have bought into it because they don't see the benefits.

Middle and upper managers below the executive level have enough autonomy to run their area in a way that makes most sense to them. Anything that poses a threat to that autonomy, such as taking away their ability to pick their own projects, will be resisted.

Quite often, they will not be overt in their resistance, but you will hear phrases such as: *Our high-priority project was rejected so it's obvious the process doesn't work.*

Part of your work is to understand that this will happen and be prepared for it with a strong OCM effort and sufficient communications.

1.8 MegaNews International

In the following two chapters, we will follow the project analysis and selection process for the fictional company MegaNews International.

MegaNews International

MegaNews International (MNI) is a multinational conglomerate with over 50,000 employees worldwide. 2019 revenues were over $25 billion US dollars, operating income was $3.9 B, cash and cash equivalents were $6 B, and they had $34 B in assets worldwide. Net income from all operations was $2.8 B. This was a 6 percent growth over 2018.

MegaNews worldwide holdings include ownership or has significant interest in 10 movie studios, 50 television stations, 25 cable channels, 5 satellite TV channels, 100 newspapers, 10 magazines, one publishing company, and various other associated enterprises such as real estate development and holding companies.

MegaNews International management has spent the past 6 months determining what the strategic goals are for the next 3 years. Its primary goals are the following:

1. **Financial**
   1.1 Increase net revenue by increasing profit margins by 5 percent per year
   1.2 Increase sales by 10 percent per year
2. **Customer Relationship**
   2.1 Develop stronger customer relationships
   2.2 Become a full service news provider
3. **Internal Process**
   3.1 Achieve operational excellence through a strong emphasis on process improvement and process ownership.
   3.2 Achieve project management excellence
   3.3 Improve our internal customer relationship processes

4. Employees
   4.1   Build a high performance corporate culture and values
   4.2   Recognize and accept change as a necessary part of the industry

In addition to their strategic goals, MegaNews is required to abide by the local and national laws and regulations in every country in which they deliver the news. The corporate CIO of MegaNews returned to her office after the 2019 strategic planning session was done and examined the list of proposed projects. Her calculations and analysis begin in Step 2.

Step 1 Summary

In this initial step of the process, we discussed the mental process of making decisions and how a well-designed EPMS can help identify the projects that are most beneficial to the overall organization instead of just a single part of it.

We also discussed many of the challenges of implementing a new system that will impact how projects are selected. Typical challenges in an organization include organizational politics, not having enough resources for projects, changing priorities, and the interactions of projects, programs, and portfolios as well as other challenges.

We moved into discussing how to identify the primary decision makers in an organization and how the priorities change as you move up the organization's hierarchy. Once we know who those people are, we looked at how we can identify their goals and expectations of the EPMS. This last step is critical to implementing a system that will meet their needs.

We then discussed how the business case should be developed to gain approval for the project, how we can "sell" the benefits of an EPMS to management, and by applying organizational change management how we could gain buy-in from the entire organization.

We ended this first step by introducing a fictional organization, MegaNews International, to use as an example of how to develop the filters necessary to identify the most beneficial projects for the organization.

STEP 2

Designing the Enterprise-Level Portfolio Management System

Step 2 Introduction

Alice: What road shall I take?
Cheshire cat: Where are you going?
Alice: I don't know
Cheshire cat: Then any road will do!
—From Alice in Wonderland, by Lewis Carroll

Now that the organization is ready to accept change, it's time to decide what types of projects will be part of the portfolio and how to select and prioritize them. We need to determine this before we can design the system. To do it, we need continuous feedback from the decision makers so that we can select the right filters and prioritize the projects properly to support strategy just as they would do if these decision makers were perfectly rational and objective.

This is not quite as simple as it sounds for two reasons. The first reason is that many of the executives will not agree with each other on what is most important. People at this level are used to having their decisions carried out, and your EPMS will remove their ability to pick and choose their pet projects. There will be a lot of discussion about the "right" filters to use so that pet projects are approved as well as discussions about excluding projects from the system that don't make the cut but are politically important.

We can accommodate this by developing an approach that handles different types of projects differently. We'll look at the possible categories of projects and decide how much to fund each category.

The second reason is that the strategic goals will change over time and the portfolio has to continually adapt to the changes, so the EPMS must be designed to accommodate changes. It is very rare for decision makers to kill projects even if they no longer make sense. The reasons for keeping dead projects walking is purely emotional. The EPMS will remove the emotional buy-in and more quickly kill projects that are no longer needed and tie up resources that could be better used elsewhere. The second reason is more challenging, but its impacts can be mitigated by developing a flexible approach to the selection process.

Why should we worry about the requirements of the filters? Because the filtering criteria we will build into the EPMS reflect the values of the executive level. They want to select the projects that will provided the greatest value to the organization and reject the projects that provide little value.

But, value is relative. What is highly valued to one person may be a low-value item to another. The executives will have to determine what value means before you can create the filters. The following Table 2.1[1] shows the different types of value that are important to the executive level:

Table 2.1 *Values important to executives*

Value Type		Benefit definition Financial	Examples	
			Financial	Non-financial
Tangible	Defined	Value can be predicted with certainty.	Cost reduction	Less steps in the process
	Expected	Value can be forecast based on historical data with high degree of confidence.	Increase in sales	Fulfilling the tasks more rapidly
	Anticipated	Benefits are anticipated, but its value cannot be forecasted with certainty.	Lower insurance premiums	Higher customer satisfaction
Intangible		Can be anticipated but not substantiated. Proxy (indirect) measures can be used to verify their realization.	Image enhancement. (evidence: higher number of positive comments in the press)	

We'll talk about requirements in more detail in the next chapter, but we'll discuss them here at a high level to get you started thinking about them.

There are two major cautions here:

First, DO NOT get too detailed. The EPMS should not cure cancer or bring about world peace. Keep it simple or you will get so stuck in trying to do everything that you will accomplish nothing. Because your company's infrastructure, applications, and projects have become so intertwined, you do what seems natural: You try to untangle the mess at the root.

A lot of companies have tried the same kind of "detailed, bottom-up" approach to project and portfolio management. Very few are successful. As Gartner analysts explained:[2]

> [many early customers] believed they must implement PPM* software automation at painful levels of detail (such as task- and assignment-level time reporting).... Unfortunately, many initial PPM software investments failed when this bottom-up approach to project portfolio management was chosen, due mainly to the high levels of complexity, low levels of adoption and extensive organization change management required to get the entire execution side of a project organization using the same system.

In other words, a "bottom-up" effort at PPM gets mired in the tactical details, where many hands touch projects and many infrastructure components collide, and where change is, therefore, difficult to enforce.

Second, do not include "exploration" projects in here. Exploration projects are those that lie somewhere between pure research and detailed development. This projects have a history of being high risk with a low probability of successful financial return. By contrast, the small percentage that are financially successful tend to be very successful, with large benefits from new product development and new markets. Any normal "filtering" process is much more likely to kill these projects than to approve them[3].

Finally, there are also operational aspects that need to be included during the design effort. These are covered in Step 3.

---

* Project and Portfolio Management

Step 2.1 Find the Real Needs

2.1.1 You Need Requirements

Is it important to have the requirements before you start? Only if you want to be successful and give the organization something it will actually use. In the implementation of major software systems such as Enterprise Resource Planning (ERP) applications, there is an extremely high failure rate due to new business processes being put in place but nobody using it. (Recall our section on implementing changes in an organization). Kimberly–Clark ($14 billion, 64,000 employees worldwide) installed SAP. After one week, they had fewer than 30 problems reported worldwide. Their 24/7 customer support center for the project was cut back after only two days due to the low volume of problems. Why? Because their strong requirements traceability process ensured all requirements were captured and managed. The project manager understood what the need for the new system was and satisfied those needs.

We're going to go into more detail in requirements in the next section.

Story

During one ERP audit at a US Government agency the author was leading, the audit team was asking questions about how the requirements for the new system were determined and managed. The different agencies involved each set up their own requirements teams to determine what their specific needs were and created cross-agency teams to determine common requirements such as security and access. The implementation team captured and tracked these requirements in the tool Rational Rose. They got good audit points for their disciplined approach

(Unfortunately, when we asked for a current copy of the requirements for our records, we were told that the entire requirements database was stored on one contractor's hard drive and the hard drive had crashed two weeks before. All of the data was lost because there was no digital backup. The only data available was on the last printout.)

Requirements gathering is NOT documenting what the users want, because they often do not know. Requirements gathering IS helping the users determine what they need and want.

If you cannot identify what people expect, then you cannot deliver it. In this situation, the project should be shut down immediately, rather than wasting more time and effort. A significant cause of the high failure rate of technology projects is that they cannot deliver a final product that people will actually use.

Law of Project Management
Users will start to change the requirements as soon as they understand what it is they originally asked for.

As just stated, this is the process of gathering and analyzing the business requirements. We're doing this for the business, not just to implement something new. So, our primary responsibility is to identify what those needs and expectations are and plan for how we can satisfy them.

Let's start out by defining what a requirement is. For our purposes a requirement is a specific statement of a need, sufficiently detailed that there is no misunderstanding about what is being said. Business requirements are very high level and, from the viewpoint of an engineer or a programmer, are very vague and unspecific. These high-level requirements are then taken down into much greater levels of detail in a process called requirements decomposition to the point where the technical people can design solutions to satisfy them.

When most people think about requirements, they focus on what the end product is supposed to be or to do. Is it an e-commerce website? A new car or plane? A hospital? These requirements are called functional requirements. They are directly tied to the goal of the final product. But, there are many other types of requirements. In most projects, these nonfunctional requirements will be the majority of the requirements you have to identify and manage.

At the highest level, we have the business needs. We obtain these in a variety of methods that we'll talk about shortly. The next level down is where we break out the functional requirements (what is it that this end product should do) and a variety of nonfunctional requirements:

"ilities"—Maintainability, reliability, upgradability, sustainability, and so on. For the EPMS, we really don't care about these, except as they apply to any tools we might buy or build.

Performance—How well does this new system perform? If I send a request for information, how fast and how accurately does it respond to my request? Is the system available 24/7, or are there planned outages for maintenance? This is a really critical category for the users.

Privacy and security—How secure is the data? Are there levels of security so that different users have different levels of access? Are there built-in privacy protections?

Usability—This is the interface between the users and the system itself. While many developers consider this a low-priority requirement, the reality is that most complex systems (such as ERP systems) fail because the users won't use the system once it is installed. It is actually a very high-priority requirement to make the system easy to use.

Health and safety—For the purposes of defining the EPMS requirements, we don't have to worry about this category.

Environmental—Another category we won't worry about for our EPMS. It will not have any environmental impact.

For the PMO itself, the requirements tree might look something like this:

These are the requirements that you must discover through the requirements gathering processes we will talk about later. Once you have a good handle on these, now you can start designing the system and assessing any commercial tools you will purchase. Having collected this level of requirements, now you can decompose them into more details and document the more detailed and more technical requirements:

- Specific business processes
- Detailed architecture and technical design requirements
- Integration and Test (I&T) needs
- Interface requirements (internal to the EPMS and between the EPMS and the organization)
- Implementation requirements showing how you're going to put the system into operations

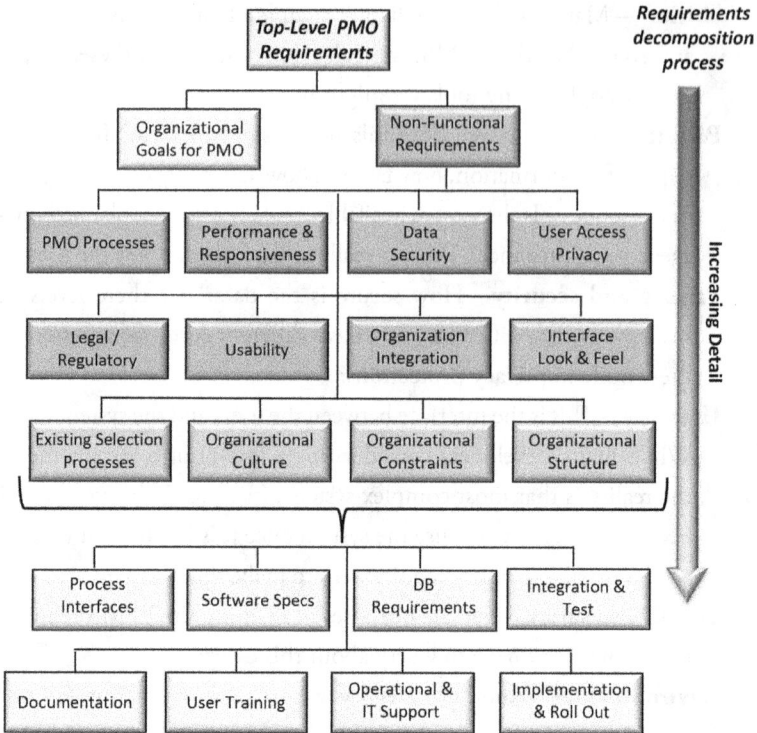

Figure 2.1-1 Requirements decomposition tree

And then finally, how are you going to document the system? How are people going to operate it? How are you going to train them in the system and in their new jobs?

Notice that there are requirements here in the form of constraints. When designing the new EPMS, you must take into account the existing processes for selecting and prioritizing projects. If the new EPMS gives radically different results than the existing system, it will be dismissed as useless. Organizational constraints, such as the communications culture or resource limitations, also need to be included in the design. The organizational structure is another area to consider. An EPMS designed for a fully projectized organization is very different than one in a purely functional organization.

Each EPMS must be designed with regard to the existing organization, its goals, its culture, and its constraints. This varies by industry and by the specific organization. Each is different. Let's look at the large construction/engineering industry for example. The projects owners engage in are generally high value (therefore very risky organizationally) and long term (increasing the risks). What are the evaluation criteria and constraints they typically concern themselves with in selecting which projects to accept?[4]:

Financial
- Life cycle return on investment (ROI)
- Return on assets employed
- Net present value of cash flows (NPV)
- Payback period
- Total capital expenditures
- Product/project gross margins

Market
- Market share
- Market growth and duration
- Period of profitable production product flexibility
- Customer impacts

Strategic
- Flexibility
- Resiliency
- Contribution to overall portfolio performance
- Enablement of Strategic Business Objective (SBO) achievement
- Enablement of other portfolio projects
- Critical resource utilization

Sustainability or triple bottom-line-focused criteria
- Economic

Social
- Community impacts
- Capacity building
- New industry/business creation

- Stakeholder support
- Workforce impacts
- Environmental, health and safety
- Airborne emissions
- Water consumption
- Discharge water quality
- Environmental degradation
- Worker health and safety
- Public health and safety

Risk

- Economic or market uncertainties
- Other event risks
- Financing uncertainties
- Cost uncertainties
- Schedule uncertainties
- Labor risks
- Stakeholder risks
- Sovereign and legislative risks
- Political risks
- Technology risks
- Intellectual property risks
- Business model risks
- Project execution risks

You can see why the BOGGSAT approach mentioned in the Preface would have severe limitations in selecting which projects to do when you take into account all of the constraints and our limited decision-making capabilities.

2.1.2 Requirement Priorities

Once you have gathered the needs of upper management, you take the answers you're given and compile and analyze them. Did they give you needs that you can satisfy? Do any of the needs given by different managers contradict needs from other managers? Are there needs that are duplicated? Once you have removed the duplicates and resolved any conflicts, meet as a group with the managers again and present the list of requirements for their approval.

At this point, you will start prioritizing the requirements. They will want everything they told you, but almost never is there enough time and resources to do everything. So, the requirements need to be prioritized into:

Mandatory

A mandatory requirement is an essential feature of the EPMS. Failure to implement the requirement means the system will not meet management's needs. All mandatory requirements must be implemented in the first planned release.

Highly Desirable

A highly desirable requirement describes a requirement that is important to the effectiveness and efficiency of the system. The missing features cannot easily be provided by software or processes.

Lack of inclusion of an important feature may affect management's satisfaction with the EPMS, but the planned release will not be delayed due to lack of any highly desirable feature. Think about implementing these in the first upgrade if you can't do them now.

Desirable

A desirable requirement describes a management need that, if implemented, will have a negligible impact on the functionality of the system.

Desirable requirements would be more likely than highly desirable requirements to be deferred or deleted if time or resources become scarce.

Optional

An optional requirement describes a requirement or features that will be used less frequently, or for which reasonably efficient workarounds can be achieved. The planned release will not be delayed due to lack of an optional priority feature. It's a "nice to have" feature, rather than something that is absolutely needed.

Some consultants use the simple "MoSCoW" rule. The acronym stands for Must, Should, Could, and Would:

- M—Must complete this requirement to meet management's needs
- S—Should do this requirement if possible, but project success does not rely on it
- C—Could do this requirement if it does not affect anything else on the project
- W—Would like to have this requirement later, but cannot be done now

Priorities must be determined through constant coordination with the top-level decision makers. It is their priorities that have to be built into the EPMS. But, they must be made to understand that there are compromises that will be necessary.

If management tells you that all their requirements are equally important, push back and ask them what could be cut out if there are schedule problems or cost over-runs? As a general guideline, no more than 25 percent of the requirements should be mandatory. These are the core requirements. These are the ones you concentrate your resources on implementing.

One common approach, when you have too many requirements to satisfy with the resources and schedule you have, is to develop the EPMS in multiple stages. This is a highly recommended approach. Satisfy the primary requirements first, then once the basis of the EPMS is implemented, develop a follow-on project to satisfy remaining requirements. This has the benefit of providing a more useful set of requirements during the follow-on project because people now can see what they got in the first rollout.

2.1.3 Requirements Documentation and Management

Law of Project Management
Always document your requirements, a verbal requirement isn't worth the paper it's written on.

Requirements *must* be documented. This is not negotiable. Never accept a verbal request for a requirement or a change to a requirement. If you do, in six months, what you remember will be different than what the requestor remembers. And, because they own the requirements, not you, you will have implemented the wrong requirement. If a stakeholder meets you in the hallway and asks you for a new requirement, always follow up the conversation with an e-mail documenting what you heard. Even better, ask them to fill out a requirements request sheet. That way it is in their own words.

Story

At one US Federal government organization the author led an audit team doing an independent review of an ERP package that was being installed. When interviewing the CIO the question was asked: "Do you accept verbal requirements?" The CIO emphatically said no, only written requirements were accepted by the project. The next day the author interviewed the project manager and asked the same question "Do you accept verbal requirements?" The project manager's reply? "Sure, we get them all the time. No problem."

There is one additional advantage to having stakeholders fill out a request sheet if they want to add or to change a requirement. Software history shows that as much as 50 percent of requirements requests go away if they have to fill out a document to request it!

It is best not to put all the requirements into one document. There should be a business requirements document that captures the pure business-level requirements (functional, performance, and maybe some other requirements). This document is best developed as a joint effort between the project manager (or project team members) and Business Analysts. This document is signed by upper management before any architecture or design work is done.

For each requirement, managing it requires the following information be captured and documented:

- Type of requirement—functional, performance, security, and so on

- Design implementations—in hardware, software, processes
- Priority of the requirement—mandatory, highly desirable, or desirable
- Source of the requirement—who gave you the requirement (in case you ever need clarification of it)
- What change requests have been opened against it
- Which test cases test it
- What is the current status—implemented, in process, not started
- Which phase it will be implemented in (for a multiphase implementation)

This can be done very simply in a requirements management tool, a small database, or even in a spreadsheet. Note that documenting and maintaining this will require some administrative resources. This tracking can be done in a Requirements Traceability Matrix that captures not only this information but in which the requirements are numbered in such a way it is easy to identify which requirements have been decomposed from higher-level requirements.

Requirements are critically important, because everything else in the project is based on capturing, managing, and understanding them. We'll talk more about requirements for our EPM system in the next step.

Step 2.2 Design Considerations

In designing the EPMS, we will take into consideration all work in the organization, not just projects in specific areas such as information technology (IT). Why? Because there is work outside of projects that can significantly impact project success. Blichfeldt et al.[5] have shown there is an impact due to projects that are outside the EPMS:

Although companies manage project portfolios concordantly with project portfolio theory, they may experience problems in the form of delayed projects, resource struggles, stress, and a lack of overview. Based on a research project compromised of 128 in-depth interviews in 30 companies, we propose that a key reason why companies do not do well in relation to project portfolio management (PPM) is that PPM often only covers a subset of on-going projects, while projects that are not subject to PPM tie up resources that initially were dedicated to PPM projects. We address and discuss the dilemma of wanting to include all projects in PPM, and aiming at keeping the resource and cognitive burden of doing PPM at a reasonable level.

There are going to be a lot of different considerations that you will take into account as you design the EPMS. One of the major design influences is the type, or types, of project that the new system will be dealing with. Once we understand the types of projects, we can decide on the filtering criteria to filter in all possible project types and the scoring system to select the most beneficial projects within the different types.

Obviously, not all projects are the same or even the same type. This is important because different types of projects will require different justifications and filters that we need to build into our system. In order to obtain the largest number of beneficial projects across multiple parts of the organization, part of what we need to do is to balance out the different asset classes, from short-term IT projects to expensive, strategic capital expenditure (CAPEX) projects.

In Section 2.2, we're going to cover some of the core topics in the design of the EPMS—how to balance out the different classes, types of projects, criteria for filtering them, and finally, determining how to score them. We will go into the detailed design of the system in Chapter 3.

It is important to ensure that the portfolio is balanced among the different types of projects. According to Kendall and Rollins[6],

Every organization has two constraints that limit how many projects can be active at any point in time. One is the amount of money the organization has or is willing to invest in change. The other is the organization's strategic resources – the one most in demand across many projects or the most heavily loaded resource across most projects. This determines how many projects can be active at any point in time.

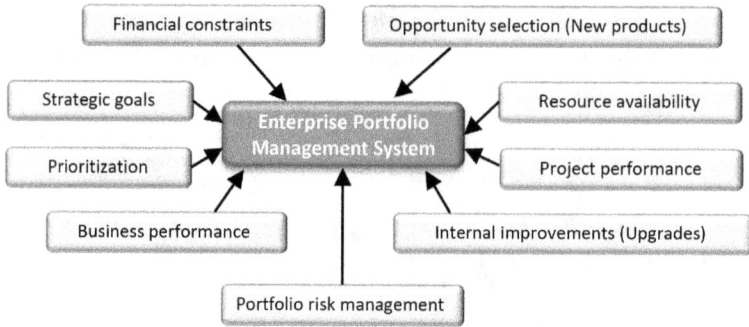

Figure 2.2-1 EPMS inputs

Each portfolio, whether at a business unit or at the top-level organization, should be reasonably well balanced to minimize risk. Some parts of the organization, such as the IT department, are going to have lower-level portfolios that are exclusively within one area. The larger organization should provide more overall balance to the portfolio.

By inputting the data required by the EPMS, you are expanding on the business case for each proposed project. One decision that must be made early in the selection effort is to determine whether the effort is worthwhile for every project. While this may sound strange because the whole purpose of the EPMS is to select projects, there may be circumstances where it may not be worthwhile.

If the project is below a certain dollar or effort amount, it may not be worthwhile to filter it through the EPMS. For projects under 100 hours, as an example, the overhead associated with the EPMS may not be worth the effort.

Other projects, such as those mandated by regulatory requirements, are guaranteed to be done regardless of the financial benefits. However, they should still be entered into the portfolio so that their risks and impacts to other projects can be identified.

Some projects are research-oriented projects that may, or may not, produce a marketable-able result. They take time and resources, but it is extremely challenging to schedule them or prioritize them. We will discuss these types of projects in more detail later. These are sometimes called innovation or exploration projects and can produce highly innovative new products. Despite their management challenges, they can be the most critically important for the organization's future.

The categories of projects must be decided by management in the way that makes most sense for the organization. A software development company will select and prioritize projects that make the most sense from their business perspective. Other organizations will select different categories and priorities. The international mining company Anglo-American has created the following categories for their own projects as shown in the following table.

Table 2.2 Anglo-American project categories

Anglo definition	Category	Subcategory	Description
Major Project	Expansion		Material expansions or increase in production capacity
	Replacement		Replacement of existing production capacity
Stay in Business Project	Replacement (of equipment)	General replacement— simple	Replacement of existing commodity equipment— single item as part of planned maintenance or potential failure or legislated upgrade
		General replacement— complex	Replacement of existing equipment/groups of commodity equipment across multiple sites as part of planned maintenance or potential failure
		General replacement— systems and plant	Replacement of existing systems and plant that my involve multiple vendors and/or design and/or construction

(Continued)

Table 2.2 (Continued)

Anglo definition	Category	Subcategory	Description
	Risk	Safety risk	Replacement of plant and equipment (including IT systems) that has failed or is proved to be about to fall and/or will materially impact safety
		Legal risk	Replacement of plant and equipment (including IT systems) that is no longer legally complaint
		Business risk	Replacement of plant and equipment (including IT systems) that has failed or is proved to be about to fail and will materially impact operations
	Business improvement	Business improvement—plant and equipment	New or replacement of plant and equipment with alternatives intended to improve business efficiency/effectiveness
		Business improvement—business processes	Any nonoperational initiative intended to improve business efficiency/effectiveness or achieve a strategic priority objective
IT projects	IT system development	IT system development	Any IT initiative intended to improve business efficiency/effectiveness or achieve a strategic priority objective

In order to minimize the influence of strong stakeholders who are primarily interested in advancing projects that benefit only their part of the organization, a questionnaire should be developed for each asset class that identifies and prioritize those projects that best support the overall organization. An example of such a questionnaire is shown in Appendix 2.2.

2.2.1 Asset Classes

In business, assets are everything of value that is owned by an organization. The two major asset classes are tangible assets and intangible assets. Tangible assets are items such as financial assets and fixed assets. Financial assets include accounts receivable, bonds, stocks and cash, and other monetary items; fixed assets include such items as buildings and equipment.

Intangible assets are nonphysical resources and rights that have a value to the firm because they give the firm some kind of advantage in the marketplace. Examples of intangible assets are goodwill, copyrights, trademarks, and patents.

From a portfolio standpoint, we are interested in any project that needs to be funded and completed by the organization. Some of the projects are going to produce tangible assets such as new facilities or a new product for sale. Some of the projects are going to produce intangible assets such as a new IT infrastructure or business process improvements. All of them take time and resources.

Projects, regardless of what type of asset they produce, are part of the portfolio and must go through the project selection process. The only exceptions are mandatory projects that we will discuss later.

We are going to classify the universe of projects into four categories: infrastructure projects, operations-related projects, new product development (NPD) projects, and capital investment projects. There are other approaches to categorizing projects, and not all of these categories may apply to your particular organization. That's alright. Select the categories that apply to you. Delete the others from the analysis, and add any new ones that are not covered by these. For example, the U.S. National Aeronautics and Space Administration's (NASA) Jet Propulsion Laboratory (JPL) in California has five criteria for filtering projects[7]:

1. New capability
2. Maintaining existing capability
3. Innovation projects
4. Visionary projects
5. Compliance projects

The projects are reviewed on an annual basis and adjusted to meet organizational priorities. The distribution of JPL's effort is shown here:

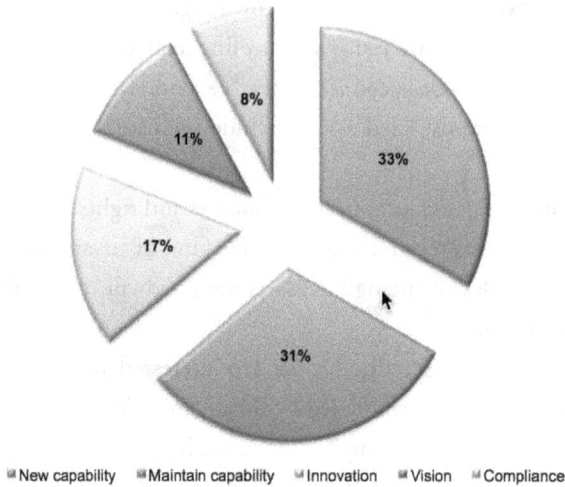

Figure 2.2-2 JPL's project distribution

JPL is a government organization heavily devoted to research and engineering projects. For categories normal to private industry, let us look at four categories and draw them visually:

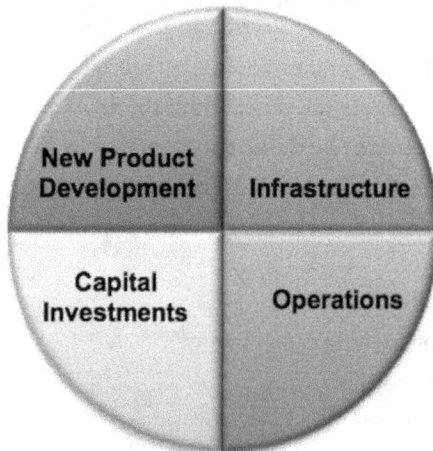

Figure 2.2-3 Business project categories

Infrastructure projects are crucial to the efficient running of the organization. This class includes both IT projects and non-IT projects, such as facility maintenance projects or equipment maintenance projects. For many organizations, the majority of infrastructure projects are IT projects. These are also the most likely to be challenged and to suffer scope creep, schedule slippage, and cost over-runs. We'll talk more about all of these later.

Operational projects are projects for specific operational groups such as marketing, HR, or legal. Marketing projects can improve brand image and corporate visibility and have great potential benefits, but they tend to be high cost projects with "soft" benefits—benefits that are difficult to quantify. Human resource (HR) projects are lower cost and low risk, but may be mandated by regulation and will fall into the type of project we will later call "mandatory."

Other classes of operational projects include business process improvement projects. These can be highly beneficial, but are also very risky due to impacts on how people work.

New product development (NPD) projects are those that produce a new product that the company can market. These are highly risky, with up to 90 percent of new products failing in the marketplace. But, they can also be highly rewarding, with the 10 percent of products that are commercially successful compensating for those that fail. This is an especially critical area for new technology-based firms (NTBFs)[8], which tend to be entrepreneurial, do not have a long history of operational development, and tend to use project management techniques far more readily than old established organizations.

Projects for NPD follow the company's NPD philosophy: first to market, fast follower, or low-cost leader. Companies that produce a brand-new product can obtain very high profits from it, but also face high development costs for a product that may not be successful. Companies that use a fast follower approach wait until a competitor comes out with a new product and waits to see if it is commercially successful, then comes out with a competitive product. Think of Apple's iPod followed by Microsoft's Zune.

Companies that utilize a low-cost leader approach wait until a product's market matures, and then undercut everyone on price. This is low risk, but also highly competitive because many other companies will be doing the same thing. Companies that use this approach rarely add any new features, but are highly skilled at cost-cutting the manufacturing of products.

Capital investment (CAPEX) projects that those that cost a lot of money with no short-term payback. These are the projects that produce new manufacturing factories, new aluminum plants, or new oil refineries. They cannot be justified in the same way that an IT upgrade is justified. We'll talk more about these later in this chapter.

2.2.2 Balancing Asset Classes and Capital Rationing

If every asset were equally important to the organization, the portfolio may be represented as shown in this figure:

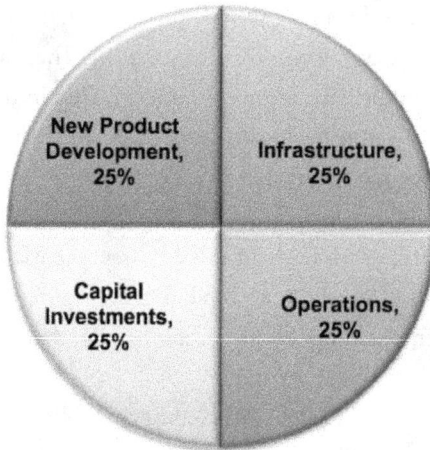

Figure 2.2-4 Balanced portfolio

However, we know that no organization will ever have a completely balanced portfolio, except temporarily by accident. Upper management, when they are laying out the annual budgets, will emphasize those areas that support the organization's strategic goals.

Removed from the following calculations are the money allocated for daily operations. In most organizations, the operations money will require the majority of the funds. These are funds that must be expended just to keep the organization going and are not available for projects. We're going to take operational budgets out of any consideration and only concentrate on budgets allocated for project work.

All projects cost money and people, and there is a limited supply of both. Investments in projects are balanced out with investments in less risky financial instruments such as investing in certificates of deposit (CDs) or bonds. How the organization rations its capital is an activity that takes a lot of time and effort by the executives to ensure that the risks inherent in projects is balanced out by the more assured returns of safe investments. Part of capital rationing is also involved with just what types of projects the money should be spent on, the topic of much of this chapter.

The executives in the finance department are charged with spending the organization's money in a way that provides the greatest benefit while balancing risk. If all financial decisions were left to the accountants, the money would be invested in savings accounts, Certificates of Deposit (CDs), and in safe financial investments. Rarely are these people comfortable in investing in projects whose outcome is uncertain and which have higher risks. Fortunately, the financial department is only one voice in how the organization allocates its financial resources. If it were left to the finance department, the organization would never create new products because there are safer places to put the money. Organizations that put too much of their money into "safe" investments eventually lose out to more innovative competitors.

The money needed for operations is highly dependent on the outside business environment and is, therefore, reactive to changes in that environment. In a growing economy, organizations put more money into growth and select more projects. In a downsizing economy, organizations pull money away from growth-related projects and use the money to improve internal efficiencies, to simply survive, or not spend money on projects at all. The COVID-19 crisis caused most organizations to stop spending money on anything except survival.

Graphic representations of the portfolio are more informative to management than simply stating "We're putting 30 percent of our money into infrastructure projects." They show quickly when the portfolio is not balanced in the way management thought.

2.2.2.1 Growth-Oriented Portfolio—Version A

An organization that is interested in future growth might take more of the project funds away from operational areas and safe investments and use the money to fund NPD or for increased capital expenditures. The pie chart looks like:

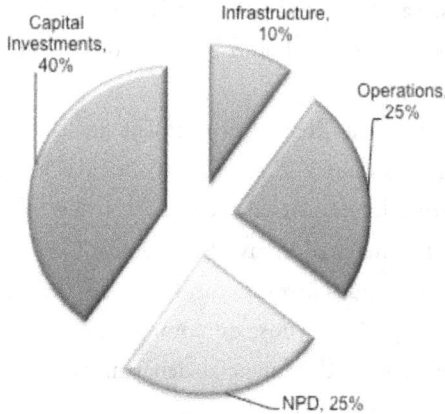

Figure 2.2-5 Growth-oriented portfolio Option A

In this allocation, money has been moved to new product development by reducing the funding for operational projects. Infrastructure and capital investment projects have been left at existing levels. Unfortunately, many organizations tend to be short-sighted when it comes to decreasing expenses and tend to reduce departments such as HR or corporate training. Good in the short term, not so good in the long term. Blindly removing money from operations to put it somewhere else just increases inefficiencies in those parts of the organization that have been cut back. If money is to be taken from operations, it should be done by increasing operational efficiencies and using the savings to fund other works.

2.2.2.2 Growth-Oriented Portfolio—Version B

A company that is growing rapidly because of high sales volumes on its existing product line just needs to expand its facilities. These are capital investment projects and are expensive. They can be high risk or low risk depending on whether the economy is moving up or down.

The allocations might look like this:

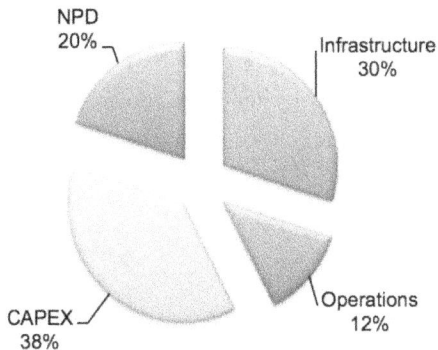

Figure 2.2-6 Growth-oriented portfolio Option B

2.2.2.3 Growth-Oriented Portfolio—Version C

In the allocation shown here, both operational projects and infrastructure projects have been reduced, with more emphasis being placed on NPD and capital investments.

This is a typical arrangement in a rapidly growing economy, where companies are going to heavily fund NPD and as well as new facilities.

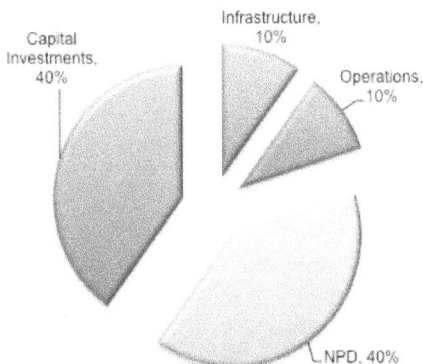

Figure 2.2-7 Growth-oriented portfolio Option C

2.2.2.4 Cost-Savings-Oriented Portfolio

When the economic conditions are on a downward slope, organizations have shown a strong tendency to reduce funding for NPD and for new facilities and either cut out all projects totally or put money into projects that increase internal efficiencies and produce cost savings. Or, as mentioned before, simply cut all project work no matter how beneficial. While the short-term financial benefits of cutting all costs are easily quantifiable, the long-term damage to the organization is less quantifiable but no less real. Multiple studies have shown that organizations that emphasize cost-cutting during economic downturns do significantly worse than their competitors once the economy starts picking, up as it always does.

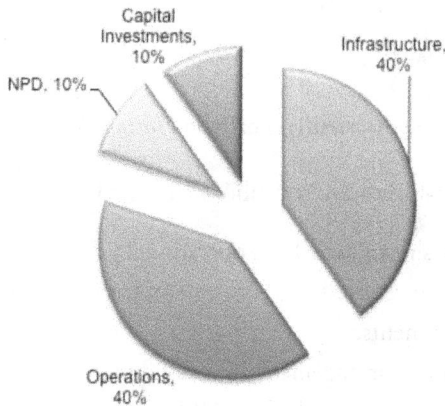

Figure 2.2-8 Cost-savings portfolio

Portfolio Alignments

The aforementioned allocations are generic and could be considered starting points for discussions with the decision makers. The exact allocations will be determined by the executive committee and will be dependent on both strategic goals and current economic conditions. As either one of these changes, the portfolio will be adjusted as needed.

2.2.3 Three Project Priorities

While there are a large number of projects that an organization can do within each asset class, we can divide them into just three basic types:

1. Regulatory-driven ("killer" projects)
2. Maintenance projects
3. Discretionary projects

Each asset category mentioned earlier can contain any one of these types of projects.

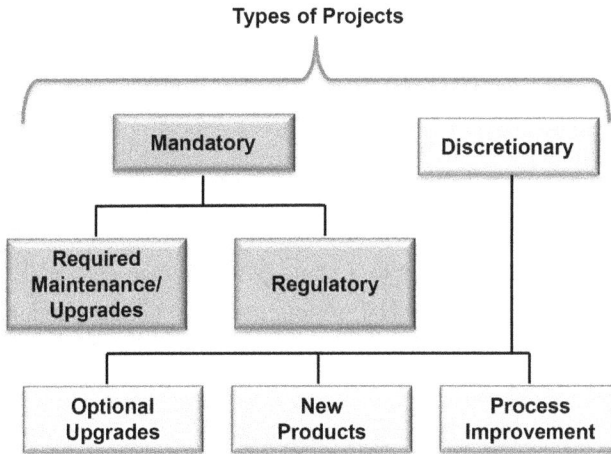

Types of Projects

```
                    Mandatory              Discretionary

        Required                Regulatory
      Maintenance/
        Upgrades

        Optional        New              Process
        Upgrades      Products         Improvement
```

Figure 2.2-9 Project types

2.2.3.1 Regulatory-Driven Projects

Mandatory projects are "must-do" projects. We have no choice. They disrupt our carefully planned existing work. Regulatory-driven projects are driven by changes in laws and regulations and are mandatory if they apply to you. Consider the HIPAA (Health Insurance Portability and Accountability Act) legislation that was passed by the U.S. Congress in 1996. Part II of HIPAA required that a patient's privacy be protected in several ways, one of which was their medical data. This mandated that all companies providing medical-related services, including insurance companies, had adequate security and privacy processes in their IT system to protect patient medical data. Implementing this new requirement disrupted the existing planned project work. With the passage of the Affordable Care Act (Obamacare), the industry faced many more mandatory projects as the full effects of the law are understood. Worse, as the act was being debated in the courts and with a proposed repeal by the subsequent administration, there is a great deal of uncertainty about whether companies should comply or not. The massive failure of the Enron company in 2001 led to mandatory changes in forcing executives to approve all of the financial statements, leading to significant process and IT changes in publicly owned organizations.

Regulatory changes can have unexpected consequences, so be prepared to make changes to the prioritized list of projects when those unexpected consequences are discovered. Because HIPAA made your medical data private, what is the impact of new technologies, such as wearable wristwatches, that monitor blood pressure, heartbeat, and other personal medical data and upload it to a cloud-based storage service? Does the storage service have to meet HIPAA requirements? Changes to long-term priorities can happen in cases like this, and those changes can be disruptive to our careful plans.

U.S. credit reporting companies such as Experian, Trans Union, and Equifax are subject to national-level legislation through federal legislation as well as dealing with separate legislation from each of the 50 states. Because these rules are coded into the software (leading to hundreds of business rules that must be checked for every credit report request), any change to any of the regulations leads to a considerable amount of work to find out where that existing rule is coded in the software and determine if the new change impacts any of the other hundreds of rules.

Companies that are subject to any regulatory-related controls must be aware of the possibilities of such interruptions and prepare accordingly. Regulatory-drive projects are sometimes referred to as killer projects because they basically kill any projects you already have in work or as "Orange Jumpsuit" projects because orange is the color of many jail uniforms—you don't do the project, you go to jail, or at the least, pay heavy fines.

The right solution to the problem of disruption is for organizations that are subject to frequent changes in laws and regulations to compensate by not selecting so many projects that their personnel are allocated 100 percent of the time. They should leave some schedule room so that when a regulatory project comes in, they can start on it with minimal disruption to existing work. However, politically, this is often not palatable to upper management. They feel that people should be working on as many projects as possible and just deal with the schedule disruptions created by regulatory changes and the loss of morale caused by canceling a lot of projects when the regulations change.

2.2.3.2 Maintenance Projects

Maintenance projects fall between regulatory-driven projects and those that are completely discretionary. Some maintenance projects are mandatory. These include work such as commercial aircraft maintenance and refurbishments of processing lines in chemical plants. Both of these types of projects are required to ensure that the equipment remains safely operational for long periods of time. These types of projects are predictable and preplanned and therefore not disruptive to planned work.

Other maintenance projects fall into the category of discretionary. An IT department that plans on upgrading Windows or implementing the latest Oracle updates has a choice as to whether it does so and, if it chooses to upgrade, when the most appropriate time is. These types of maintenance projects can be preplanned and again are not disruptive to planned work. They should be included in the selection, prioritization, and planning processes that we will discuss next for discretionary projects. The cost justification for these projects must be done carefully so that only really needed projects get approved. Because these types of projects are not strictly mandatory, they are simply cost sinks and do not generate any new revenue. The best that can be said about them is that they may improve productivity, a thing that can be very hard to quantify. The maintenance projects that are discretionary should be treated as all other discretionary projects are and justified as to their benefits.

Emergency maintenance projects, such as equipment breakdowns, are those that are required to be done immediately to fix a problem. They are often highly disruptive to planned work but are unpredictable and so do not figure into our discussions here. However, in an environment where such breakdowns happen, such as a steel mill, a complex chemical processing plant, or even a complex IT network, the best approach again is not to overload people with planned work, so there is some overhead in the schedule to accommodate outages.

Story

The author spent some time helping develop project management processes at the Qatar Ammonia and Fertilizer Company (QAFCO) in Messaieed, Qatar. QAFCO is one of the world's largest producers of urea and ammonia, both used in fertilizers. There were three major sets of processing lines, called trains, that took the locally abundant natural gas and processed it into the final products.

The processing required high temperatures and pressures of corrosive gases and liquids to produce the urea and ammonia. The job of the Systems Engineering department was to plan regular outages to replace major pieces of processing equipment before they wore out or broke to keep the trains processing as efficiently and as safely as possible. However, each train had a senior manager in charge who was bonused based on the train's output. Their goal was to keep the trains running as hard and as long as possible. As you would expect, there were a significant number of arguments about when maintenance should be scheduled.

2.2.3.3 Discretionary Projects

Discretionary projects are mostly what this book is about. These are the projects that an organization has full choice as to whether it does them or not. Categories of discretionary projects include:

- Capital investment projects
- NPD projects
- Infrastructure projects
- Operational projects

- Process improvements
- Discretionary maintenance projects
- Dedicated marketing, HR, and other department-specific projects

Capital investment projects include items like new facilities, property purchases, or major machinery and equipment purchases. These are high-cost purchases and are usually done during good economic times to increase capacity. New facility projects are also long-term investments that will tie up funds for several years. The cost of these is generally large enough that only top-level management can make these commitments. These tend to be low-risk projects that will provide substantial returns as long as economic conditions stay stable during a period long enough to justify their expenditures. If economic conditions change rapidly, these projects can lead to equally substantial losses.

Capital investment projects are sometimes referred to as CAPEX projects because of their high dollar value (hundreds of millions or billions of dollars) and long return on investment (often years). These projects are better managed using program management techniques rather than pure project management techniques. Industry terminology is confusing by often referring to these efforts as projects rather than their true descriptions as programs. Despite the confusion, we will follow industry practices and refer to them as projects. You should be able to tell from the context whether it is a simple project or a true program.

These kinds of projects consume large amounts of money and a lot of organizational resources. They are typically approved only at the very top levels of management, and the filtering criteria need to be design to approve them in stages. The first approval should be for the project overall as a strategic goal, and later approvals should be for each individual stage gate to decide whether or not the financial numbers look good enough to proceed compared to the risks.

This size/complexity of project is susceptible to being killed any time the numbers don't look promising. In Fall 2013, Anglo-American Mining backed out of a joint venture to develop a gold/copper mine in Alaska at the end of Phase 3 because the risks of doing the project and the long timeframes for revenue did not look promising. They backed out of the project after spending $500 million in the early stages. That takes more courage than most executives have.

NPD, including research and development (R&D) projects and other exploratory projects, are highly risky and initial revenue from such projects may not happen for years if ever. History shows that the majority of new products do not become financially profitable. However, the small percentage that do can provide enough profit to more than make up for the losing projects. Some companies, such as Minnesota Mining and Manufacturing Company (3M), devote a large proportion of their financial assets to supporting NPD projects. Only a small percentage of them become profitable, but many of those become highly profitable (think of Sticky Notes). 3M typically spends about 5.5 percent of its operating expenses in R&D projects, but that is 5.5 percent of U.S. $3 billion in income from operations, a significant amount of money[†]. Google is another organization that allows people to work on their own pet projects, leading to many of the newer products that Google has released.

Of course, it's not just how much money you spend, it's how you spend it. Between 2004 and 2009, Apple Computer obtained a 72 percent growth in revenues from their $4.6 billion R&D investment[‡]. By comparison, Microsoft Corporation spent $31 billion during the same period and obtained only a 32 percent growth from R&D, Cisco spent $19 billion and got a 25 percent growth, while Intel Corporation spent $23 billion but received no revenue growth from their R&D investment.

How did Apple do so much better than these other companies? A strong NPD culture and processes allow them to filter among many possible projects to select the best ones. Google also has such a innovation-oriented culture. Most of its new product have come from individual research by employees who came up with an idea and were given the freedom to work on it. In 2019, their R&D spending had grown to $16.217 billion.

Best practice in the NPD arena is to use a stage-gate process. On a regular basis, during the early phases (called stages) of the project, a review is held to assess whether the project will satisfy strict profitability criteria.

[†] 3rd Quarter 2008 SEC 10-Q filing.

[‡] http://informationweek.com/blog/main/archives/2010/04/post_23.html

If not, the project is killed and the resources allocated to more promising projects. Each project must go through several of these gates in order to continue. It is not unusual for a company to kill 50 percent of their projects at the early gates. This winnows down the large number of projects to those that are most likely to be winners in the consumer market.

As Maniak[3] points out, there are actually two benefits to these risky exploration projects. The first benefit, and the most obvious one, is that the final product that comes out of such a project is often highly innovative and can produce significant market advantage to the company. At least for a while, it is the only company producing such a product, and anyone who wants the product must buy it from them and only them. Examples include personal electronic devices such as the Sony Walkman or the much more recent Apple iPod.

Infrastructure projects can be reasonably divided into IT projects and non-IT projects. There has been a strong interest shown in portfolio management by many IT departments in the past few years because of the increasing amount of IT work being done as projects. According to research[9] performed by PriceWaterhouseCoopers, IT-related productivity has been declining since the early 2000s even while the costs of IT have been increasing. More and more IT spending is going to maintain existing systems rather than benefiting the organization. This makes justifying IT projects much more difficult.

A strong emphasis on reducing costs has led to more projects to improve IT effectiveness but with no increase in the personnel to do the projects. More people are multitasking with concomitant reductions in productivity and an increase in the percentage of IT projects that are late and over budget. Portfolio management is a perfect solution to this type of an environment. Fewer, but more critical projects will be selected, waste and duplication will be reduced, costs will be reduced. Fewer mistakes will be made, quality will improve as will schedules and costs, and a higher percentage of projects will be completed successfully. No wonder, IT departments have been looking so strongly at EPM systems.

Non-IT infrastructure projects include anything required to keep the organizations facilities and equipment operating and usable. This category will include facilities upgrades and equipment repair/maintenance/ upgrade projects. It may also include equipment purchase and installation projects that are not sufficiently large to be considered a major capital expense.

Operational improvements form another category of discretionary projects. These are done to improve operations by increasing efficiencies or to support one particular department. The marketing department, for example, runs marketing and sales campaigns as a project—identifying the goals, planning out the work and the budget, assigning resources, and monitoring how successful the effort is.

Included in operational improvements are Business Process Improvement (BPI) projects. In the past 25+ years (since the re-engineering trend in the early/mid-1990s), these have become increasingly important to companies. These are efforts to improve internal efficiencies in how we operate, especially since the economic downturn that began in 2008.

These are a peculiar type of project compared to more "normal" projects such as IT projects or NPD projects. These can be very complex, long-lasting projects and can be fraught with dangers. There are two reasons BPI projects have problems: the first is that business processes affect how people work, and any time you change people's work, you will face resistance as we talked about earlier (remember the story about the utility in the last section?). The second is that all business processes link to other business processes. There is no such thing as an isolated business process. If you change one, you have to change the other processes that interact with it, and your project will very quickly grow out of control unless you put strict boundaries around which processes you are changing and which ones you are not. This is needed so that people will not assume you are changing processes that you are not. In the project charter, you should have a section on project exclusions specifically stating what process you are changing and whether or not you are changing the interfaces to other processes.

We see that there is a large variety of projects an organization can undertake, but they fall within just a few broad types. The type of project that lends itself best to being managed through portfolio management techniques is the discretionary project. The organization has a full choice whether to do this project or put its money somewhere else.

The following insert is about a fictional company, MegaNews International, whose motto is "We don't just report the news, we create the news!" The Corporate chief information officer (CIO) has just returned from the annual strategic planning session held at corporate HQ in Australia and finds a list of projects on his desk. How does he select the "right" projects?

Table 2.3 MegaNews project options

MegaNews International
As stated at the end of Step 1, the CIO of MegaNews has been given a list of proposed projects for her IT department to complete. She has called her senior staff together and lays out the following projects:

A. New privacy laws that will take effect in 12 months in Europe require us to strengthen our website registration database.

B. A new law in California requires us to change our website so that viewers must "opt-in" to receive our e-mail newsletters rather than "opt-out" from receiving it. This must be completed within three months.

C. Corporate finance wants to install a data warehouse to manage all of the financial information. No given timeframe.

D. We want to have a new website to compile news from other sources and allow viewers to buy it from us.

E. We are opening new U.S. headquarters in Los Angeles and need to tie their LAN into the corporate network. The construction schedule says it will be ready for IT within four months.

F. United Press International, a major news feed for us, is upgrading their news distribution network within the next six months, and we need to modify our IT infrastructure to tie into it.

G. We need a new service to allow us to deliver user-customized financial news via iPhones, iPads, and PDAs with wireless connections.

H. We are going to put news screens into each Starbucks Coffee Shop in the United States showing news headlines from around the world. This will be done over the next three years.

I. Our website is currently written in English, we intend to internationalize it by creating versions in multiple languages.

J. Half of our employees are using Macintosh computers, the rest are using Windows 8. The Windows component needs to be upgraded to Windows 10 once it has been tested for compatibility, a 12-month effort. This will improve productivity of the Windows side by 2 percent after the initial loss of productivity that follows any major upgrade.

Using MegaNews as an example, let's discuss what criteria should be used to select projects.

2.2.4 Filtering Criteria

Now that we have a picture of the types of projects we might be dealing with, how do we score and prioritize them so that they most strongly align with organizational strategy? Everyone in management has their own interpretation of what the priorities are, a situation that usually leads to conflicting priorities, confusion, subversive stakeholders, and sometimes outright conflict. "Decibel decision making" may have worked in the past, but it always suboptimizes the organization's effectiveness as well as reducing morale.

Simple or complex criteria?

How should we select and score the projects? It depends on what is important to our organization. There are several approaches that can be taken.

The United Kingdom's Cabinet Office's Office of Government Contracting has developed a Portfolio Management Guide. In it, they propose some very simple filtering criteria (Figures 6.3 and 6.4 from the Final Public Consultation Draft, 2009).

The proposed projects are then compared against each other after going through the filtering process. These are very simple criteria and apparently adequate for the process they were designed for.

For a more complex, and therefore more thorough, set of filters, we also have a number of choices. Cooper[10] has proposed the following scorecard for NPD:

Factor 1: Strategic fit and importance
- Alignment of project with our business strategy
- Importance of project to the strategy
- Impact on the business

Factor 2: Product and competitive advantage
- Product delivers unique customer or user benefits
- Product offers customer/user excellent value for money (compelling value proposition)
- Differentiated product in eyes of customer/user
- Positive customer/user feedback on product concept (concept test results)

Table 2.4 UK OGC criteria

		Contribution				
		Weight	None	Some	High	Score	Total
	Prioritizing change criteria						
1	Supports at least one strategic objective	20%	0	5	10	10	2
2	Realizes significant benefits in a short time with low risk	20%	0	5	10	5	1
3	Contributes to external targets	10%	0	5	10	0	0
4	Complies with a legislative requirement	25%	0	5	10	10	2.5
5	Addresses an area of under-performance	5%	0	5	10	5	0.25
6	Improves efficiency	5%	0	5	10	5	0.25
7	Mitigates against corporate risk	10%	0	5	10	10	1
8	Honors an existing contractual obligation	5%	0	5	10	10	0.5
Change priority score							7.5

Factor 3: Market attractiveness
- Market size
- Market growth and future potential
- Margins earned by players in this market
- Competitiveness—how tough and intense competition is (negative)

Factor 4: Core competencies leverage
- Project leverages our core competencies and strengths in:
- Technology

- Production/operations
- Marketing
- Distribution/sales force

Factor 5: Technical feasibility
- Size of technology gap (straightforward to do)
- Technical complexity (few barriers, solution envisioned)
- Familiarity of technology to our business
- Technical track record on these types of projects
- Technical results to date (proof of concept)

Factor 6: Financial reward versus risk
- Size of financial opportunity
- Financial return (NPV, ECV, IRR)
- Productivity index (PI)
- Certainty of financial estimates
- Level of risk and ability to address risks

Part of your job in designing the EPMS is to identify which of these factors, or others, are most important to your upper management. They cannot all be equally important, they have to be prioritized (we will talk about how to do that later).

Not everything that is important can be measure financially. Our goal here is to create a set of objective filters that focuses on the organizational strategic goals while still giving some flexibility to management. That flexibility is important to allow growth in an area where we might not have a strong product presence, but rounds out our product line.

The majority of our filters will be oriented toward the project's financial benefits and the project risk. However, nonfinancial benefits should also be taken into account when appropriate.

As shown in the scorecard just listed, many of these factors are not financially measurable. For example, the IT department of the Project Management Institute uses "benefit to members" as a major criterion for selecting projects. How can this be done if we're not calculating the financial benefits? For projects where nonfinancial criteria are important, the steering or governance committee should pick the perceived benefits from a range of 1 to 5 (or 1 to 10 if that is more customary in your organization), where 5 is highly beneficial, 4 is mostly beneficial, 3 is neutral, 2 is somewhat detrimental to the organization, and 1 indicates the project may harm the organization if performed. All projects in this category go through the same ranking process.

So, other types of benefits are possible, but for most projects, the filtering criteria will be financial ones. Projects are paid for by money, and it is the responsibility of the executives to spend the organization's money as wisely as possible. In the next chapter, we will discuss the details of various financial filters, such as ROI (ROI—an annualized rate of return expressed as a percentage), internal rate of return (IRR), payback period, and others. However, the purely financial approach has limitations, and some very worthwhile projects, such as R&D projects, will never pass a purely financial filter. This is one of the biggest limitations of most EPMS implementations and a major reason why the approach often fails after being tried.

Research done in the field of NPD[3] shows that financial filters are only one of a series of criteria used, and are not the most important. As shown in the next figure from that article, strategic fit outweighs financial benefits:

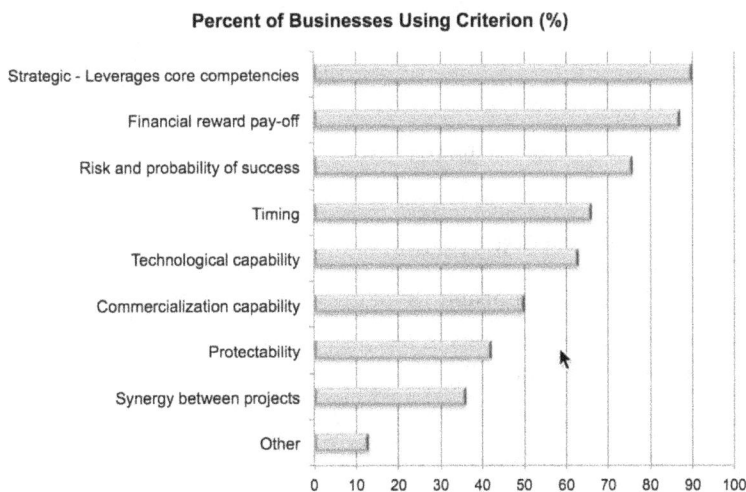

Figure 2.2-10 *NPD filter criteria*

For example, the major manufacturers of small digital cameras try to have a variety of products at different price points so they can compete directly with each other. They might approve a project to develop a new camera that fits a price point they do not already cover, knowing that they will never be the market leader at that price point.

According to the following figure from the same research, over 24 percent of companies engaged in NPD do not use financial methods at all. So, other, nonfinancial criteria need to be developed for them.

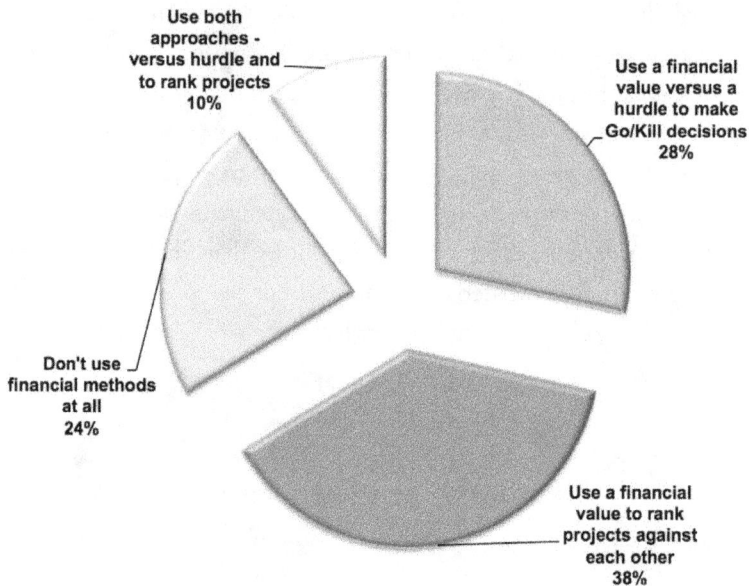

Figure 2.2-11   Financial metrics versus hurdle

2.2.5 Detailed Scoring

Now that we have a reasonable list of questions that will allow us to filter and score the proposed projects, just how do we score them?

If you are developing the software internally instead of purchasing commercial software, create a database for each of the questions. As each question is answered by clicking on the appropriate box, it is automatically scored.

Here we have designed-in the possibility that sections may have different weights. If annual revenues are much more important than the initial investment, you would put in an appropriate weighting factor. These weighting factors can be changed easily in response to the feedback obtained during the initial pilot project. If the list of projects presented to the steering committee for feedback doesn't reflect how they would make decisions, this is the place to adjust the scores to more accurately reflect how decisions should be made.

The total scores are then presented, along with the project risk assessment, as a rank-ordered list to the steering committee. Because the numbers we present them are rough numbers, they should be allowed some flexibility in selecting projects that are close to one another. For instance, if two projects are within 50 points of each other and have similar risk profiles, they should be considered equivalent investments.

2.2.6 Weighting Criteria

Many authors such as Wood[11] suggest weighting the criteria to avoid the limitations inherent in a purely financial approach. We might first identify the criteria themselves as follows:

- ROI
- Risk
- Confidence level of benefit delivery
- Impact to other projects

These do not have to be the same for every category of project, and in fact, should be different for every type of project. For capital expenditures on a new manufacturing facility, ROI would be a reasonable filter. For new product development, one filtering factor may be whether the new product differentiates us in the marketplace and gives us a sustainable advantage.

The next step is to weight each filter. For example, we might give the following weights to the criteria we listed above.

- ROI = 50 percent
- Risk = 20 percent
- Confidence level = 20 percent
- Impact to other projects = 10 percent

These are examples of types of criteria, there are others that might be used depending on what is important to the organization. For example, a professional organization might give a high weight to "benefits to members." Or, a filter that might be used in new product development might be "increase in market share."

Now we can go a step further and, for each project, give them a score between 1 and 10. A score of 10 shows the project will provide a lot of that criteria such as a strong ROI, and a score of 1 indicates it will not.

Except for risk and impact. These are negatives. Because the risk score identifies how risky the project is, the risk score should be done from 10 to 1, just the opposite of how the others are scored. A low risk project would get a score of 8, 9, or 10. A high-risk project would get a score of 1, 2, 3, or 4, and a medium risk project would get scores of 5, 6, or 7.

Similarly, a project that has a high impact to other projects in work would be scored in the range of 1 to 4, medium impact 4 to 7, and low impact 8 to 10. We multiply these scores by the weights, add them up, and this gives us an overall score for the project.

Table 2.5 Project weighting example

	Weight	Project 1		Project 2		Project 3		Project 4	
		Score	Adj. Score	Score	Adj. Score	Score	Adj. Score	Score	Adj. Score
ROI	0.50	5	20.50	4	20.00	2	10.00	7	30.50
Risk	0.20	3	00.60	5	10.00	9	10.80	4	00.80
Confidence level	0.20	5	10.00	8	10.60	8	10.60	3	00.60
Impact	0.10	9	00.90	8	00.80	4	00.40	4	00.40
Total	10.00		50.00		50.40		40.80		50.30

Based on this approach, Project 2 would score the highest and has the best chance for approval. Its ROI score is only moderate, but we have a high degree of confidence we can do it. By comparison, Project 4 has a very good ROI score, but it is moderately risky, and we are not sure we can successfully accomplish it.

It is important to have consistency in decision making. Everyone who looks at a project should score it reasonably the same. Otherwise, one member of the steering committee might say the project has a very high risk, while another member says the same project has a very low risk. During the design period of the EPMS project, some definition of what the criteria are should be established and agreed-upon by the executives. For example:

Table 2.6 Sample weights

ROI Range	0-5%	5-10%	10-20%	20-25%	25-30%	30-40%	40-50%	50-100%	100-150%	>150%
Score	1	2	3	4	5	6	7	8	9	10

An ROI range above 50 percent may seem high to a financial person, but venture capitalists often demand ROIs above 100 percent to compensate for the high risk of their investments. Your own breakdown will be determined by what is normal for your company. These numbers should be adjusted to the different types of projects being considered. In the next chapter, we will talk more about ROI and about the hurdle rate.

Because no scoring system is perfect, the executives should be given the latitude to select two projects that have scores relatively close together. Projects 2 and 4 in our example score close to one another and either one could be selected.

2.2.7 Determining the Scores

So, how do we determine what those scores should be? The best way is to derive those scores from a series of questions that each proposed project must answer. These questions are then given a score based on the answers to the questions.

Many of these answers are a best guess right now. You haven't done the newly proposed project, so we don't have real numbers to analyze. In order to minimize the possibility of wildly inaccurate guesses, make the questions and possible answers as detailed as possible so that the person answering it has to think about it.

For example, instead of asking if the project will increase customer retention, phrase it as follows:

Does or will the project increase customer retention?

1. Not at all?
2. By 0–5 percent?
3. By 6–15 percent?
4. By 15–20 percent?
5. By more than 20 percent?

And, then weight the answers. Answer #5 would have a higher weight than Answer #1 because increasing customer retention is very important.

MegaNews International Projects

Now let's return to MegaNews International. We left the corporate CIO facing a series of proposed projects, wondering which ones to approve. The first thing he noticed was that two of the projects were mandatory because they were in support of regulatory changes. These projects were:

New privacy laws that will take effect in 12 months in Europe require us to strengthen our website registration database (Project A).

A new law in California requires us to change our website so that viewers must "opt-in" to receive our e-mail newsletters rather than "opt-out" from receiving it. This must be completed within three months (Project B).

So, these two were moved immediately to the approved list. Project A is estimated to cost $1 million and requires 10 people for six months. Project B is estimated to cost $500,000 and requires 2 people for two months. The executives will approve these projects because they must be done. But, the CIO is worried about how many resources these projects will tie up that will not be available for other work.

Let us now look at Project F: United Press International, a major news feed for us, is upgrading their news distribution network within the next six months, and we need to modify our IT system to tie into it. While this is not a regulatory project, if MegaNews International wants to stay connected to a major source of news in the future, it must upgrade its own IT infrastructure, so this really falls into the category of a "must do" project. It is estimated to cost $3.5 million and requires three people for four months.

To make intelligent decisions on the remaining projects, the CIO will need more information. After sending e-mails to the people who proposed the projects and getting more details, the CIO now had the following information:

C. Corporate finance wants to install a data warehouse to manage all of the financial information. No given timeframe.

- Estimated cost: $2.5 million
- Estimated benefit: $50,000 per year in improved productivity by corporate finance
- Resources required: 10 people for six months.

D. We want to have a new website to compile news from other sources and allow viewers to buy it from us.

- Estimated cost: $4 million
- Estimated benefit: $1.5 million/year
- Resources required: 10 people for six months.

E. We are opening new U.S. headquarters in Los Angeles and need to tie their LAN into the corporate network. The construction schedule says it will be ready for IT within four months.

- Estimated cost: $0.5 million
- Estimated benefit: $100,000 per year
- Resources required: five people for three months.

G. We need a new service to allow us to deliver user-customized financial news via iPhones, iPads, and PDAs with wireless connections.

- Estimated cost: $5 million
- Estimated benefit: $2 million/year from advertising
- Resources required: 25 people for six months

H. We are going to put news screens into each Starbucks Coffee Shop in the United States showing news headlines from around the world. This will be done over the next three years.

- Estimated cost: $20 million
- Estimated benefit: $10 million/year from advertising
- Resources required: six people for 36 months

I. Our website is currently written in English, we intend to internationalize it by creating versions in multiple languages.

- Estimated cost: $6 million
- Estimated benefit: $2 million/year from advertising
- Resources required: 25 people for six months

A. Half of our employees are using Macintosh computers, the rest are using Windows 8. The Windows component needs to be upgraded once it has been tested for compatibility, a 12-month effort. This will improve productivity of the Windows users by 5 percent.

- Estimated cost: $5 million
- Estimated benefit: unknown
- Resources required: 10 people for 12 months

The calculations for this last project, the Windows upgrade, has a lot of assumptions and soft numbers that are needed. How can you judge how much productivity will increase because of an operating system upgrade? How can you even judge whether it will increase or decrease? For the purposes of performing the calculations, let's make the assumption that productivity will decrease by 10 percent for the first six months until people are familiar with the new software, then it will increase by 2 percent. After one year, we can reduce the Help Desk and IT headcount by 25 people.

2.2.8 Stakeholder Involvement

The scoring questions should cover enough areas to determine the development costs of the project, the future benefits from it, impacts to other projects, and its risks.

But, there is no one group in the typical company that can answer all of these different questions. So, how do we get them answered?

The answer is that we have to involve other parts of the organization. Each section of our questionnaire is answered by someone in the group that has the best information.

Once the EPMS accepts a request for a new project, there is a specific sequence of steps to process that request. We'll look at it in more detail in the next chapter. At a high level, this can be shown in the following flowchart:

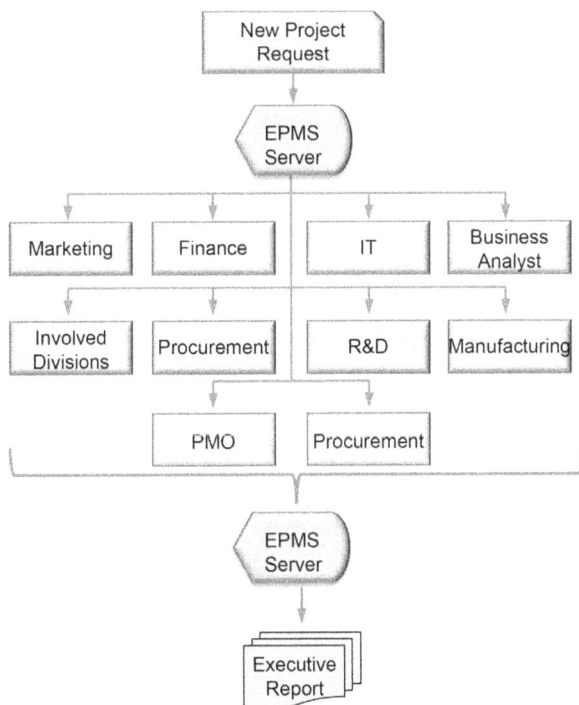

Figure 2.2-12 Organization components involved

The initial request comes from anyone in the company. The computerized form is filled out and routed to the EPMS.

The EPMS then routes the different parts of the form to different departments to fill out their portions of it depending on the specific project: finance, IT, engineering, facilities, procurement, marketing, a business analyst, and so on. Each person fills out the portion of the form that they can best estimate the data for. For example, a request for a new software product may route to the following groups:

Each has their own area to complete on the form.

- Finance: rough estimate of the overall cost of the project
- IT: the level of IT effort to develop the product
- Procurement: the costs of any purchases for the project
- Marketing: potential future financial benefits of the product
- Business analyst: impacts to the business

If the project will require resources that are currently scheduled on other projects, the form should be routed to the PMO for assessment of the impacts to the other projects if this project is approved.

Since most projects are approved or rejected based on financial data, the most important areas in the form are related to the costs of the project and to the possible future financial benefits.

Cost Data

If part of the project involves the mechanical engineering department, the head of mechanical engineering should appoint one of the engineers there to be the point of contact for determining project costs. Similarly electrical engineering, software engineering, IT, and any other groups involved in the project should include their own costs for the project. The financial department and procurement department may have to be involved in this part of it, as well as HR providing the salary bands for the expected staffing levels.

Benefits Data

The engineers are really good at identifying a range of costs for the project. Not so good at identifying the future revenues. For this information, we have to turn to another group, usually marketing. They are often involved in calculating the possible range of future revenues from new products.

If the future benefits of the project are primarily cost savings, as they would be in business process improvement projects, then some estimates of the reduced headcount or increased productivity need to be made to allow calculations of future cost savings.

Benefits are more difficult to quantify than costs are. There are a lot of assumptions and guessing in deciding how much revenue a new product will give us in two, five, seven years. Each assumption is uncertain and may or may not prove to be true depending on what the future really holds. If there is enough time, these calculations should be performed under different assumptions about the future.

Other departments may involve manufacturing, the PMO, IT, procurement, and any other department or division that may be affected by the new project.

Once the data are filled out, the results are summarized, a risk analysis is done on the proposed project, and the final score is sent to the steering committee for review and either approval or rejection of the project.

2.2.9 Designing the Human Interface

One crucial aspect of defining the requirements is to understand how people want to interact with it. It is very difficult to design a software interface that is both highly functional and flexible and yet is intuitive and easy to use. Those are two extremes of the design effort. High functionality and flexibility are the antithesis of an intuitive interface. Not many software programs achieve both, and the developers will be forced to make tradeoffs based on the requirements you capture.

This part of the requirements and design effort cannot be emphasized highly enough. The ease of use of the EPMS will make people either want to use it or turn people aware from it, rendering your entire effort useless. People who use software do not care what happens beyond the screen and the keyboard, but how they interact with the software is core to their acceptance of it.

The historical approach to developing software was borrowed from other more advanced project management fields such as construction and aerospace. You gather all of your requirements before you design and then build the project plan around satisfying those requirements. This doesn't work in software, and it hasn't worked since the 1960s when software development on mainframe systems began to accelerate.

Software users rarely know how to describe "how" they want to interact with the system in such detail that the developers can produce exactly the right interface. It's not the fault of the developers, it's because users can only think in terms of what they already know how to do.

This is why, a much better approach to developing software products has been accelerating since the early 2000s. A variety of "agile" approaches has been developed in which the developers work closely with the users, showing them what the interface looks like and making rapid changes based on the users' feedback. This allows the users to effectively design the interfaces in a way that is easy for them to use.

One piece of advice: Never let the developers design the human interface. (For an interesting discussion of the difference between software engineers and normal users, see the book *The Inmates are Running the Asylum by Alan Cooper.*) Developers tend to be rational, linear thinkers who want to put in every possible combination of functions into the product and who enjoy complexity. A word processing program such as MS Word has millions of lines of complex code and includes functions that 95 percent of users will never use. Start the EPMS with basic functions and add more later on as people gain experience with it and request additional capabilities.

Input to the EPMS

Your stakeholders will primarily interface with the EPMS in two areas: the initial project request form and the outputs generated by the EPMS.

Employees who have an idea for a new project will fill out the online project request form (PRF). This should be designed so that it is easy to fill out and provide enough information to allow the EPMS to analyze the project.

The PRF should include at a minimum:

- The person requesting the new product: Name, organization, title, contact information
- The current problem the product will resolve or the new opportunity it will provide
- A description of the proposed solution

- The benefits it will provide
- Any known risks associated with doing the project
- The different divisions/departments/groups that will be involved

One possible format for a PRF is the first pages of the Toyota Selection Process, shown in Appendix 2.2. Executives should have an input into what they need in the PRF. Don't underestimate the importance of a user-friendly request form. The easier it is to use, the more likely people are to use it. If the programmers make it too challenging, it reduces the desire to use it.

Outputs From the EPMS

The outputs generated by the EPMS will be of three primary types: the rank-ordered list of projects that the steering committee will use to select new projects, the dashboard used daily by the portfolio manager, and the regular status updates on the current state of the projects in the portfolio. Each one has different users and requires a different design.

For the steering committee, they want enough information to make an intelligent decision on which projects to approve. No numerical scoring is perfect, so the committee should be given some flexibility in which projects to approve while still knowing what the analysis shows.

When properly designed, it is possible to drill down into more details on any project just by clicking on the project or on one of the colored indicators. The dashboard is difficult to design and implement. This is one area where commercial products have an advantage over in-house development. But, repeating an earlier comment, tracking projects already in work is not necessarily part of a portfolio management system, it really belongs to a PMO.

The format for the reporting should be both detailed enough to provide management the information they need, but not so detailed that it overwhelms them with details. Sometimes, a simple spider (or radar) chart shown here is adequate for a single project.

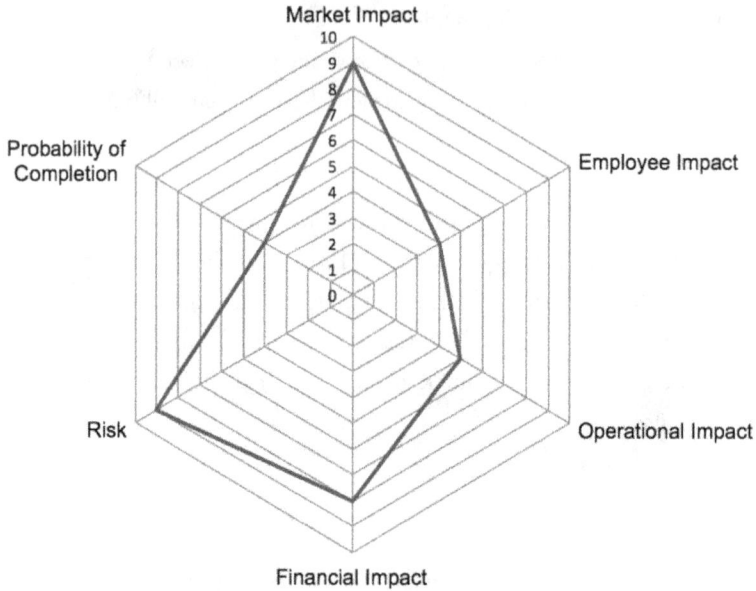

Figure 2.2-13 Reporting project priority to management

If there are multiple projects to be compared, a spreadsheet or a database will work better that allows showing the multiple projects under consideration. The information to be reported should include:

1. Project
    1.1 Project name
    1.2 Requester
    1.3 Department
    1.4 Departments impacted by the project
2. Mandatory (Yes/No)
3. Required upgrade (Yes/No)
4. Internal improvement
    4.1 Employee productivity
    4.2 Customer relations
    4.3 Process improvement
5. Financial scores
    5.1 Initial investment
    5.2 Annual revenue
    5.3 Annual expenses

6. Overall score

7. Risk score

2.2.10 Design Considerations for Tracking Projects in Work

Once projects have started, they will be monitored during the execution phase. This means the developers must incorporated tracking software tied to the project's schedule so that proper governance can be applied to the project. If the project is seriously behind schedule or over budget, this should be obvious in the EPMS reports to management so that they can make an intelligent decision to keep the project going or to kill it and free up resources for other projects.

Another consideration is that projects are approved based on their business case justification. If the scope of the project changes during execution (not an uncommon situation), at what point has the scope changed so much that the project no longer satisfies the business case? This needs to be flagged by the EPMS so that management can decide to kill the project. Unfortunately, this is much harder to do than tracking schedule/cost issues. It is often a judgment call whether the business justification has been violated or not.

Step 2.3 Doing the Financial Calculations

Not everything that counts can be counted, and not everything that can be counted counts

—Albert Einstein

Companies that rely mostly on financial metrics obtain "unbalanced portfolios" that are not well matched to the strategy of the firm

—R. Foti[12]

We could get very sophisticated about the financial calculations that could be applied to the project selection process. We could hire economists and do a lot of detailed mathematical modeling. But let's be honest—at this point, we really don't know accurately how much the projects are going to cost or how much benefit they're going to provide. We're guessing about the future state of the environment, and even many stock market analysts, who earn a great deal of money predicting the future, have a fairly low success rate.

For products that we are going to sell, part of the goal of the marketing department is to identify future benefits from these products. Even though they do a lot of consumer surveys, product testing, and gather as much information as they can, their numbers are only rough guesses as to what the future profits will be. Productivity improvements due to changes in business processes are in the same category. These are "soft" numbers, educated guesses, often overly optimistic guesses, rather than the "hard" numbers that can be assigned to the costs of the project.

Hard numbers are those things you can measure and expect to be validated after the project is completed. For example, project costs and revenues. Soft numbers are benefits that are hard to accurately quantify, but you can make some estimate of: reduction in order backlogs and billing errors, decrease in future maintenance requirements, improvements in supply chain management, and so on.

So, rather than try and attain an accuracy of three decimal points, let's set up the financial calculations so that we can quickly assess the costs and the risks within 25 percent or so. For complex engineering projects, we may not get closer than ±50 percent. (If the project is approved and a proper amount of planning is done, this number should be within 10 percent, but for now, 25 percent accuracy is about as good as we need to do.) The goal of the financial analysis is to give the decision makers enough information to allow an intelligent decision as to how this project compares against the others and whether this project is worth doing or not. If the project justification uses a lot of soft numbers, examine the assumptions very closely and do not select the project if there are too many assumptions being made. This is part of preparing a business case for the project.

Having said how rough and approximate the numbers are, upper management has more trust in any numbers, hard or soft, than they do with not having any numbers at all.

Economist Kenneth Arrow was a statistician during the Second World War. One of his jobs was analyzing weather forecasts made months into the future. The forecasts, he found, were pretty much useless.

*When he warned his commanders against taking them too seriously,
he received a legendary response: "The Commanding General is well
aware the forecasts are no good. However, he needs them for planning
purposes."*

We quoted Albert Einstein earlier because we need to keep in mind
when we're filtering projects, that some of the most important projects may
be difficult to assign hard numbers to. Anything that improves employee
morale and productivity is a worthwhile project. But, how do you assign
numbers to a small increase in morale? You really cannot, so it becomes a
best guess. A soft number. But, we can still make our guesses reasonable.

Borrowing a thought from the Elihu Goldratt's theory of constraints,
to gain the greatest benefits, internal projects should concentrate on
improving the constraints, the bottlenecks, in the organization, whether
that constraint is poor business processes, poor technologies, poor product development processes, limited skilled resources, and so on. But, it is
very difficult to quantify the financial benefits of doing these projects. If
I improve business processes, how much of a productivity improvement,
and thereby a financial benefit, can I expect? 2 percent, 5 percent, 10
percent? It's hard to nail down these numbers.

Let's now concentrate on how we assign numbers and do the financial
calculations that will help management select the projects.

Along the effort to determine the financial benefits of doing a project, another concept besides the traditional ROI, NPV, or other typical
calculations, consider using an Economic Value Added (EVA)[13] analysis as an additional ROI-type approach: most simply, this refers to the
amount earned that is in excess of the cost of doing the work. If the cost
is $100,000 and you earned $110,000, the $10,000 difference between
the cost and the amount earned is the EVA.

2.3.1 Building the Business Case for Proposed Projects

We talked about the business case extensively in the previous chapter and
showed how to justify the EPMS project itself. The justification for the
projects that will be added to the portfolio will be different depending on
the type of project. Creating a reasonable business case for the project will

be done by the project sponsor who wants this project approved or by someone on their staff. If it is a new product development, this will likely be done by someone in marketing. If it is an internal improvement project, the business case will be done by the sponsoring organization usually by a business analyst reporting to a particular division.

The emphasis on the business case for most projects is financial benefit. While many executives will claim that something they want is "a strategic investment," that statement is insufficient to justify a project. By comparison, if we can say *"We're a $10B company with an accounts receivable average age of 75 days. This project is going to get it down to 60 days. Reducing the collection period by 15 days is going to free up $75M in working capital."* That type of detailed justification will get a project approved. That is what you want to capture in the business case. You don't want some high and mighty strategic goal that can't be measured against. Force the decision makers to put numbers on the success criteria.

For internal projects such as process improvements or IT projects, before writing the business case, the person who submits the project request should spend time meeting with management to identify exactly what is expected from the product. The outcome of the meeting(s) is a list of high-level business requirements that define the end result. What is requested in the business case should not be a high-end, gold-plated product. It should be what is required to solve the business problem but no more.

Because the IT department in many organizations is a large financial cost sink and IT projects historically have a high failure rate, upper management has become very leery of approving them. In the business case for an IT project, a best practice is to offer three versions of it, doing the financial calculations for all three:

- Bare-bones version, just enough functionality to solve the worst problem only and at lower cost
- Middle-of-the-road version, with the functionality to satisfy all of the business needs but at a higher cost
- Gold-plated version, to enhance functionality, benefits, user-friendliness, and future growth, usually at a much higher cost

At this point, the costs are very rough guesses, so don't spend a lot of time on them. Just come up with reasonable estimates, but make them as detailed as you can. It will help sell the project to management.

For example, an online company has large data centers that require very large amounts of electricity. Online companies typically run their facilities at maximum capacity around the clock, regardless of the actual demand. As a result, data centers can waste 90 percent or more of the electricity that is used to run them. The head of facilities for your company has done some analysis and shows the following benefits of improving the energy consumption of the 5,000 square-feet data center consuming 1,127 kW of power (numbers from a white paper by Emerson Network Power[14]:

Table 2.7 ROI calculations for energy project

Energy-saving action	Energy logic savings with the cascade effect		ROI
	Savings (KW)	Savings (%)	
Low-power processors	111	10%	12–18 months
High-efficiency power supplies	124	115	5–7 months
Power management features	86	8%	Immediate
Blade servers	7	1%	TCO reduced 38%
Server virtualization	86	8%	TCO reduced 63%
Higher voltage AC power distribution	20	2%	2–3 months
Cooling best practices	15	1%	4–6 months
Variable capacity cooling	49	4%	4–10 months
Supplemental cooling	72	6%	10–12 months
Monitoring and optimization	15	1%	3–6 months

While these numbers are under optimal conditions, they show the level of detail that you will need to provide management to make a decision on whether to approve the project or not.

If part of the project requires purchasing software, we will point out later why you should never use the financial numbers given you by vendors for the product's benefits. As already mentioned, IT projects have a historically high failure rate so many company executives have learned to distrust the wonderful ROI numbers that are stated in the business case. For IT projects, you can increase the probability of having the project selected by doing your own financial calculations and perhaps include case studies from other companies that have implemented the same product.

Example: Let's say our CIO wants to implement the Software Engineering Institute's Capability Maturity Model (Integrated) (SEI CMMI) into the IT group. This is expensive and will take several years, but the benefits have been shown to be worthwhile in the long term.

Should he (or she) just verbalize the benefits of the CMMI processes? Will that convince the executives to put money into it? Probably not. But, if the CIO can show strong financial benefits, then the project stands a much better chance of being approved. For example, SEI Tech Report 2001: CMM ROI showed the following:

Table 2.8 ROI for software process improvements

Cost of S/W Process Improvement per engineer	$1,375
Productivity gain/year	35%
Improvement in defects discovered prior to formal test	22%
Yearly reduction in time-to-market	19%
Reduction in postrelease defect reports	39%
Value returned for every dollar spent on SPI	$5

In other words, the CIO can show a ROI, and ROI, of $5 for every $1 spent on the project. That is the kind of number, and justification, that will help the project get selected.

It is absolutely necessary to have a strong business case for the proposed projects? The research shows that industry leaders in the area of new product development do a lot of front-end work to ensure that they have good numbers that go into the financial analysis. The following chart[15] shows the percent of businesses that do analysis prior to starting projects:

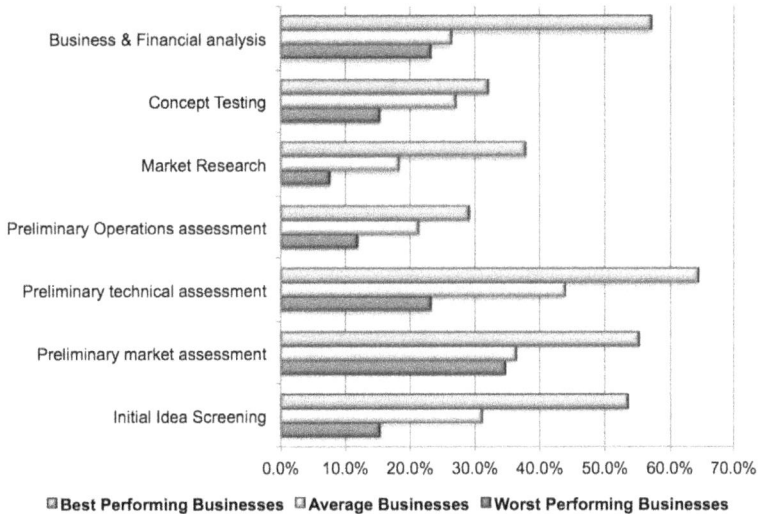

Figure 2.3-1 Analysis done prior to project approvals

It shows clearly that top performers do a lot of work getting the numbers right before proposing a project. The best performing businesses do market research and market assessments, financial analyses, preliminary technical assessments, and screen out ideas much more than even average companies.

In IT, there are problems other departments do not have. Too many CIOs made promises for years that the next investment will clear up all the current IT problems, without actually delivering on that grand promise. Top executives have recognized that they have been pouring a lot of money into IT and still not getting what they want. According to a study by the Panorama Consulting Company[16] of 1,300 ERP implementations across the globe, 79 percent of them delivered less than half of the expected business benefits. Similarly, *Information Week* found that only 25 percent of IT projects will have delivered hard monetary benefits.

Another study by *Information Week* found that 65 percent of ERP projects go over budget, and 93 percent take longer than expected. Further, a significant portion of the participants in the study admitted going 50 percent or more over budget. These numbers have not improved since then. While these studies are on ERP implementations (which have a long history of troubled projects), similar results have been found for other complex IT implementations such as client relationship management (CRM) projects and supply chain management implementations.

2.3.2 The Business Case for Different Futures

If we had perfect information about the future the decision which projects to pick would be very simple. (The future being defined as the number of years that management has told us to do the calculations for.) However, we have limited information about the future. We can only guess at how well our new products will do or how much more productive our employees will become.

While we cannot know for certain the future, we can divide the future into futures we're certain about, futures we're somewhat certain about, and futures that are totally unknown. Military organizations have for many years (probably hundreds or years or longer) divided their future guesses into three categories:

Known–knowns: We know with a great deal of certainty what the future at some point will be, such as the known composition and deployment of enemy forces. We can make predictions and plans based on relatively certain knowledge in this scenario.

Known–unknowns: We know what the general state of the future will be, but we do now have any details, such as knowing the enemy is there, but now how big their forces are or how they're deployed. In this case, we can develop reasonable estimates based on what we know.

Unknown–unknowns: We cannot even predict what the future will be because we have virtually no knowledge or information. We don't even know that the enemy is out there, let alone how big they are or how deployed. We're blind and deaf.

Hugh Courtney (Courtney)[17] has provided a simple framework for thinking about the amount of uncertainty surrounding the future:

Level 4: True uncertainty
No known range of possible
futures. (Unk-unks)

Level 3: Range of futures
Range of possible future
outcomes

A   *Level 2: Alternative futures*
B   Limited set of possible future
C   outcomes, one of which will occur

Level 1: Clear future
Single view

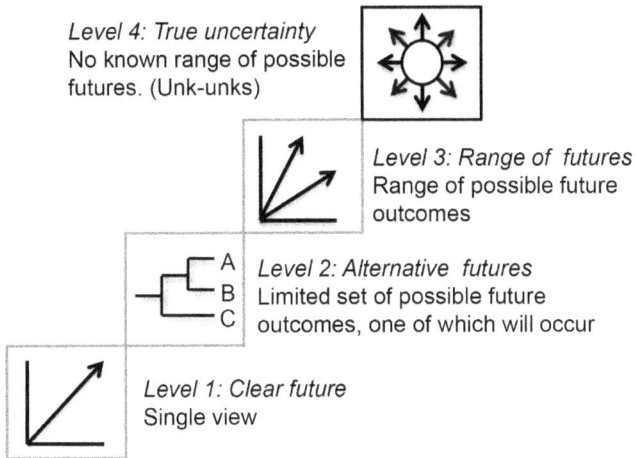

Figure 2.3-2 Possible future states

If the future is clear (Level 1), then our financial calculations are very straightforward and need only be done once for each proposed project. This is accurate out to a year or so. If there are well-defined possible futures (Level 2), then we should do our project calculations for different possible future environments. This would be the situation in a 1 to 3 year timeframe. Further out, say 3 to 5 years, there is a wide range of possible futures (Level 3) and all of our calculations become less certain. We should perform our financial calculations within well-crafted scenarios that describe our assumptions about the future. If we are working at a Level 4 state of uncertainty, more than five years in the future, then we are wasting time doing any calculations, and we'll need management to provide us with the possible future states they want us to work within.

Because every calculation you do depends on your assumptions about the future, for Levels 2 and 3 of Courtney's framework, the cost justification section of in the business case should be built three times using three different assumptions about the future:

- An optimistic financial future—the case that only occurs
  10 percent of the time

- An expected financial future—the situation that will occur 80 percent of the time
- A pessimistic financial future—the case that will only occur 10 percent of the time

How can we do this? We use a decision tree with three possible scenarios. This allows us to deal with Courtney's Level 2. Let's say that in an optimistic future, this project will produce a net revenue of five million euros. We expect the future to be moderate, and the project will produce a new revenue of three million euros. If the market turns down and the future becomes pessimistic, it will produce a new revenue of only one million euros.

Now we build our decision tree to determine the value that we expect from this project. If a possible event has a 25 percent probability of occurring, and if it does occur, it will benefit me by $10,000, then the expected value of the event is: $0.25 \times 10,000 = \$2,500$.

To take this one step further, a possible future event has a 10 percent chance of happening. If it happens, I will gain $10,000. If it does not happen, and there is a 90 percent probability it will not, I will lose $5,000. My expected value becomes:

$$0.10 \times 10,000 + 0.90 \times (-5,000) = 1,000 + (-4,500) = -\$3,500$$

We can now use these calculations and develop possible future outcomes based on how likely we think the different scenarios are. If we think the most likely future has an 80 percent probability of occurring, and the pessimistic and optimistic futures each have a 10 percent probability of occurring, then the expected revenue in each one is:

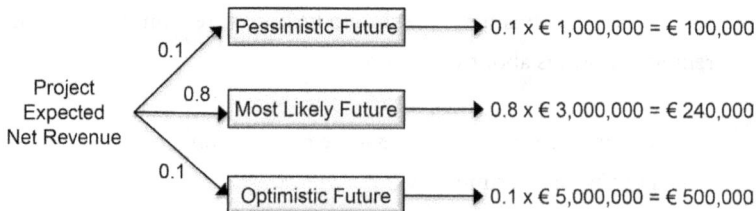

Figure 2.3-3 Decision tree analysis

Adding the three possible future outcomes and dividing by three gives us an expected value for the project of 280,000 euros. This then is the value we use when doing the later financial calculations. If you had the time to be really thorough in your calculations, for each of these three possible outcomes, you would perform the calculations for the three different versions of the product: bare-bones version, middle-of-the-road version, and gold-plated version, thereby doing nine separate calculations. A lot of work, but it will give you, and the decision makers, a much better view of possible outcomes.

As our EPMS does the cost calculations and compares the cost of the product with the expected revenues, it will subtract the cost of the project from each of the possible future revenues and calculate the net expected monetary value (NEMV) of the project. If this number is negative, that is, if the project costs more than any possible future revenue, the project should be rejected.

Let's see how this works for the MegaNews International projects. The CIO, working with the Marketing Department, has determined projections for the following projects based on their assumptions of strong market response and weak market response:

How did we arrive at the net revenue or savings? Let's take one example.

Project C: $(0.8 \times \$250,000) + (0.2 \times -\$75,000) - \$2,500,000 = \$2,315,000.$

So, we took the probable savings and subtracted the cost. The other calculations are similar. Using this approach, we see that the most beneficial project is H—putting news screens into Starbucks Coffee Shops and collecting the ad revenue.

Like every projection out into the future, there are a lot of assumptions that must be made, and a lot of these numbers are best guesses. How did we decide the probabilities of strong and weak response? It's our best guess. How did we come up with the figures for the revenues? Again, it's our best guess. These are subjective numbers, and you will find them heavily challenged when you present your analysis to the decision makers. In defense, you should have strong justification for where the numbers came from. The Marketing Department can help you here because they make these future guesses frequently.

Table 2.9 *MegaNews project options*

Project #	Project	Estimated cost	Probability of strong response	5-year revenue or savings if strong response	Probability of weak response	5-year revenue or savings if weak response	Net revenue or savings, or (loss)
C	Corporate finance wants to install a data warehouse to manage all of the financial information.	2,500,000	80%	$250,000	20%	-$75,000	($2,315,000.00)
D	We want to have a new website to compile news from other sources and allow viewers to buy it from us.	4,000,000	75%	7,500,000	25%	1,250,000	$1,937,500.00
E	We are opening new U.S. headquarters in Los Angeles and need to tie their LAN into the corporate network.	500,000	95%	$500,000	5%	$125,000	($18,750.00)
G	We need a new service to allow us to deliver user-customized financial news via smartphones, tablets, and PDAs with wireless connections	5,000,000	60%	10,000,000	40%	2,500,000	$2,000,000.00
H	We are going to put news screens into each Starbucks Coffee Shop in the United States, showing news headlines from around the world.	20,000,000	50%	50,000,000	50%	15,000,000	$12,500,000.00
I	Our website is currently written in English; we intend to internationalize it by creating versions in multiple languages.	6,000,000	65%	10,000,000	35%	2,500,000	$1,375,000.00
J	Half of our employees are using Macintosh computers, the rest are using PCs running Windows 8. The Windows component needs to be upgraded to Windows 10.	5,000,000	10%	22,500,000	90%	-5,000,000	($7,250,000.00)

In the financial environment that began occurring around 2007 and got progressively worse during 2008 and 2009, the projects that you would have picked would fall into the pessimistic scenario. These are likely to include survival projects to just keep the organization going rather than to develop new products. As the financial environment deteriorated, the portfolio should have been re-examined under the new future and adjustments made to the projects in work. In Ram Charan's book[18] on how to manage in these difficult times, he says: *"Projects that once were evaluated on the basis of their return on investment now must be judged in terms of how much cash they consume and can generate, and how soon they can bring in cash."* If the economy has improved since our original numbers, the most optimistic case is more likely and those numbers become more accurate.

2.3.3 The Project Manager's Uses for the Business Case

While the business case is initially used to sell the project to the organization, it does not get put on a shelf and forgotten. It has uses later on during the execution phase of the project. It should be used to guide the project manager's decision making to ensure that the original goals of the project are kept in focus.

When creating a business case, you should start with the end in mind—how does the end result benefit the organization? One way to approach this is to ask a related question—what does success look like? How will we know when we have delivered what the organization needed? Part of the business case should contain success criteria that are agreed-to by the major stakeholders.

Once success has been defined for the project, metrics are built around that definition of success. The metrics should be as detailed and as quantitative as necessary to ensure that we accurately measure how we're doing against the goal of the end product. If the end product is going to eliminate production-line shortages or reduce cycle time, then the success criteria are built around those expectations.

As an example, let's say that the project is going to build a data warehouse to replace a mix of older legacy data systems. How responsive should data queries be? (Recall our discussion of nonfunctional requirements earlier. Performance requirements like this are a key input to the design of a product.) If a request for data is sent and the answer comes back in two seconds, is that a successful response? How about 10 minutes for a complex query, or 24 hours? While most business people would not be happy with a 24-hour turnaround for information, it is up to the project manager to define exactly what the product's detailed success criteria are and measure against those during the project. Being told "as fast as possible" is not an acceptable answer. You cannot measure against that.

Defining those detailed success criteria is done by the primary stakeholders, those who have the most to gain from the end product. These types of success criteria are not necessary in the business case to justify the project, but need to be added later as the project management planning process develops the details of the project.

Keep in mind that any project that assumes future income is subject to the future financial environment. If it changes, the product that was produced may not be considered successful through no fault of the project manager. When you perform the financial calculations, *clearly* state what assumptions you are making about the future.

2.3.4 Impact of Change Requests During the Project

One difficulty that exists in most projects involves change requests. All projects are subject to changes. The goal of a formal change management system is to minimize the impacts of any changes. The most devastating types of change requests involve adding requirements (leading to scope creep) and deleting functionality in order to meet the schedule.

Both of these types of changes will lead to the project no longer meeting its original business case. What should happen, but almost never does, is the project's business case numbers should be recalculated to see if the project still satisfies the original request. If additional scope is added what is the impact on the project's cost and schedule, and how does that impact the ROI? If scope is deleted to meet schedule, what is the impact to the end product, and how does that reduced functionality impact what was promised?

In some cases, the project, if it deviates from the business case, needs to be brought back into alignment with what the original goals were.

In the situation where a change improves the business case, the business case should be adjusted with all major stakeholders approving the changes. The business case is not a static document. Make changes to it when it makes sense to do so (but always keep a copy of the original business case for comparison).

If a major change request is made, it makes sense to revisit the business case and check the impacts. Experienced project managers are pretty savvy about identifying and controlling major change requests. Yet, projects are much more likely to suffer from multiple small changes, and in this case, only rarely is the business case re-examined and recalculated. At what point has the project changed so much that it no longer makes sense? At that point, the project should be killed and a new project defined. We mentioned success criteria should be part of the business case. The document should also identify kill criteria—under what circumstances should the project be canceled.

In the construction industry, any changes that impact scope, cost, or schedule after construction begins will almost never cause the project to be canceled. Once the building starts, it will complete whatever the cost is with few exceptions (such as during a severe economic downturn). This is not true in IT. Just because the developers have already started coding does not mean that change requests for new functionality will stop, or that the architecture of the software will not change. People who would never dream of asking for a building redesign after construction starts have no problems with asking for additional functionality after coding starts. In the IT industry, it is particularly important to revisit the business case during the execution phase of the project.

There are methodologies in the IT world to attack this common problem. The Swiss government first attacked the problem of IT projects with the Hermes methodology in the 1970s. More recently, Projects in Controlled Environments (PRINCE) is a methodology that was funded by the British government, specifically for IT projects in the public sector. The PRINCE approach (now up to PRINCE II) requires that the project be constantly compared to the original justification to ensure that it still makes sense. This is a best practice.

Another approach that has evolved in IT is the use of agile development approaches. When IT began discovering the benefits of project management, they copied existing methodologies that developed in the areas of aerospace and construction, and quickly found these approaches don't work. They don't work because in aerospace and construction, the basic requirements don't change very much, particularly after the development phase starts. But, IT never learned to define the requirements ahead of time and lock them down, so developers are constantly having to deal with changing requirements.

This led to the growth of agile development approaches that can adapt to changing requirements. Historically, agile-type approaches were first recommended for IT in a presentation back in 1970[19]. The same presentation nicknamed the traditional approach as a waterfall approach, the first recorded instance of that name.

In IT, the problem of change requests is a common one and often poorly dealt with. Other industries have learned how to deal with it better. Both the Construction Industry Institute (CII) and Independent Project Analysis, Inc. (IPA) emphasize a methodology for large-scale engineering projects called front-end loading (FEL). This is a process by which a company develops detailed definition of a capital project to meet business objectives. *"Benchmarking data in the oil and gas industry, …, shows conclusively that effort spent (up to a point) on front-end definition (so-called 'Front-end Loading' – FEL) correlates positively with project outcome performance"*[20].

Using an FEL approach, the requirements are defined and locked down months before any detailed planning is performed. This approach allowed Saudi Aramco to develop a U.S. $2 billion gas field project in the middle of the Saudi Arabian desert, and to complete it six months ahead of schedule and for 27 percent under budget. The total percentage of change requests 2 percent, and all of them safety-related. This project was awarded Project of the Year by PMI in 2004. There are similar examples from other oil and gas projects.

2.3.5 Some Basic Financial Terminology and Concepts

Before we can set up the financial filters, we need to understand some basic financial concepts. This is a very simplistic background, and when you develop the calculations for your own EPMS, you should get someone from the financial department to help you with the more sophisticated calculations.

The goal of financial analysis in a portfolio is to invest in projects where the value of the future returns is greater than the cost. If the future value is greater than cost, the extra value enhances company's bottom line (and the stockholders'). We want to select projects with *highest value* of future returns *and* greatest probability of *success.*

There are multiple methods of calculating the expected financial benefits of different projects. Each has its own strength and weakness. No one method is perfect. Often financial officers use multiple methods of calculation for each project to find the "best" average answer.

What is more important than the specific method used is that the same financial methods be done for all projects of the same type and to the same number of years in the future. All IT projects should be compared by the same financial methods. All capital investment projects should be compared by the same financial methods. You cannot compare a construction project that has a cost–benefit justification with one that has a NPV justification. Be consistent and use the same approach for both.

Once the financial calculations have been carried out, the specific approval justification should also be dependent on the type of project. Compare a project with similar projects. A BPI project requires different approval gates than does a new manufacturing facility. Each type of project should have distinct and unique justification criteria.

It is important to remember that nothing in the future is certain. Both costs and future cash flows must be estimated. It is easier to estimate costs, so future revenues are generally more uncertain than development and manufacturing costs. Several methods can be used to compute the advantage in an investment when the cash flows are certain, but none can guarantee success. By doing the appropriate calculations, there are ways to understand the implications of risk, but there no ways to eliminate uncertainty. If there were, the stock markets would be much more predictable than they are, and we would all be living on yachts!

The ***time value of money*** is a concept used to understand the investment implications of a project, that is, the investment of money related to expected interest. This is based on the premise that money has the most value when it is invested and receiving interest or can produce more money in the future.

One of the people who sits on the organization's executive committee is the Chief Financial Officer (CFO). This person's responsibility is to ensure that the organization gets the greatest value for its money compared to the risk. Should the organization invest its cash in stock or buy CDs? Should the organization invest in projects that expand it or save its money? These are questions the CFO gets heavily involved in answering. A risk-averse CFO is more likely to recommend investing the money in CDs or bonds. A more risk-tolerant CFO is more comfortable with investing the money in risky projects.

Future value (FV) measures the future amount of money that a given amount of money is worth at some specified time in the future assuming a certain rate of return.

The opposite of Future Value is **present value (PV)**, the PV of an amount that will be received in the future. It is also called discounted value. The calculation is just the reverse of FV. How much do I need to invest today to obtain $1.21 in two years? The answer is $1.

Other financial terms we need are:

Capital rationing: Selecting best group of projects without going over budget. Because all organizations have limited budgets for projects, how do they allocate the money across multiple projects? This is a topic we discussed heavily in the previous section.

Benefit/cost analysis: A formal discipline used to help assess the case for a proposed project by comparing its benefits to its expected costs.

Discount rate: The rate used to calculate the PV of payments

Discounted cash flow (DCF): Reducing cash flow to account for the time value of money. As an example, a $10 million lottery ticket paid over 20 years with a discount rate of 6 percent is worth about $5.73 million today. If you won the lottery and asked for all of your money up front, you would receive $5.73 million and not $10 million. If you invested that $5.73 million at the 6 percent interest rate assumed in the calculation and took out one-twentieth every year, at the end of 20 years, you would have collected $10 million.

Interest rate: The cost of borrowing funds. NOTE: For our Islamic students, the Quran prohibits making money on money, that is, it prohibits paying interest. However, the concept of compensating a lender for the risk of the investment is still valid. It is simply handled in a different way. The results are the same.

Internal Rate of Return (IRR): The interest rate at which the PV of project revenues and costs are equal. This is a completely artificial interest rate calculation and is only used for comparing different projects. The project with the highest IRR is usually the one selected.

Opportunity cost: The value of the next best alternative that has been given up as the result of making a decision. It implies the choice between desirable yet mutually exclusive results. For example, if I select project A instead of project B because the NPV is better *and* I cannot do both, the "opportunity cost" is the cost of not doing project B.

Net Present Value (NPV): The present value of the expected future benefits minus the present value of the cost.

Payback period: The period of time required for the return on an investment to "repay" the original investment. The payback period is considered a method of analysis with serious limitations. It does not properly account for the time value of money, risk, financing, or other important considerations such as the opportunity cost.

Return on Investment (ROI), also known as rate of return (ROR) or sometimes just return, is the ratio of money gained or lost on an investment relative to the amount of money invested.

Which ones are most commonly used? Payback period has a lot of limitations due to its simplicity. Benefit/cost analysis is most effective on projects where the benefits are not quantifiable, such as infrastructure or large engineering projects. The most common calculations are ROI and NPV (and its inverse, the IRR). For the majority of the projects in the portfolio, these are the calculations that are most useful. Now that we have learned these basic definitions, lets look at how we do the financial calculations to select the more financially beneficial projects.

2.3.6 *Financial Filtering Methods*

2.3.6.1 Payback Period

Payback is a very simple calculation that tells us how long it will take to recover our initial investment. A project costs $10,000,000 initially. You expect to receive $3,000,000 per year. What is the payback period?

So, how do we do this calculation? It is a very simple calculation (and therefore very limited in its usefulness). It is no more than estimated costs divided by expected annual benefits. For our MegaNews International projects, the calculations look like this:

A special note for project J: This type of calculation requires a lot of rough assumptions. Let us assume that 20,000 people are affected with an average salary of $80,000/year. A 10 percent reduction in productivity is like adding 2,000 people to the workforce, resulting in a six-month cost of $40 million.

A 2 percent increase in productivity over six months would result in a benefit of $8 million or an annual benefit of $16 million. Let us assume that the total annual savings is created by laying off 25 IT people, resulting in a saving of $2.5 million.

Running out the savings on a monthly basis, we see that we break even on the project around 27 months after we complete it.

From the standpoint of a payback calculation, the CIO can immediately see that corporate finance's data warehouse is not going to give the corporation any benefit for 50 years, long after it has been replaced with newer technology. She can throw that one out immediately.

Project E, the Los Angeles offices, is marginal from a payback period. Most financial officers demand a payback period no longer than three years for an IT project. Let's see how this project does in the other financial calculations.

Quick Notes

Don't bother doing financial calculations beyond a cost estimate for mandatory projects unless directed to do so. Since you have no choice but to do these projects, the return is irrelevant.

Table 2.10 MegaNews project payback period calculations

Project	Project	Estimated cost	Annual benefits	Payback period
C	Corporate finance wants to install a data warehouse to manage all of the financial information.	$2.5M	$50,000	50 years
D	We want to have a new website to compile news from other sources and allow viewers to buy it from us.	$4M	$1,500,000	2.67
E	We are opening new U.S. headquarters in Los Angeles and need to tie their LAN into the corporate network.	$0.5M	$100,000	5.00
G	We need a new service to allow us to deliver user-customized financial news via PDAs with wireless connections. The revenue will come from ads.	$5M	$2,000,000	2.50
H	We are going to put news screens into each Starbucks Coffee Shop in the United States, showing news headlines from around the world. The revenue will come from ads.	$20M	$10,000,000	2.00
I	Our website is currently written in English; we intend to internationalize it by creating versions in multiple languages. The revenue will come from ads.	$6M	$2,000,000	3.00
J	Half of our employees are using Macintosh computers, the rest are using PCs running Windows 8. The Windows component needs to be upgraded to Windows 10.	$5M		27 months

All financial projections need to be carried out to the same number of years in the future, called the planning horizon. You cannot compare two projects if one is calculated out for three years and the other for five years.

When accounting for costs in internal projects such as BPI or IT upgrade costs—two major costs that are often left out of these projects are the cost of training for the employees and the costs associated with OCM, the organizational change management activities we discussed earlier. These are necessary costs of delivering a successful project that will be used by the people affected by it.

An additional quick note is to determine whether the "costs" of the project are only the design and development costs, or will they include the lifecycle costs (Total Costs of Ownership—TCO). For many projects, this will make a significant difference in the resulting analysis. Whichever way you calculate costs, project-only or lifecycle, all projects of the same type must be calculated the same way so that they may be compared in a consistent manner.

A final quick note is to include any significant contingency funds identified during risk analysis into the financial calculations. A high-risk project may very likely require a lot of money to reduce the risks to an acceptable level, and these funds should be included in any ROI, NPV, or other financial analysis.

2.3.6.2 Return on Investment (ROI)

How much money am I going to get back for the money I'm expending on this project? ROI includes predicted future financial benefits.

What is the "best" ROI? There's no answer to this, and different types of projects should be judged against different ROIs. As we have said before, developing a new manufacturing facility has a completely different ROI than does a BPI project, yet they may both be worthwhile projects. Upper management must choose a reasonable ROI as a bottom filter that projects must overcome to even be considered. Once that minimum ROI is met, the projects that provide the highest ROI should be chosen after assessing for risk. These bottom filters will be different for each different type of project. Note that some projects, such as mandatory "must do" projects will have a negative ROI. This is acceptable for those projects, and the other weighting factors will have to overcome a negative ROI.

In the world of financial portfolio management, there is a concept call a "hurdle rate." This is the minimum ROI a company requires for investments. It is more common in some industries, like manufacturing, than in industries like consulting. In setting the hurdle rate for a financial portfolio, there is some account taken of risk, at least in theory. Higher-risk projects, as many IT and NPD projects are, are given a higher hurdle rate. In practice, these hurdle rates are set by management's "best guess" at how much return they expect for their invested project dollars.

One additional comment about performing ROI calculations for IT projects: never use the ROI numbers given you by the vendors, as we've said before. These are highly inflated values for an "ideal" situation and are designed to sell a product, not to improve your business. Spend some time and do your own ROI calculations.

Returning to our MegaNews projects, the ROI calculations are as follows (note, we have left off the mandatory projects):

Assuming management tells us to use a five-year planning horizon. We multiply the annual benefits by five, subtract the cost to get the profits, and then divide by the cost. So for project D, we have ROI = (5 × $1.5M − $4M) ÷ $4M = 0.875.

The calculation for project J is somewhat tricky, and we have to identify carefully the assumptions used. Remember what we said before about it:

We assume that 20,000 people are affected with an average salary of $80,000/year. We expect a 10 percent reduction in productivity as people get used to working with the new software. This 10 percent reduction in productivity is like adding 2,000 people to the workforce, resulting in a six-month cost of $40 million.

After six months, we expect productivity to increase by 2 percent. A 2 percent increase in productivity over the next six months would result in a benefit of $8 million or an annualized benefit of $16 million. Let's assume that the total annual savings is created by laying off 25 IT people, resulting in a saving of $2.5 million.

We take the benefits that we have calculated for J, divide by the cost, and come up with an ROI of $6.4 million over our five-year planning

Table 2.11 MegaNews project ROI calculations

Project	Project	Estimated cost	Annual benefits	ROI
C	Corporate finance wants to install a data warehouse to manage all of the financial information.	$2.5M	$50,000	–$0.9M
D	We want to have a new website to compile news from other sources and allow viewers to buy it from us.	$4M	$1,500,000	0.875
E	We are opening new U.S. headquarters in Los Angeles and need to tie their LAN into the corporate network.	$0.5M	$100,000	$1M
G	We need a new service to allow us to deliver user-customized financial news via PDAs with wireless connections. The revenue will come from ads.	$5M	$2,000,000	$1M
H	We are going to put news screens into each Starbucks Coffee Shop in the United States, showing news headlines from around the world. The revenue will come from ads.	$20M	$10,000,000	$1.5M
I	Our website is currently written in English; we intend to internationalize it by creating versions in multiple languages. The revenue will come from ads.	$6M	$2,000,000	$0.67M
J	Half of our employees are using Macintosh computers, the rest are using PCs running Windows 8. The Windows component needs to be upgraded to Windows 10.	$5M	(see the following discussion)	$6.4 M

horizon. So far, this is our most favorable project from an ROI calculation. But, we had to make a lot of assumptions to do the calculation.

When we graph these results over a 10-year planning horizon, we obtain the following figure:

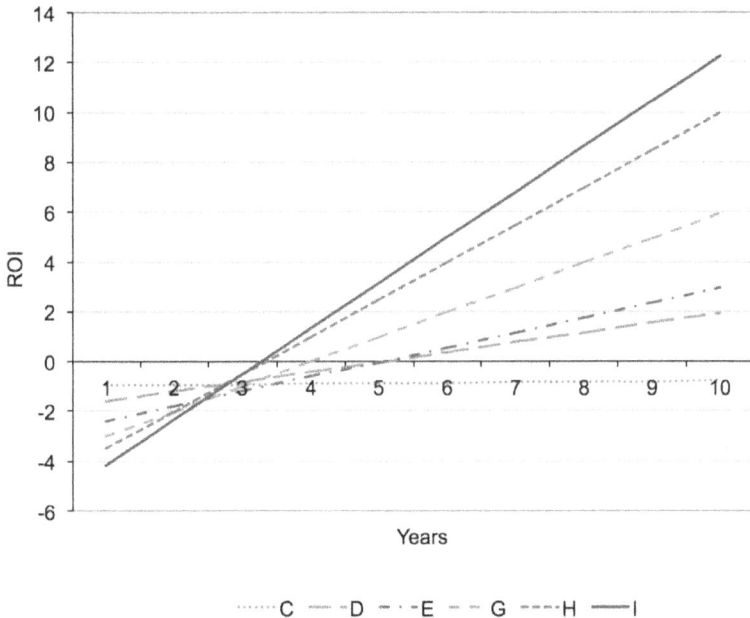

Figure 2.3-4 **ROI** *over 10-year planning horizon*

But 10 years is a much longer planning horizon than is justified for an IT-related or a process improvement project. Nobody wants to wait that long. A much more reasonable timeframe to compare projects is 5 to 6 years. Project E, the Los Angeles headquarters, looks to be a strongly positive return. To show the sensitivity of ROI calculations to the planning horizon, the CIO has plotted out ROI for these projects from 1 to 6 years to obtain the resulting figure:

We can immediately see that all projects have a negative ROI for the first two years. They cross the zero axis showing increasing returns somewhere between 2.5 and 5 years. The exception is the data warehouse, which never becomes profitable within the planning horizon.

Net Present Value (NPV)

The NPV is the present value of the expected future benefits *minus* the present value of the cost. This is a quick and easy selection approach. If the NPV of the project is less than zero, the project should be rejected because it will cost more than it will provide in benefits.

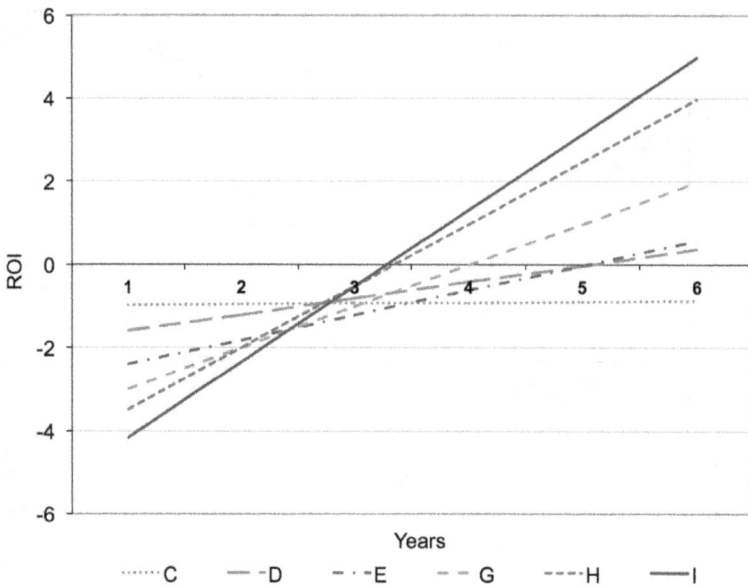

Figure 2.3-5 ROI over six years

If NPV is greater than zero, then benefits exceed costs and the project should be considered. When using NPV to compare different projects, the one with the *largest* NPV should be selected (all other things being equal). Note that the calculation is highly dependent on the planning horizon. A project that could be highly profitable in six years might not be considered if the planning horizon is only five years. When you are doing the calculation, if a project is even close to being profitable, recalculate it for another year out. See if it becomes much more profitable in the slightly longer timeframe. This is an example of a sensitivity analysis.

Returning to the overworked CIO of Megaprojects, he assumed an interest rate of 8 percent and has now calculated the following:

Projects H and J show really good NPV. Based on this alone, those two projects should be approved. Project C ended up again showing really poor numbers. This is consistent with what the CIO has already concluded about the financial data warehouse—it is not a viable project. Project E is also showing a negative NPV, so from this standpoint, it is not a good project.

Table 2.12 MegaNews project NPV calculations

Project	Project	Estimated cost	Annual benefits	NPV
C	Corporate finance wants to install a data warehouse to manage all of the financial information.	$2.5M	$50,000	−$2.13M
D	We want to have a new website to compile news from other sources and allow viewers to buy it from us.	$4M	$1,500,000	$1.84M
E	We are opening new U.S. headquarters in Los Angeles and need to tie their LAN into the corporate network.	$0.5M	$100,000	−$93K
G	We need a new service to allow us to deliver user-customized financial news via PDAs with wireless connections. The revenue will come from ads.	$5M	$2,000,000	$2.76M
H	We are going to put news screens into each Starbucks Coffee Shop in the United States, showing news headlines from around the world. The revenue will come from ads.	$20M	$10,000,000	$18.45M
I	Our website is currently written in English; we intend to internationalize it by creating versions in multiple languages. The revenue will come from ads.	$6M	$2,000,000	$1.8M
J	Half of our employees are using Macintosh computers, the rest are using PCs running Windows 8. The Windows component needs to be upgraded to Windows 10.	$5M		$34.13M

Just as he did for the ROI calculations, the CIO has also plotted out for six years the NPV calculations at an 8 percent interest rate to see where each project can become profitable.

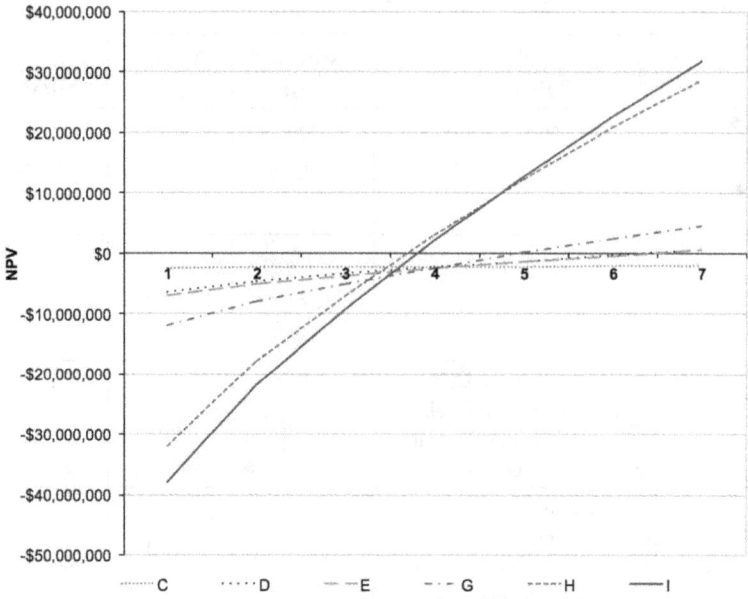

Figure 2.3-6 NPV at 8 percent interest rate

Our highly intelligent CIO knows that these calculations are sensitive to interest rate assumptions, so he also plotted the NPV assuming a 10 percent interest rate.

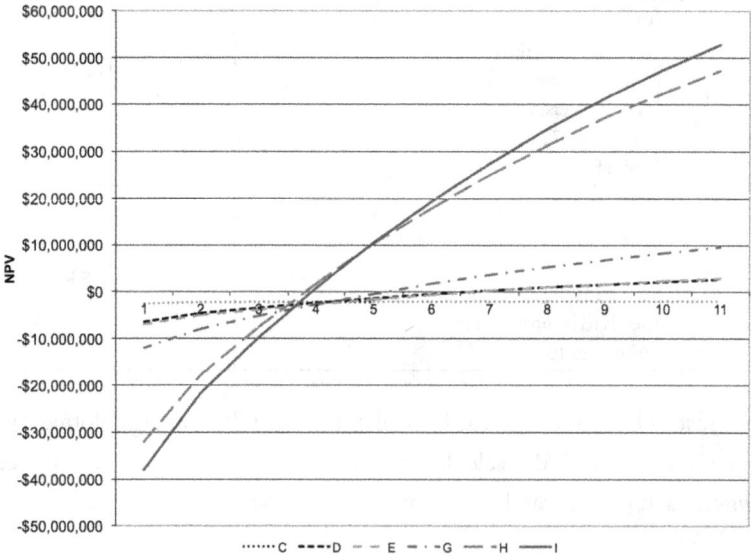

Figure 2.3-7 NPV at 10 percent interest rate

Note that assuming a worse interest rate, 10 percent, means that no project will be selected within the five-year planning horizon except for projects H and I. Earlier, we stated that a business case should be built around three possible states of the future: optimistic, expected, and pessimistic. Applying that approach to NPV calculations, the CIO should perform calculations at interest rates of 5, 8, and 10 percent (or even higher) and compare the resulting answers.

2.3.6.5 Benefit/cost Analysis

This is the ratio of expected costs to expected benefits. A hallmark of CBA is that all benefits and all costs are expressed in money terms, and are adjusted for the time value of money, so that all flows of benefits and flows of project costs over time (which tend to occur at different points in time) are expressed on a common basis in terms of their "present value." What benefit am I going to gain for the money this is going to cost me? It is often used when expected benefits include items with fluffy numbers, such as productivity improvements or employee morale.

The actual calculation is done by dividing the expected benefits with the expected costs (the benefit cost ratio (BCR)). Using revenue as the benefit is a potential negative, as revenue is not the same as profit. It is better to do the calculation using expected profit and thereby include the project costs within the calculation.

- At BCR < 1, costs greater than revenues.
- At BCR = 1, revenues equal costs.
- At BCR > 1.3, you should consider doing this project.

Why a BCR of 1.3 or better to approve the project? Why not a BCR greater than 1? Because the numbers in this calculation are so vague and so roughly done that it is better to be safe and ensure that the project will be profitable.

Unfortunately, this type of calculation is commonly used in public works projects, and it is highly subject to optimistic guesses as to future benefits. Political organizations rarely have this capability in-house, so they normally hire consultants to do this type of analysis. Consultants are always eager to keep their clients happy so as to obtain future contracts, so the results of the analysis are historically optimistic. In fact, a study of the accuracy of cost estimates in transportation infrastructure planning found that[21]: for rail projects, the actual costs turned out to average 44.7 percent higher than estimated costs, and for roads projects, 20.4 percent higher.

Another study[22] found that actual rail ridership was on average 51.4 percent lower than the original estimates when justifying a new rail or subway line. For roads, it was found that for half of all projects estimated traffic was wrong by more than 20 percent. There is a very strong tendency to exaggerate the benefits and minimize the costs and risks. In southern California, during the early part of this century, several major toll way projects were heading rapidly toward bankruptcy because they based their tolls on traffic projections, which turned out to be overly optimistic.

For the MegaNews projects, the CIO has again used a five-year planning horizon and calculated:

These calculations are similar in results to the ROI calculations. Which makes perfect sense when you realize that the benefit/cost ratio is the inverse of the ROI. Projects G and H are showing strong here and would be selected if benefit/cost were the only calculations performed.

The real standout in terms of benefits is project J—the MS Windows upgrade. It is showing a very strong cost to benefit ratio. However, remember that we used a lot of very fuzzy numbers when calculating it, making assumptions about productivity gains. Be very cautious when selecting projects that require productivity assumptions and use multiple calculation methods before you select them.

2.3.6.6 Internal Rate of Return (IRR)

The IRR is the rate where the discounted cash flow(DCF) exactly equal the initial investment. That is, IRR is the interest rate where NPV = 0. So, we use our NPV formula, set the equation equal to zero, and back-calculate to find the interest rate that gives us that result.

Warning: This is a totally artificial rate and is only used for comparing investments.

Example of IRR:

Table 2.13 MegaNews project benefit/cost analysis

Project	Project	Estimated cost	Annual benefits	Benefit/ cost
C	Corporate finance wants to install a data warehouse to manage all of the financial information.	$2.5M	$50,000	−0.01
D	We want to have a new website to compile news from other sources and allow viewers to buy it from us.	$4M	$1,500,000	−1.88
E	We are opening new U.S. headquarters in Los Angeles and need to tie their LAN into the corporate network.	$0.5M	$100,000	1
G	We need a new service to allow us to deliver user-customized financial news via PDAs with wireless connections. The revenue will come from ads.	$5M	$2,000,000	2
H	We are going to put news screens into each Starbucks Coffee Shop in the United States, showing news headlines from around the world. The revenue will come from ads.	$20M	$10,000,000	2.5
I	Our website is currently written in English; we intend to internationalize it by creating versions in multiple languages. The revenue will come from ads.	$6M	$2,000,000	1.67
J	Half of our employees are using Macintosh computers, the rest are using PCs running Windows 8. The Windows component needs to be upgraded to Windows 10.	$5M		7.40

2.3.6.7 Comparing Different Methods

Table 2.14 *Comparison of different calculation results*

Method	Advantages	Disadvantages	Best used when
NPV	• Most realistic of the 3 methods. • Uses time value of money. • Allows for various scenarios as far as cash flows.	• Is complex. • Requires assumptions to be made about rate, likelihood of cash flows.	The investment will be over several years, and the discount rate is likely to change over this time period. There are negative and positive cash flows. NPV or payback period should be used if discount rate cannot be determined and must be assumed.
IRR	• Is simple. • Uses one discount rate.	• Is often not realistic; the discount rate usually changes over time. • Does not work for positive and negative cash flows. • May not know discount rate. • Expresses return as a percentage—most companies set their goals in monetary terms (e.g., sales increase of $2M). IRR will prefer 500% of $1 to 20% return on $100.	Best used when cash flows move from negative to positive, and remain positive.
Payback period	• Is simple. • Is easily understood.	• Does not account for time value of money. • Does not recognize timing of cash flows—yet earlier is better than later. • May lead to excessive investment in short-term projects. • Does not differentiate between projects with same payback period but with other factors that are different: For example, investment required.	Is for project of relatively short duration: a few years maximum. Discount rate should be low. For example, in a developing country with high inflation, using the payback period method may be misleading. (NPV or payback period should be used if discount rate cannot be determined and must be assumed).

Table 2.14 (*Continued*)

Method	Advantages	Disadvantages	Best used when
ROI	• Is simple. • Can be used for a variety of benefits depending on how benefits are calculated.	• Not a true calculation method, merely a way to identify your returns depending on how you calculate benefits using one of the other methods.	Not a method. Used in conjunction with NPV, IRR, or payback to determine your overall return.

2.3.7 Summary of MegaNews International Projects

Now that we have seen how to do the calculations, lets compare the calculations for the MegaNews International projects.

Now we have all the data on one sheet and can compare the results. Projects A, B, and F we determined were mandatory, we have to do them regardless of the costs or benefits.

Project C, the data warehouse, ranked poorly in all of our calculations. There is no rational reason for ever doing this project with the current numbers.

Project D, the new news website, has a good payback period, but a poor ROI and a poor benefit/cost ratio. This project should be shelved until there are stronger benefits to it.

Project E, the Los Angeles U.S. headquarters, doesn't look either good or bad from an ROI or benefit/cost ratio, and the payback period is long. But, it is a relatively low-cost project and should probably be approved from an infrastructure standpoint.

Projects G and H look reasonable. H has better ROI and benefit/cost numbers, but is also much more expensive. Both of these projects assume future advertising revenue, and so are subject to fluctuations based on how solid those assumptions are. Some additional research on future ad revenues might be done to provide support for the numbers.

Project I is also subject to the same assumptions as G and H, but the numbers for this project are poor in comparison, so the decision makers will probably not choose this project.

Project J proved to have surprisingly good financial justifications. A short payback period, a good ROI, and a better benefit/cost than the other projects. However, J is also very sensitive to the assumptions made. Always

Table 2.15 *MegaNews project benefit/cost analysis*

Project	Project	Estimated cost	Annual benefits	Payback period	NPV	ROI	Benefit/ cost
A	New privacy laws that will take effect in 6 months in Europe require us to strengthen our website registration database.	$1M	N/A	N/A	N/A	N/A	N/A
B	A new law in California requires us to change our website so that viewers must "opt-in" to receive our e-mail newsletters rather than "opt-out" from receiving it. Due in 3 months.	$0.5M	N/A	N/A	N/A	N/A	N/A
C	Corporate finance wants to install a data warehouse to manage all of the financial information.	$2.5M	$50,000	50 years	−2.13M	−0.9	−0.01
D	We want to have a new website to compile news from other sources and allow viewers to buy it from us.	$4M	$1,500,000	2.67	$1.84M	0.875	−1.88
E	We are opening new U.S. headquarters in Los Angeles and need to tie their LAN into the corporate network.	$0.5M	$100,000	5.00	−$93k	1	1
F	UPI is upgrading their news distribution network, and we need to modify our system to tie into it.	$3.5M	N/A	N/A	N/A	N/A	N/A
G	We need a new service to allow us to deliver user-customized financial news via PDAs with wireless connections. The revenue will come from ads.	$5M	$2,000,000	2.50	$2.76M	1	2
H	We are going to put news screens into each Starbucks Coffee Shop in the United States, showing news headlines from around the world. The revenue will come from ads.	$20M	$10,000,000	2.00	$18.45M	1.5	2.5
I	Our website is currently written in English; we intend to internationalize it by creating versions in multiple languages. The revenue will come from ads.	$6M	$2,000,000	3.00	$1.8M	0.667	1.67
J	Half of our employees are using Macintosh computers, the rest are using PCs running Windows 8. The Windows component needs to be upgraded to Windows 10.	$5M		27 months	$34.13M	6.4	7.40

be very cautious of any benefits that depend on productivity increases. They are very hard to measure outside of a manufacturing process.

Step 2.4 Rate the Project Risks

In this section, we're going to talk about how to assess how likely the projects are to be successful. It makes no sense to approve an expensive project with only a 10 percent probability of successfully completing it. This is the area project managers call risk analysis. In the next chapter, we're going to look specifically at the risks of the EPMS project itself.

According to research[23], the costs of portfolio risk management are difficult to quantify in advance, requiring assumptions about the productivity improvement it will bring. By comparison, managing the overall risk of the portfolio (as contrasted with individual projects within the portfolio) has more easily defined benefits and ensures that the organization is not subject to extremely high risks overall[24].

A broader viewpoint is that managing uncertainty in the portfolio is more important than managing risk. You can identify the risks that might impact individual projects, but the risk of the portfolio is the product of the risk of the individual projects due to cascading effects of problems on one project often impacting others.

For this reason, and because a portfolio of projects has risks that individual projects do not as well as living in a more dynamic environment, it's a better approach to think about managing uncertainty than risk. Uncertainty is a much broader term that captures all the variability in the environment the portfolio exists in. When you do risk analysis, keep in mind that there is uncertainty in the outside world that may impact the project and is not being captured in the detailed risk analysis.

All project managers are taught about risk. We are taught to think, from the very beginning of the project, about things that can impact the project later so we can prepare for them. Risks are specific events that can either cause damage to some part of the project (threats) or can improve the project (opportunities).

Asking "What are the risks on this project?" and "How risky is this project?" are two totally different questions. Knowing the individual risks on the project does not mean you know how risky the project itself is because of the influence of the environment external to the project. Similarly, knowing the risks of each project in the portfolio does not tell you the overall risk level of the portfolio for the same reason. This is especially true on larger and more complex projects.

The uncertainty in the portfolio can be considered a combination of the individual risks of the projects, the uncertainties in their interactions, and the uncertainties of the outside environment. Leifer[25], in talking about NPD projects, suggests four categories of uncertainty:

- **Technical uncertainties** include issues related to the completeness and correctness of the underlying scientific knowledge, the technical specifications of the product, manufacturing, maintainability, and so on.
- **Market uncertainties** include issues related to customer needs and wants—either existing or latent forms of interactions between the customer and the product, methods of sales and distributions, the relationship to competitors' products, and so on.
- **Organizational uncertainties** refer to the capabilities required from the project team, their relationships with the rest of the organization, changing priorities, the level of support from management.
- **Financial uncertainties** include access to funding for the projects, both internal funding or external funding, including partnerships and joint ventures.

While not all of these uncertainties apply to our portfolio implementation project or even to all of the projects within the portfolio, it indicates that we should think about all of the uncertainties in our efforts in addition to the individual risks inherent in the project itself.

2.4.1 Introduction to Portfolio Risk

Why are we talking about risk for projects that are being proposed? We have not even started them yet, how can we know what their risks are?

Part of the goal of an EPMS is to balance out risk and reward. It is generally true that the greater the benefits of the project, the higher the risk, and the greater the chances of failure. Low-risk projects almost always provide few benefits but are more likely to be successful. Low-risk projects that provide large benefits exist primarily in college textbooks on portfolio theory.

Each of us, including your managers, has a maximum amount of risk we're willing to take (our risk tolerance). We must identify the risky projects so that we can balance them out with less risky projects. We can do this at a very high summary level, or we can do it at a more detailed level depending on how much effort management wants to put into the pre-approval risk assessment.

Project risk analysis begins when the project is first being considered for approval. If the project is approved, a more detailed risk analysis is done by the project manager and is revisited regularly during the execution phase of the project. We said in the last chapter that we cannot predict with great accuracy either the cost of the projects or their future benefits. We just don't have enough accurate detailed information to do that. The same applies to assessing the projects risks—we cannot predict them perfectly. But, we can do it well enough to determine if this is a risky project or not.

So, even without knowing the detailed risks of the proposed projects, we can assess at a high level which projects are risky by looking at the typical risks for the *type* of project and our own history in doing those projects. A company that has a strong background in developing manufacturing facilities has a good history of what the risks are in building a new plant. A company that does a lot of software programming understands those risks pretty well. A pharmaceutical company has a thorough understanding of the huge risks in developing a new drug compound. A construction company that decides to develop its own project management software is creating a high-risk project, because they just don't have the background or experience to do it. This level of risk understanding is adequate for comparing new projects against each other.

Portfolio-level risk has four aspects to it:

- Developing the wrong products
- Delivering products that are likely to be too late or too much over budget
- Wasting resources working on low-priority projects
- Wasting resources by working on duplicate projects

Developing the wrong product is obviously a waste of the organization's time and money. This is something that a portfolio management system cannot prevent if the management wants to try it. But, the EPMS can point out the dangers in doing so by allocating it a high risk.

Delivering the final product too late or too much over budget will have a negative impact on the financial justifications done for the business case. If the product is completed very late, there is lost opportunity for the planned benefits. If it is significantly over budget, the ROI will not be as good as it was initially calculated to be. This is where our preproject risk assessment can help. If we don't have experience with this type of project, the risk analysis will point this out as a high-risk project.

Wasting resources by working on duplicate projects is something a portfolio management system is very good at identifying and in avoiding, and in fact, this is a major source of the cost savings provided by an EPMS. Don't believe your organization does duplicate work? In a large enough organization, there is not only the possibility of duplicate/overlapping work, but there is a high probability of it. During the late 1990s, Hewlett–Packard discovered that there were seven divisions all developing business printers in competition with each other. Waste of money.

2.4.2 Project Risk Assessment

PMI[26] defines risk as an uncertain event, which, if it occurs, will have an impact on at least one project objective, such as time, cost, scope, or quality. That is, a risk is something that can happen in the future that will have an impact on the project either negatively or positively. Because we're not worried about any positive risks for each project at this point, we will just concentrate on the negative risks, the threats, that might cause our projects to not be successful. (Professional risk managers also look at positive risks as opportunities to do better than planned. Most project managers barely have time to worry about things that can harm their project, let alone things that can help it.)

A risk has three components:

- An unplanned-for event
- The probability of that event happening
- The impact on the project if it does happen

What is the likelihood of something happening, and what are the impacts if it does?

Because the project has not been approved yet, we do not have any detailed information on what its specific risks are, the kind of information that comes out of the risk analysis effort after the project is approved. Yet, we need some idea of how risky the project is before we even approved it.

In Section 2.4.3, we'll discuss in more detail the types of areas that should be looked at during this preliminary risk assessment. At its simplest, the approach used is to identify the project risks at a very high level by:

Identifying the external risks such as uncertainties in the marketplace or in the economic environment

Identifying our organization's experience in doing this type of project

Identify risks that are unique to this type of project, such as OCM risks to our business process project, regulatory risks to our drug development project, or political risks to our new refinery project

Identify whether the work will be outsourced or done internally

Other risk factors as required for the specific industry

We want to answer the question: What is the probability that the end product will be successful. Not just the project success, but the success of the end product produced by the project. This is difficult to measure quantitatively. The most common approach is to have experienced management people make the determination, primarily by the marketing department. This can be done by having them individually, and apart from each other, make an estimate on what the risk is based on a scale of 1 to 10 (1 being no risk, and 10 being high risk) and then average the results. This is similar to a Delphi approach. The other approach is to have the governance or steering committee assess the project's risk, also based on a scale of 1 to 10, and then agree on what the number is.

The other part of the risk, the organization's experience in this type of project, is easier to determine. Projects that your organization has no experience with are highly risky, projects that are done often have lower risk associated with them. Again use a scale of 1 to 10 and have the part(s) of the organization that will be involved in the project assess the risk.

When you average these numbers, you have a reasonable assessment of how risky the project is without actually starting the project. If the project is approved, then once the project manager completes the initial risk analysis, you can take that number and plug it back into the portfolio risk.

For example, we can build a small matrix like the following one and give it to the right stakeholders (questions are indicative of risk and only examples):

Table 2.16 Risk ratings

Risk	Low risk		Medium risk					High risk		
	1	2	3	4	5	6	7	8	9	10
Are there market risks for this product?										
Are there risks due to our experience with this type of project?										
Are there risks unique to this type of project?										
Are there risks due to outsourced work?										
Are there other risks on this project?										

This is the simplest risk assessment possible. We'll talk about more detailed ones later in this section.

Some types of projects are inherently more risky than others. Projects in the pharmaceutical industry have a high failure rate between the initial concept of a specific drug and the completion, years later, of the final clinical trials and approvals. NPD projects have a high failure rate, many of them are unsuccessful in the market after spending a great deal of money and personnel resources to develop. It is often said that 90 percent of new products will fail to be financially successful, but the other 10 percent will make up for them.

Projects in the large construction industry are generally high risk with the primary risks being cost/schedule overruns, safety risks, environmental/regulatory risks, and sometimes market risks for a construction project built on speculation like a new shopping mall. If the completed building does not sell or rent, the entire project will not fulfill the business case nor make a profit.

Story

One of the stories that is often told in architecture classes is the history of the Empire State Building in New York City. Groundbreaking occurred on Jan 11, 1930. When it was completed one year, 45 days later (almost 5 months ahead of schedule) it was the tallest building in the world. A distinction it held for many years.

The original planned budget was close to $50 million. It was completed for $41 million, nine million dollars under budget. Why was it completed so far under budget? Because between the time the building was planned and the time it was completed the Depression occurred. This made both workers and materials much less expensive than planned.

But, also because of the Depression, the building sat largely empty for 50 years and was often referred to as the Empty State Building. The owners turned the lights on in the upper floors so it would look more rented than it really was. It was not fully rented until 1951. Successful as a project, but not a business success until much later.

In the construction and engineering industries, there is a survey form called the Project Definition Rating Index (PDRI) developed by the Construction Industry Institute (CII)[§]. This is a series of questions designed to draw out the amount of risk on the project. The answers to the questions are weighted for importance, and projects that score well are more likely to complete on time and on budget:

- The basis of the project decision, including the business strategy
- The basis of the design
- The execution approach

The highest weighted risks are in the first group, the business area. Poor decisions made here will have a much larger impact on project success than decisions made later by the engineers, the contractors, and the project managers.

[§] http://www.construction-institute.org

Story

The author was working with a client in Dubai in fall of 2008. During his visit, the new Dubai Mall opened to a lot of fanfare and heavy publicity. This is the largest mall in the United Arab Emirates by store count, about 600 stores. It included a large indoor aquarium and an Olympic-size ice skating rink. Due to continual design changes the project was a year late, and instead of opening during a financial boom time it opened just as world economies started to implode and people stopped shopping. The mall was opened despite the fact that only one third of the stores were open for business. Most stores were boarded up, making the brand new mall look like a ghost town. The mall cost US$3 billion, and there was a $US1 billion construction claim against it.

Because of their comparatively small size and short duration, management considers IT projects to be low risk compared to manufacturing facility projects, and yet they have a high failure rate. In reality, there is much management research that shows that IT projects in general are more risky than they appear to be, and that this should be taken into account when an IT project is selected for the portfolio. As Dewan[27] phrased it: *"... The authors find that IT investments are substantially riskier than ordinary capital investments, and that IT risk is associated with a substantial risk premium. This risk premium is driven in part by the lost option value of making irreversible capital investment decisions."*

"A key implication of the findings is that managers should apply a substantially higher discount rate when evaluating IT investments relative to other types of less risky capital investments. Furthermore, the results suggest that the timing of IT capital investment is a critical factor in managing both the risks and returns of IT investments."

Once the project has begun, one of the first steps the project manager should undertake is to begin the detailed risk assessment. All stakeholders are involved and each identifies the risks that might occur on the project. These are documented in the project's risk register and ranked as to the probability of the risk happening and the impact on the project if it does. This process leads to a rank-ordered list of risks.

This is a much more detailed risk analysis than was done to approve the project. If, after doing the project risk analysis, it is determined that the project is much more risky, or much less risky, than initially thought, the new risk number should be inserted back into the portfolio's risk calculations to see if the overall risk level of the portfolio has changed. If a project is significantly more risky than was thought, the steering committee should review it again with the new risk number to see if it still makes sense to do the project.

The simplest approach to determining risks, and it works well for smaller projects, is just to give each risk a numerical ranking, 1 to 5 is common, for the probability of it happening. A risk scored "1" is unlikely to happen. while one scored "5" is highly likely to happen ("highly likely" can be as little as a 25 percent chance of occurring). In a similar fashion, the impact of the risk, if it happens, is also scored 1 to 5. A score of "1" means the risk will cause little damage to the project, a score of "5" means it will cause significant risk to a project objective. Once these numbers are assigned, they are multiplied, and the result is the risk score for the project. The list of scored risks is then rank-ordered, and the highest risks are mitigated to the extent possible. Contingency plans are written for any risks deemed high after mitigation approaches.

This probability × impact (P-I approach) is sufficient for the level of risk detail we need here. If the projects are complex, like oil refineries or new aircraft development, there are much more sophisticated ways of identifying risks and scoring their impacts.

Project risks can be categorized as technical risks, external risks, organizational risks, and project management risks, as shown in the following drawings for a software project and for a construction project:

All of these are potential risks on every project and should be considered during the detailed risk assessment. Project managers tend to concentrate on the technical risks that impact the project, yet these are often the most controllable. More significant risks are those outside the project manager's control—external risks and organizational risks. These are the

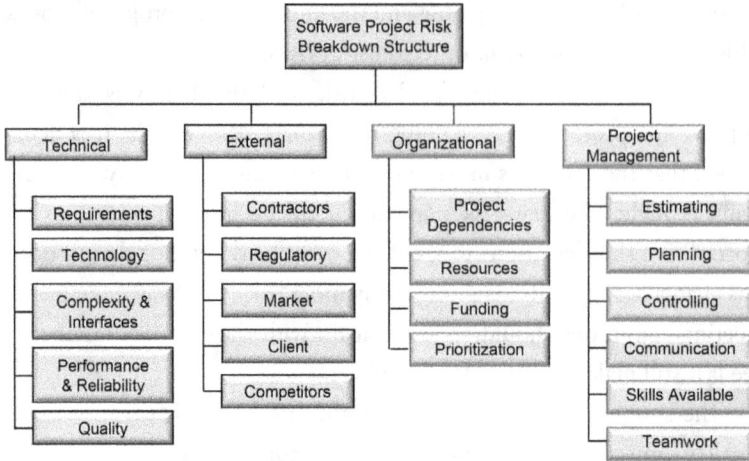

Figure 2.4-1 Risks in IT

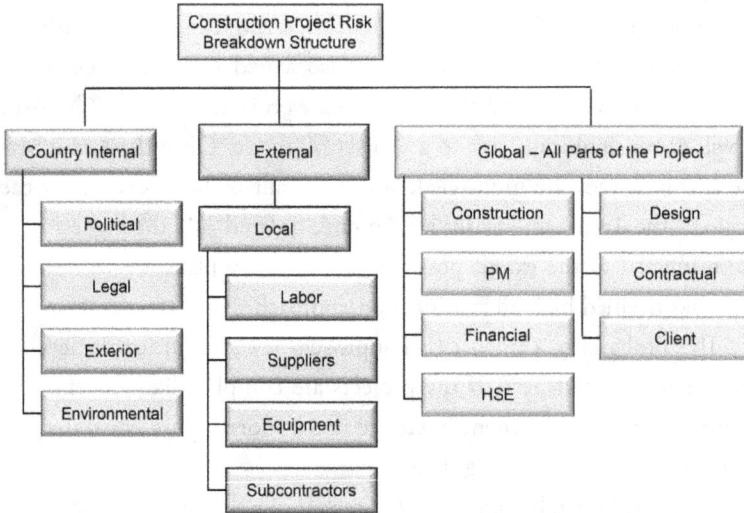

Figure 2.4-2 Risks in construction

risks that can do far more damage to the project than the purely technical risks inherent in the project. These other risks can be identified by getting the right stakeholders involved such as clients and upper management.

One aspect of doing the risk assessment in the beginning of the project is to set aside contingency funds to pay for the risks that happen. As we assess the risks of projects that are being considered for the portfolio, any really significant risks that are identified even at this early stage should initiate the set-aside of funds to pay for risks. These funds should be considered during the financial analysis so that the ROI and other measures include project risk in the results. There is some judgment and experience that is required here. Too little money set aside for risk will not cover the costs of the risks, and the project will go over budget. Too much money set aside for risk will reduce funds that might have been available for other projects.

The portfolio manager should have a bucket of money set aside she can use for projects that are over-running their budget. This bucket can be requested separately from management, or it can be taken out of the management reserve from all the projects in the portfolio and used where needed.

2.4.3 Portfolio Risks

The portfolio risk is the average of the individual risks of all the projects in the portfolio. We risk-score each project individually, add up all the risk scores, and divide by the number of projects. This part is simple. What is not simple is determining how much risk the steering committee is willing to take in exchange for benefits. As we mentioned earlier, the more risky the project, the greater the benefits, but the higher the risk of failure. The projects that are low risk generally provide low benefits also. A survey performed by eQuest Consulting[28] of project portfolios in Australia and New Zealand companies found that, on average, most projects were divided between low risk and medium risk:

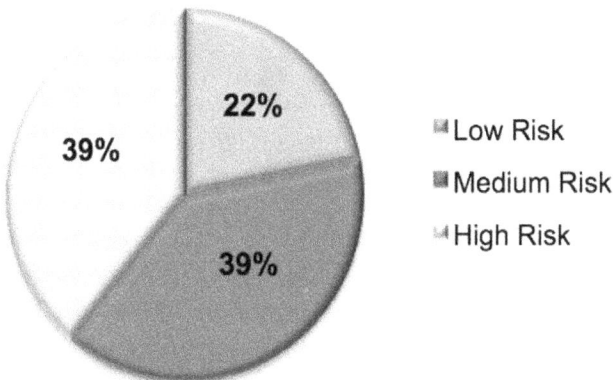

Figure 2.4-3 Division of risky projects

The portfolio risk is determined primarily by the risks of the individual projects that are included in the portfolio, but it is also influenced by outside factors. Any resources, such as staff, that any one project shares with other projects increases the portfolio risk. If our portfolio is a collection of public works construction projects, the risk of the whole portfolio is increased when the price of steel doubles (as it did in 2007–2008). This new level of risk is now the baseline for judging new projects. If our portfolio is the collection of all IT projects in the organization, then the risk is multiplied by the fact that one group of IT developers is working on all projects. A good EPMS will allow for input to common project risk factors independent of any one project. This allows for continually updating the risk level of the portfolio due to factors outside the individual projects.

In portfolio risk management, there are risks that can multiply under the right circumstances. If multiple projects within the portfolio utilize the same resources, then care must be taken to ensure that those resources are available to all projects as needed. If one project in the portfolio runs behind the expected schedule and ties up critical resources, that has a ripple effect on the other projects in the portfolio that need that resource. Portfolio management tools can help identify those risks that impact multiple projects so that they can be avoided. A scarce resource is a danger point in projects, whether that scarce resource is a person with particular skills, a piece of equipment that many projects need, or a shortage of materials. If there is only one construction crane available for three projects, then the schedules must be built around its availability, and it should be identified as a risk item.

Story

Lowe's[29] enterprise risk management group uses a prioritization matrix for every new project it considers. The group, which comprises the company's top seven executives, examines four components of each project: business returns, strategic alignment, process impact and risk. Risk is a negative score, so the greater the technological or other risk, the lower the overall score will be, says Steve Stone, CIO at the home improvement retailer. Therefore, a risky project needs to score high points in the other categories to get a green light.

In addition to the risks in each project and the risks inherent in a multiproject environment, there are additional risks that can occur in a portfolio environment. Changes in the strategic direction of the company put all projects at risk, as do major organizational changes such as mergers and acquisitions (M&As) or downsizing due to economic environmental changes.

Toyota Financial Services asks about risk in six key areas as part of its project approval process. These questions, or similar ones, are at the level that we need to ask in order to do the risk assessment. These questions can be broken down into five different categories:

- Market and external risks
- Management and user-level support
- Scope-related risks
- Project-related risks
- Organizational experience
- Outsourcing risks

While the specific questions will differ for each organization, these categories are fairly typical for all types of projects.

Market and External Risks

- These are questions designed to drive out the external risks. If we're putting up a new shopping center, will the future economic environment allow it to be profitable? If we're creating a new type of personal entertainment device, will enough people buy it that we'll recoup our heavy R&D expenses on it?
- Is this a new product in the marketplace?
- Is this a new product for us?
- How much competition is there?
- What is the economic environment?
- What are the barriers to entry for new competitors?
- Is there reasonable external funding available for this project?

Management/User-Level Support

These are questions designed to determine if upper management is strongly behind this project. If it is a product to be used internally, such as process improvements, IT upgrades, or a new ERP system, will the employees actually use it once it is delivered? Too many internal projects, particularly IT-related ones, are completed from a technical standpoint and then end up being a waste of time because the employees or managers will not use the product.

- Are all the stakeholders supportive, or are there subversive stakeholders?
- Does the designated project sponsor strongly support the effort?
- Are subject-matter experts available to work on the development?
- Will process owners providing adequate time and/or support?
- Has the project requester identified the need for OCM as part of the project?
- Will all the required organizational resources been made available for the project?

Scope-Related Risk

These are questions that apply to anything related to scope or requirements. The larger the project is, the riskier it is. The more parts of the organization that are affected by the project, the riskier it is.

- What is the objective of the project?
- How many end users are affected by the project?
- How many internal organizations are impacted?
- Are business requirements accurate and complete?
- How well do purchased products satisfy our business needs?

Project Management-Related Risk

While it would be nice to think that there are no significant risks related to the project manager's abilities, we know there are many risks that are associated with each project related to skills, experience, project structure, and other project-specific areas.

- Do we have enough time to plan the project properly?
- Do we have enough time and resources to gather and analyze the requirements?
- Estimated total cost of the project?
- Will adequate time allocated for the project, or is there a desire to rush it?
- Approximate project working team size?
- Impact on other projects in work?
- Do we have enough of the right skill/experience levels?
- How many different geographical work locations is the project going to spread across?
- Are project team members going to come from outside agencies?
- Are any project team members coming from an offshore vendor?
- Is the project using the appropriate project management approach and methodology?

Organizational Experience

Any type of project that our organization has little or no experience with is automatically risky. If we have always outsourced our IT infrastructure and are now bringing it back in-house, any IT projects are going to be risky. If we're the architects of a new building and the owners want us to be the project managers also, that is highly risky.

- Do we have sufficient knowledge of how to manage this type of project?
- Is this technology or process new to the industry or to our organization?
- Was a proof of concept done for the project?

For some types of projects, other categories must be included. For example, if we are looking at doing internal process improvement projects, we would include questions arranged around finding out if the organization was ready for the changes that will come. Some of these questions might give us the following information:

- How many business units and business divisions will be impacted by the project?
- How many end users will be affected by the project?
- What is our history of accepting unapproved change requests?
- Are OCM resources allocated to the project?
- Have all the stakeholders agreed to the OCM approach and associated impacts?
- How confident are you of the project estimates?
- How many external entities to the company are likely to be involved in the project (e.g., governmental agencies, other companies, vendors, and so on)?
- Are there any constraints that may limit the successful implementation of this project?

There are also obviously risks related to different industry categories. The construction industry worries a lot about safety risks and about financing risks. The risk assessment should be done taking these risks into account along with the other risks we have already talked about.

Risks in Outsourcing

Any work done by another company under a contract or a purchase agreement adds additional risk to the project. No matter how tight the contract, we have less control over outsourced work than we do over our own internal resources. You have less transparency with a contractor than you do with internal employees. The contractor could be running into serious problems and you will never see them.

In some industries, such as construction, the risks are well documented and should be included in any preapproval questionnaire. In fact, the PDRI mentioned earlier does exactly this. In other industries, such as IT, the risks do not have as long a documented history. Since the current outsourcing trend began in the late 1990s and early 2000s, there have been a few outsourcing success stories but a lot of failures. Treat any work done outside the organization walls as risky.

In fact, the history of outsourcing problems has grown so large that the decision makers in your company will be very leery of any project that requires significant outsourcing. There should be a higher risk assigned to it, as well as stronger financial justifications than a similar project would have that does not require outsourcing.

Outsourcing is problematic in all industries, and the risk depends on the maturity of an organization's outsourcing approach and history. A good example is the airplane manufacturing industry. Boeing released the 787 Dreamliner late and hugely over budget, causing billions of dollars in overruns and contract cancelations and penalties. Why? Because they convinced themselves that they could save a great deal of money by outsourcing virtually all of the major components. This is an easy financial calculation to do just by comparing labor and material rates in different countries with labor and material rates locally in the state of Washington where their main plant is located.

But, just because it is an easy calculation to do does not mean it was accurate. Boeing experienced such several quality problems on products produced by their low-cost suppliers that the entire development effort went over budget and was three years late. Boeing had no experience outsourcing major design and manufacturing and create huge risks by doing something they had no experience in. Their previous aircraft, the 777, was a model of a well-run project by comparison, because it was done totally internal to Boeing.

By contrast, look at the history of the Airbus A380, developed during the same period as the 787 Dreamliner. Airbus is a European consortium comprised of companies in several countries. They have a lot of experience outsourcing work and did not run into any significant outsourcing problems. The A380 was also years late and significantly over budget, but the problems were related to management decisions, poorly thought-out attempts at cost cutting, and technical problems, not outsourcing issues.

What you should ask are:

- What is our experience with outsourcing?
- What parts of our organization will be involved with the outsourcing?

- How much experience does the outsourced organization have with organizations similar to ours and with the work we are hiring them to do?
- What is the success record of the outsourced organization?
- What is the financial status of the outsourced organization?

Example of Risk Analysis—IT

Even though the PDRI survey is becoming widely accepted within construction and engineering companies, there is no equivalent acceptable form within IT. Each company creates their own risk assessment questionnaire. The questionnaire in Appendix 2.4 was developed by the PMO in the IT unit of a major California utility company. The risk areas that are identified include:

- Project size
- Project structure
- Technology
- Outside risks

This is a reasonable example of how to do a risk analysis on an IT project without actually having started the project. By answering these questions, it creates an understanding of what the risks are on the project. The numbers are a best guess and should be answered mostly by the IT staff, with a few questions (mostly related to user acceptance) to be answered by middle management.

MegaNews International Example

Lets take one of the MegaNews International projects and run it through a different version of the IT risk assessment questionnaire. Let's pick project G, the news downloads to iPads, PDAs, and smartphones.

25 people for six months is 25 people × 8 hours/day × 22 days/month × 6 months = 26,400 hours of work.

We will have to interface with other organizations to determine the technical requirements for different product vendors, but there are no regulatory restrictions. The rest of the estimates are the CIO's best guesses.

Table 2.17 MegaNews risk example

Project profile item	Risk score	Risk weight	Project risk score
Size			
1. Total man-hours for the project			
a. 100 to 3,000	Low—1		
b. 3,000 to 15,000	Med—2	5	15
c. 15,000 to 30,000	*Med—3*		
d. Over 30,000	High—4		
2. Development duration estimate in calendar time			
a. 12 months or less	*Low—1*	4	4
b. 13 months to 24 months	Med—2		
c. Over 24 months	High—3		
3. The work will be performed by:			
a. Mostly by on-site personnel	Low—1	2	4
b. Significant portions by on-site personnel	*Med—2*		
c. Mostly by off-site personnel	High—3		
4. Number of departments involved			
a. One	Low—1	4	12
b. Two	Med—2		
c. Three	*High—3*		
5. Approximate number of end users			
a. Up to 25	Low—1		
b. 25–100	Med—2	1	5
c. 100–1000	High—3		
d. Over 1,000	*High—5*		
6. Number of different geographic locations in which the product will operate			
a. One	Low—1		
b. 2–4	Med—2	2	10
c. 5–10	High—3		
d. Over 10	*High—5*		

(Continued)

Table 2.17 (*Continued*)

Project profile item	Risk score	Risk weight	Project risk score
Organizational and Customer			
7. The system or product description			
a. Totally new system or product	*High—3*		
b. Replacement of an existing manual system	Med—2	5	3
c. Replacement of an existing automated system	Low—1		
8. The severity of internal process changes needed			
a. Low—1	*Low—1*		
b. Medium—2	Med—2	5	5
c. High—3	High—3		
d. Unknown	High—3		
9. The general attitude of customers			
a. Poor—anti-information	High—3	5	5
b. Fair—some reluctance	Med—2		
c. Good—understands value	*Low—1*		
10. Upper-level user management commitment to the system			
a. Unknown	High—5		
b. Somewhat reluctant	High—3	5	10
c. Adequate	*Med—2*		
d. Extremely enthusiastic	Low—1		
11. Requires organizational interface with other companies			
a. No or very little	Low—1		
b. Moderate	Med—2	4	20
c. Extensive coordination with other entities within our organization	High—3		
d. Extensive coordination with outside entities	*High—5*		

Table 2.17 (Continued)

Project profile item	Risk score	Risk weight	Project risk score
Technology			
12. Requires interface with other companies			
a. No or very little	Low—1		
b. Moderate	Med—2		
c. Extensive interfaces with other entities within our organization	High—3	3	3
c. Extensive interfaces with external entities	High—5		
13. The IT team knowledge in the proposed application area			
a. Limited	High—3		
b. Understands concept but no experience	Med—2	5	10
c. Has been involved in similar implementation efforts	Low—1		
REGULATORY RISKS			
14. Requires regulatory approval			
a. No	Low—1		
b. In one country	High—2	5	5
c. In multiple countries	High—3		

The overall score is 111. We're going to score this as a moderate-risk project. We now repeat the scoring for all similar projects under consideration. By using simple questionnaires like these, we can determine the risk of a requested project sufficiently accurately that we can take its risk into account when considering it.

A final risk comment: When a project begins and the risk analysis is completed, that risk number should replace the initial risk analysis that was done to approve the project. This means both approaches have to use the same numbering criteria. If the project's detailed risk assessment is significantly different than the initial guess, the portfolio risk level may need to be adjusted.

This is a reasonable example of how to do a risk analysis on an IT project without actually having started the project. By answering these questions, it creates an understanding of what the risks are on the project. The numbers are a best guess and should be answered mostly by the IT staff, with a few questions (mostly related to user acceptance) to be answered by middle management.

Example of Risk Analysis—PDRI Survey for Construction

We mentioned earlier the PDRI. It identifies risks on large construction projects just as the IT risk questionnaire does for IT projects.

Unlike the IT example, there is a large database behind the PDRI created by members of the CII submitting their PDRI scores and the actual results from the projects that were rated. This allows the PDRI scores to be weighted for their importance to project success. The results show clearly that the most important factors in project risk are the early management decisions.

Step 2.5 Dealing With Strategic Changes

2.5.1 Overall Strategy Changes

We said earlier that the projects within the portfolio should be prioritized according to the strategic goals of the organization. But, what happens when those goals change? While employees tend of think of strategic goals as these lofty 5- or 10-year plans that everyone is working toward, the executives realize that in this fast-paced, internationally competitive environment that companies work in they need to re-examine the strategic goals much more often than that. In fact, as noted earlier, 70 to 90 percent of strategic goals are never achieved.

Organizations live in a dynamic environment. Fitzroy and Hulbert classified the environment into three levels:

The world environment—The broad social/technical/economic worldwide environment in which the organization competes. These influences affect virtually all organizations simultaneously. While some changes can happen rapidly, the more common influences are the rise of the orient in manufacturing, population growth, and the aging of the population in the more developed countries.

The industry environment—The factors that impact a specific industry such as the construction industry or the aerospace industry. These influences can include the lack of skilled resources specific to the industry, market conditions, entry barriers, and so on.

The specific competitive environment—This is the environment created by the relationships the organization has with its competitors, its collaborators (consultants and supply chain), and finally, the organization's customers.

Organizations that live in a highly dynamic environment, such as almost any software, or technology-driven environment (think how fast smartphones have changed!) face a lot of uncertainty. Taking two years to develop a new product when the environment can change within six months is highly risky and requires a strong forecasting capability. You want your product to come out at the front end of the technology when it's released, not a year after your competitors have released their own versions.

The uncertainty about what the future is, what technologies will be available, what your competitors are doing, and even what your strategic goals will be in two years creates an environment that must constantly be reviewed and changes made to adapt.

Regular review of the portfolio by the steering or governance committee is crucial to continued success. The committee should add, kill, or reprioritize the projects in the project registry. According to McDonough and Spital[30], portfolios reviewed quarterly do better than those reviewed semiannually, although this might depend on the type of projects under review.

So, how should the portfolio react when the goals change? Your design of the EPM system has to take this possibility into account and be sufficiently flexible enough to support it. There are basically three major answers to this question, and which one is correct depends on how upper management decides they want to handle it.

When the strategic goals change, the portfolio should be re-examined for its congruence with the new goals. Projects that no longer support the new goals after being reassessed need to be identified and a decision made as to how to disposition them.

One option, if a project no longer supports the new strategic goals, is to determine if you need to create a replacement project, or if you even need to do a replacement project. If a higher priority project is facing cost over-runs, the steering committee could use the resources from the canceled project to support the overrun.

Another option is to simply pick the next higher-priority project from the existing list of proposed projects. This has the benefit of already having gone through the assessment and prioritization process.

A third option is allow the division that "owns" the canceled project to propose another project that is important to them. This communicates that a group whose project is canceled will not be punished for canceling a project. That type of decision-making freedom is beneficial to the organization. The downside to this option is that it lends itself to political manipulation in which a group can get a project done that would not have scored highly if it went through the normal assessment process.

While not a primary consideration, a canceled project also frees up resources. Sometimes, this is a consideration that should be taken into account.

If the strategic goals change, we have to reweight the new goals. Upper management must tell us (not us them) what the importance of each goal is and how much weight it has in the overall calculation. When we have each project fill out the detailed question sheet that determines its costs and benefits, we have to weight each answer so that we apply higher weights to the more important goals.

2.5.2 Back to MegaNews International

Lets look back at our fictional company, MegaNews International. MNI is a multinational conglomerate with over 50,000 employees worldwide. 2008 revenues were over $25 billion, operating income was $3.9 billion, cash and cash equivalents were $6 billion, and they had $34 billion in assets worldwide. The net income from all operations was $2.8 billion. This was a 6 percent growth over 2014. Its worldwide holdings include ownership or has significant interest in 10 movie studios, 50 television stations, 25 cable channels, five satellite TV channels, 100 newspapers, 10 magazines, one publishing company, and various other associated enterprises such as real estate development and holding companies.

The project portfolio process has selected these projects through financial calculations and risk analysis as the projects best supporting strategic goals. Look back at Table 2.15 for the results of the financial analysis.

What happens if management decides to change the strategic goals to adapt to the new financial environment? Let's compare the old goals with the new ones:

Table 2.18 Changes in strategic goals

Old strategic goals	New strategic goals
1. **Financial**	1. **Financial**
1.1. Increase net revenue by increasing profit margins by 5% per year	1.1. Increase overall revenue by increasing profit margins by 10% per year
1.2. Increase sales by 10% per year	1.2. Increase revenue from Internet operations by 20% per year
2. **Customer relationship**	2. **Customer relationship**
2.1. Develop stronger customer relationships	2.1. Become the #1 provider of worldwide news on the Internet
2.2. Become a full-service news provider	2.2. Become a full-service news provider through Internet, electronic media (radio and television), and printed news outlets
3. **Internal process**	3. **Internal process**
3.1. Achieve operational excellence through a strong emphasis on process improvement and process ownership	3.1. Achieve project management excellence
3.2. Achieve project management excellence	3.2. Improve our internal productivity by 10%
3.3. Improve our internal customer relationship processes	
4. **Employees**	4. **Employees**
4.1. Build a high-performance corporate culture and values	4.1. Treat our employees as highly skilled assets
4.2. Recognize and accept change as a necessary part of the industry	4.2. Recognize and accept change as a necessary part of the industry

We can see that there is a new emphasis on increasing revenues and profit margins and a new emphasis on Internet-based revenue. We now have a new goal of increasing internal productivity by 10 percent to save costs, among other new goals.

Since we released the additional project list, two new projects have been proposed:

Improve our internal business processes by consolidating existing processes and eliminating un-needed ones. This will cost $150 million and will improve productivity by 5 percent.

We can significantly expand our own Internet News Portal into an e-commerce site for a cost of about $2 million. This could be rolled out in phases over a period of 18 months and provide $1 million in annual revenues.

Doing the financial calculations for these two projects (Note: for the first project, assuming again 20,000 people with an average salary of $80,000, a 1 percent increase in productivity is the same as saving the work of 200 employees. 200 employees make $16 million per year), we see that:

Table 2.19 Re-analysis of projects K and L

Project	Project	Estimated cost	Annual benefits	Payback period	NPV	ROI	Benefit/cost
K	Improve our internal business processes by consolidating existing processes and eliminating un-needed ones.	$150M	$16M	9.38 years	−$79.7M	−0.467	0.53
L	We can significantly expand our own Internet News Portal to an e-commerce site for a cost of about $2M.	$2M	$1M	2	$1.85	0.15	1.00

Project K, while promising to improve our internal business processes, does not look promising in the calculations. Project L, which provides a revenue stream, looks much better and would be prioritized at the same level as existing project G.

The portfolio should be rebalanced approximately every six months. Too often and the project work is disrupted and teams get discouraged when their projects are canceled because something more financially sexy was approved. Not often enough and too much time is wasted on projects that are not as beneficial as ones waiting in the queue. Regulatory projects are very disruptive because they can interrupt projects in work to meet unexpected regulatory changes, often with tight deadlines.

2.5.3 Solutions and Recommendations

The most effective approach to designing the organization charged with portfolio management is to make it part of a Program Management Office (PMO). The PMO already has much of the structure required to manage projects and programs and so incorporating portfolio management within itself is a more efficient approach. If the organization does not have a PMO, or the PMO is structured so that it is a center of best practices rather than a management office, the EPMS should be designed as a standalone organization.

In order for the EPMS to remain effective as the larger organization evolves and changes, the EPMS must itself evolve from a localized group providing only project selection to a larger, more inclusive role including overall portfolio metrics, risk analysis, and rebalancing of the portfolio as the environment changes. More mature portfolio management offices have a broader scope of work and more responsibility than newly implemented offices.

Step 2 Summary

This step was all about identifying the details of the EPMS design and covered an extensive amount of material. We began by asking management what their requirements were for the new system. It is these requirements that will dictate the design. If the requirements are wrong or incomplete, the EPMS will not function as expected.

Once we have the requirements identified and locked down, we proceeded to discuss various design considerations such as types of projects and asset classes. We identified various different portfolios that management wants to pursue from a strategic standpoint: a balanced portfolio, three types of growth-oriented portfolios, and a cost-savings portfolio.

We divided projects into three different categories based on their priorities: mandatory ("must-do") projects, maintenance projects (we need to do them but have flexibility in their scheduling), and discretionary projects. It is this last category that the EPMS is designed to focus on the projects that we can decide to do, or not. We used the MegaNews International company to show examples of each.

We discussed the filtering criteria that management wants built into the EPMS. These filtering criteria should be the same as managers themselves would us. We then added weighting criteria that reflect management's priorities. Not only what is important to management, but how important is it relative to the other filtering criteria.

Software projects are successful, or not, depending on how easy they are for users to actually use. We discussed the various types of users for an EPMS and used them to design the forms built into the system, including data entry forms and reports coming out of the EPMS.

Once the inputs for a new project are received, the data are processed by financial filters such as ROI, IIR, and others. This section covered some basic financial concepts that are important to management, but too often unknown to developers.

Part of the project selection process is to identify how risky the project is, even before you know any details of the project. We identified how to do that and how to assess risks to the overall project portfolio.

We finished the chapter by discussing how to deal with changes in strategy using MegaNews as an example.

STEP 3

Planning and Implementing the EPMS

Introduction to Step 3

Now that we've armed ourselves with the right information to create the EPMS, prepared the organization to accept it, and designed it, we are finally ready to create the project plan to actually manage the work of developing and implementing it.

This chapter outlines a basic project management approach and then goes into details on how to apply project management to a complex information technology (IT) infrastructure project. If you are already experienced in IT project management, feel free to skip over the more basic portions. If you are a senior manager who is in charge of managing such an effort or a project manager with experience in other fields, go through each section to understand the steps involved.

As stated earlier, as a project manager, you are always being measured against the schedule and budget you create at the beginning of the project. If you are six months into a 12- month project and you're two months behind schedule, is it because you're doing a bad job managing the project? Because something unexpected happened? Or, because the plan was bad to start with? The more thoroughly you plan out the project, the less likely it is to be late or over budget.

In this chapter, we're going to walk through the development of the project plan to design and implemented the EPMS, starting with developing the scope of work and going through the detailed architecture, scheduling, budgeting, and other needed project management steps.

Before we start, it is important to determine how the EPMS will be implemented. Will it start with a pilot program in one small part of the organization and then expand from there? Will it be rolled out in a big bang to the whole organization? Will some other approach be used? It makes a difference in how the development project is planned.

The approach we recommend is to start small and then evolve the EPMS as you learn more, as people get used to it, and as the acceptance among management grows. This is similar to the recommended approach for Project Management Office (PMO) implementation. In fact, we will go through some document PMO implementations to give you an idea of various approaches.

The first step here, if you have not already done it, is to find out what projects already exist.

Story

In 2008 Catholic Health Initiatives (CHI) established an Enterprise Program Management Office for IT to implement standard practices and improve project success rates. The team identified over 800 projects, many of them were duplicates of other projects or not aligned with CHI's strategic goals. By intelligently selecting the most critical projects they brought this down to 140 projects, reducing waste, duplication, and low priority projects in the process. Their efforts were so successful that in early 2012 the EPMO was expanded beyond IT to support all types of enterprise-wide projects.

An organization of any complexity has many departments that do not fully coordinate with each other. Each department determines what is most helpful to it and develops projects to support its goals. The result is that there is often similar, even identical, projects going on in different departments. A major benefit of the EPMS is that these wasteful efforts will be identified and coordinated.

When doing this initial survey, the team members should:

- Review the organization's mission and strategic goals
  - o Identify how often those goals change due to changes in management or in the environment
  - o Review enterprise architecture plan to ensure that any development will be compatible
- Interview the appropriate managers to assemble a list of projects
  - o Projects being actively worked on
  - o Projects that are in queue waiting to be started
- Determine which processes and systems already exist to select projects
- Interview management to determine the set of reports and metrics they require, including the schedule and format for each

The results will identify the requirements for the new system and will guide the team on how to approach the project plan.

There is a complexity here, which we often see in organizations that have grown through mergers and acquisitions. The companies they purchase may already have a portfolio management system, or a PMO, in place. Trying to get everyone on to a single, unified platform will result in failure. It will not fail for technical reasons, but for political reasons. No organization will be willing to give up a system it is used to without a fight. If faced with this situation, it is easier to have the IT department in the owning organization create software, which could take the outputs of each independent system and combine them into something the decision makers can use to effectively manage the projects in the overall organization. That approach is beyond the scheme of this book.

A Note on Commercial Tools

According to research by the Center for Business Practices,[1] most organizations have developed their project portfolio management process in-house (87.0 percent). Only 13.2 percent of organizations have implemented a project portfolio management software tool.

If the decision has been made to purchase a commercially available tool rather than develop one in-house, there are many other activities regarding defining requirements and procurement processes that must be performed. Even the best commercial tools will generally satisfy only 80 percent of your criteria plan on developing internal workarounds for the 20 percent that the tool cannot provide. Hint: DON'T trust the software vendor salespeople to tell you the tool you select will cover everything you need. The tools are thorough, but probably do not operate in the way that is best for your organization.

This is an important sequence. You must determine yourself first what your organization needs before you start looking at commercial tools. Identify your current requirements for an EPMS and any future growth needs you can anticipate. Remember that once you purchase a tool, you're locked into it for years.

Pre-made tools have their own business processes built-in. While this can be advantageous, it also means that you will have a more difficult time convincing people to use the tool because it requires changing how they work today. The OCM effort need to convince employees and managers to actually use the new system will be much larger than it would be for an in-house tool that takes into account how people already work.

Implementing a commercial tool requires that you consider the tools abilities and limitations as well as your organizations when it comes time to put it into the production system. Many times, upper management expects immediate results from an expensive tool without understanding that the data you fed into the tool was the same poor data you had before the tool. Management is trying to make decisions with data that is no better than it was before.

Because of the extensive work required to configure a tool to your organization and input all the existing data, tools often get a reputation among the project managers as more overhead and bureaucracy, leading to even more resistance.

Which tool should you buy? The academic answer is "It depends." It depends on your organization's needs and expectations, and how willing people are to change how they work.

The most capable tools change year by year as vendors try and catch up with their competition. Organizations such as Gartner and Forrester review tools annually and release reports on the ones that provide the most capabilities. If you go through several years of reports, you will see that different vendors leapfrog from one year to the next.

Socio-technical systems are combinations of people, processes, and technology (PPT) to accomplish goals. When everything comes together just right, the end result is far more effective and efficient than if the different parts of the end system are done independent of each other and without consideration for the other parts.

If one part of the PPT triad is ineffective, the results are poor, and the other areas must compensate for it. If the people in the portfolio management area don't have the right tools or processes, the entire EPMS will be inefficient and not deliver the results expected. If the people themselves are inexperienced or untrained in project and portfolio management, the results will be the same—the EPMS will not deliver what was expected or needed.

In order to ensure that everything comes together just right, the EPMS must be designed for the right combination of people, processes, and technology and then thoroughly planned out just as any other project would be.

3.1 Initializing the Project

If you develop the EPMS internally, it should be compatible with the organization's existing project planning/reporting application (if one exists). This way managers and employees only have to input data once for new project ideas and it can be propagated upward into the EPMS. Of course, the systems must be able to access the same data and pull up reports at various levels. It also means that all project managers must be using the same or compatible project management tools configured to the same status metrics.

When you develop a project plan for the EPMS implementation, it's just like a project plan for any other project you manage. You will write a project management plan that may include how to manage areas such as:

- Requirements
- Schedule
- Budget
- Quality
- Human resources plan
- Communications plan
- Risk
- Procurement (if any)
- Ancillary areas
  - Benefits management
  - Stakeholder management
  - Change management
  - Progress metrics
  - OCM plan
  - Configuration management
  - Data management
  - And so on

Does a project manager need to do all of these in detail for every project? Absolutely not. You, the project manager, decide what to do, and to what extent, to make this project as successful as possible. How long will it take to write and get approved an overall management plan? Longer than you would think due to the need for review and rewrite cycles. We will offer a proposed schedule later.

For these areas, it is expected by upper management that the project management plans will be written to ensure that you have thought through exactly how you're going to manage the project. For a project the size and effort of an EPMS implementation, you don't need to write a separate management plan for each one of these areas unless your own internal project management processes require it. It should be adequate to write a single project management document that covers all of these areas. This top-level management plan would have a section for each of the previously mentioned areas. If some of the work can be done by other parts of the organization, such as quality management or procurement, just reference those areas rather than recreating a plan for each.

There are multiple consultants who have come up with critical success factors (CSFs) for successful EPM implementations. They all say pretty much the same things. Gartner[2] found seven CSFs for a portfolio management system that are common to many such recommendations:

- Making a portfolio management process work requires strong governance and holding participants accountable.
- Portfolio management is such a major undertaking that it needs to be treated as a project itself to succeed.
- It needs a process owner and a qualified support team.
- Having a disciplined process means that all proposals go through the same screening. The process is ongoing, and approved initiatives are reviewed when conditions change.
- The objective prioritization framework should include investment categories and risk-adjusted evaluation criteria.
- Communication and education programs are needed to develop stakeholder buy-in and support for the project portfolio management process.
- To facilitate the use of project and portfolio management (PPM) approaches, provide tools that make compliance easier. Tools ensure consistency and support group decision making.

All of these should be taken into account when planning out the implementation process.

In order to ensure that all projects, even existing ones, strongly support strategy, we will put all projects through the filtering process, proposed as well as existing. The advantages are that it will kill projects that no longer make sense and any duplicative projects that are wasting resources. The disadvantage is that when people learn that the projects they're working on are being re-examined, they may become less productive until they learn whether their project has been approved or not. Why work hard on something that might get canceled?

3.1.1 The Project Charter

Before you even start writing the management plan, you will need to write a project charter and get it approved. If you were involved in developing the business case that we discussed earlier, that should be sufficient to justify the project. You should consider simplifying it so that it provides useful material for discussion during the project's kickoff meeting. There is no need to swamp people with details only the decision makers need.

If there was no business case, you will need to develop the project charter. This is typically a relatively high-level document that states the following:

- Project's goal
- More specific objectives (e.g., a subsidiary goal might be to roll out the EPMS in a single IT department and then hold a lessons learned to review how well it went)
- The scope of the project as well as scope exclusions
- Rough schedule milestones and budget
- Assigned PM and his/her authority level
- Participating organizations
- Assumptions and constraints
- High-level risks

The goal of the charter is to get the primary organizations that will be involved in the project to understand what the goals of the project are, its overall approach, their own roles and responsibilities, and rough-guess schedule, budget, and risks. Once everyone agrees on it, the charter is signed and approved.

The project charter documents the project at a summary level and gives you the authority to spend the company's time and money, and use its resources, to do the project.

3.1.2 The Kickoff Meeting

The kickoff meeting is a gathering of the primary players in the EPMS development. Often thought of as being a waste of time, it is, in fact, a critically important meeting for the project manager. Yes, by now, everyone involved has heard of your project and understands the goals, but that's not the point. The meeting is important to you because this is where you take charge of the project and start making decisions. This is where you show your leadership capabilities and get the primary participants to agree on the way you will manage the project.

What should be done during a kickoff meeting? For starters, it should be scheduled for at least a day. This is a significant project and needs a strong start. This is not a meeting you can do in 2 to 4 hours. Plan on scheduling several sessions if needed.

Secondly, get a dedicated note taker to capture the major points of the discussion and decisions made as well as to capture action items or things to put into the parking lot for later resolution. You're running the meeting, if you're taking notes at the same time, you might miss something important. An outside facilitator could help the meeting move more efficiently.

What should be done during the meeting?

1. Walk through the project charter. Get everyone's agreements or comments.
2. Ask each participant what worked well on past projects and what to avoid (AKA lessons learned). As we never bother to look up lessons learned from earlier projects, this is an excellent time to capture them. Most project management knowledge is in people's heads, it's what we call tribal knowledge.
3. Ask the primary stakeholders what level of confidence they want in their schedules and costs (50 percent? 80 percent? 90 percent confidence factor?). We will talk about why this is important later.

4. Ask the primary stakeholders what their level of risk tolerance is. How much risk are they willing to take? Their level of risk tolerance helps you in making decisions in the middle of the project.

5. What does success mean for this project? What is the definition of completion? What benefits are expected out of the project? Does everybody agree on when the project is finished?

6. How do we report status to date? If the project is 10 percent behind schedule, is that yellow or red? If it is 5 percent over budget, is that green or yellow?

7. What are the CSFs that will help this project become successful?

8. What are the communications needs? (Management cares a lot about this!)

After the meeting is over, complete any action items captured during the meeting. Write up the meeting minutes and send them to everyone involved. Ask for their feedback to make sure the minutes accurately capture what was discussed and agreed-to. These minutes will form a baseline document that you can use in the future to remind management what had been agreed-to at the beginning of the project.

3.2 Developing the Scope of Work

3.2.1 Scope of an EPMS Project

We talked about the business requirements in the previous section, but now let us look at them in more detail specifically as they apply to our EPMS project. As in any project, the first big step is to define your scope of work. This includes both the final scope of the product, in our case, the EPMS, but also the scope of work needed to develop and implement it.

The *product* scope is defined by the requirements. The *project* scope includes the size of the team, the schedule, the budget, and all the work needed to be done in order to give the organization a successful enterprise portfolio management system. We can help you with defining the product scope, but identifying all of the details that will determine the project scope is situational to your specific environment.

In order to understand what the end result will look like, we have to understand what it is expected to do. This is the process of gathering management's needs and expectations. These are the requirements that we will build to. We discussed the process for gathering those in detail in the last chapter.

Now that we understand what requirements are, we can start by asking what are the functional requirements for an enterprise-level portfolio management system? Remember: the functional requirements are the things that the system should be able to do, as contrasted with how well it does them, how easy it is to use, or other constraints such as privacy and data security.

Certainly, a major functional requirement is that the system should be able to accept the requests for new projects. This requirement will be implemented by developing a process that captures each new project request. Once the request for a project is created, further processes will provide more details, prioritize the request, identify the risks in doing it (and in not doing it), and present it to the decision makers to be approved or not.

Another major functional requirement is that the system should track the status of each project in work. This implies a common set of metrics that all projects use so that the projects can be measured against management's acceptability parameters (red, yellow, green), against the business case for the project, and against each other. This can also be done if the organization is using an enterprisewide project planning tool managed by the PMO.

A third functional requirement is that the EPMS should identify the level of utilization of each resource used by all the projects. This prevents resource conflicts and allows the resources to be scheduled in the most efficient manner possible. This is also a function that can be done by the PMO if the proper planning tool is used.

The most basic functional requirement is that the system delivers a prioritized list of potential projects that:

1. Strongly support strategic goals
2. Provide the greatest benefits
3. Have an acceptable level of risk

Upon a little thought, it will be obvious that these three functional requirements are very high level. To be useful in designing the system, each of these needs to be thought through in much more detail. To implement each requirement will take new processes, new tools, maybe additional staff, and a change to the technology infrastructure to accommodate the new system.

The requirements decomposition process starts as soon as management approves the high-level requirements for the EPMS. From there, design decisions will need to be made on how to status each project. How does management want to see the portfolio status reported?

- At what point does a project turn from green (in good shape) to yellow (has some problems) to red (major problems that need to be fixed or the project killed)?
- If it is 10 percent over budget, is it yellow or red?
- If it is 10 percent behind schedule, is it yellow or still green?

These are the types of questions that need to be presented to management for decisions before any tools are configured and the system is implemented. These decisions can be made during the kickoff meeting where you have the primary players involved.

Part of the design process is understanding the technology infrastructure that will support any tools purchased or developed. If your IT network is Cisco, don't buy any tools that only run on Microsoft networks. While your IT personnel should not be involved in defining the top-level needs, you need to start getting them involved as soon as the discussion turns to what tools do you need to buy, or on the detailed design of the system.

For each organization, the answers will be different. EPM systems will have the same top-level requirements, but below that top level, the answers and the designs will be different to adapt to the organization.

3.2.2 Requirements and Stakeholders

Many of the detailed requirements will never be seen by the users, but they are important to the design and maintenance areas. In fact, we can divide requirements into three categories:

- Requirements the users care about
- Requirements they care about and don't think of until you point them out
- Requirements the users don't care about but the technical staff needs them

In the first category, requirements the users care about, we have typically the following requirements you will have to obtain from the users:

- Functional requirements
- Performance
- "Look and feel"
- Usability
- Privacy

In the second category, we have requirements that the users will care about but don't think of until you ask them:

- Data accuracy
- Data security
- Legal and compliance requirements
- Training requirements
- System documentation

In the last category, we have requirements the users don't care about but the technical people do. Without these more detailed technical requirements, the developers cannot properly design the system:

- Interface requirements among the different modules of the software
- Integration and test requirements
- Implementation requirements
- Operational and backup requirements

The requirements process takes a lot of time to do properly, but you cannot design the EPMS, understand the scope of work, or develop detailed plans until it is completed.

You will have to repeat and to customize the scope development process for each type of project that is expected to be in the portfolio, especially with regard to the filtering criteria. As we saw in the last chapter, these criteria are different for each type of project, so part of the design will be to decide the different types and then create filtering criteria for each. If your organization wants to assess 10 different types of projects as part of the portfolio, you will need to repeat the filtering criteria 10 different times and the status criteria 10 different times. A manufacturing plant that is 10 percent over budget is a much different problem than a small IT upgrade that is 10 percent over budget. Your management will need to determine these criteria.

A typical top-level set of requirements is shown in Appendix 3.2-1.

3.2.3 Capturing Requirements

Where do we get the requirements to design our EPMS? We have already captured what upper management's expectations are, now how do we get the detailed requirements we need?

In the play *My Fair Lady* by Loerner and Lowe, Eliza Doolittle's father is meeting with Dr. Henry Higgins to try and extort money from him but can't seem to get a word in. When Higgins questions him on what he wants, he replies *"I'm willing to tell you, I'm wanting to tell you, I'm waiting to tell you!"*

Unfortunately the stakeholders you will need to meet are almost universally the opposite. Normal people do not think in terms of requirements, and your stakeholders are all very busy people who rarely have the time needed to meet with you to discuss what they need from the new EPMS.

There are multiple ways to capture requirements, and you will probably use several of them depending on exactly what types of requirements you are trying to identify and what would work best in your own organization:

- Examine existing business processes
- Interviewing the stakeholders
- Other methods such as data flow diagrams or surveys

3.2.3.1 Capturing Existing Business Processes

One primary method to capture what our EPMS needs to do is to look at the existing business process—how are projects selected now? First of all, let's define what a business process is. A business process[3] is a group of logically related tasks that use the resources of the organization to provide defined results in support of the organization's objectives. Everything the organization does and everything it produces is a result of business processes. Selecting projects is a business process comprised of multiple steps.

Believe it or not, your organization already has a way to select projects. It is probably not documented. It probably was not even designed to be particularly efficient. It just grew and evolved over the years in response to what made sense to management at the time.

Each part of the organization developed its own way to select projects based on what made sense for them. This leads to projects that are selected in isolation from all the other projects the organization is doing. They are optimized for the group but suboptimized for the overall organization. Resources are spent on projects that do not support overall strategic goals.

The traditional way of understanding existing business processes is to simply observe each step in the process and document what that step adds to the process and who is doing it. By doing this, you will develop a flowchart of what the steps are in the process similar to the flowchart we presented in Step 2.2.

3.2.3.2 Interviewing Stakeholders

Because you're designing and implementing a brand-new system, the most effective way to gather the high-level requirements is to interview the major stakeholders. Upper management sees the problems that the organization has in completing projects but doesn't always see what the causes are or how to fix them. If you have gotten this far, you have already interviewed upper management and middle management to gather their expectations of what the EPMS should provide them. So, now we need to meet with them again to get more detailed requirements.

When you interview top management, be prepared with a list of the existing problems (which you can get from interviewing middle management) and how an EPMS can help manage and mitigate the problems. Rather than interview upper managers individually, it's more effective to do this in a group setting. That allows them to see what other managers need, and they can discuss their needs more thoroughly. (An additional benefit in doing it in a group setting is that while these upper layers of managers are very time-constrained and you will not typically be able to get much of their time.) This approach also has the benefits of identifying requirements conflicts early.

There are multiple ways to gather requirements from our stakeholders:

- Individual user interviews
- Group user interviews and Joint Application Development (JAD) sessions (a structured workshop setting used to extract consensus-based requirements)
- Focus groups
- Working groups
- E-mailed surveys and questionnaires

Once you have gone through this process with upper management, you will need to repeat the process with lower-level, functional managers and with the project managers, starting with the requirements that upper management has approved. Each of them will have their own set of needs that the system should accommodate as long as they do not contradict the top-level requirements given by upper management. Ask this group how they would implement these top-level requirements. This set of requirements should then also be analyzed and prioritized. At this level, you will generally find conflicts between the needs of upper management, the functional managers, and the project managers. These conflicts will need to be resolved before more detailed design work can begin. If the different types of managers cannot reach agreement on how to resolve a conflict, the problem should be escalated to higher-level management for a decision.

For the early interviews with senior executives, the recommendation is to do unstructured interviews and help them think through what they need from the EPMS. Once you have captured these and gotten their approval for them, develop a set of structured interview questions for lower levels of managers built around the requirements you obtained from the upper levels. Make everyone you talk to aware that what they tell you will shape the system. Your design will be based on what they want.

When you do more structured interviews, do not be too rigid. Allow some flexibility in the questions asked and ask "Is there any requirement you have that I didn't ask about?" Lower-level managers will live with the EPMS outputs on an operational basis, and they may have good ideas for make it more useful and effective. Any major changes resulting from these discussions may have to be elevated for approval, but don't dismiss them.

Documenting the rationale for each requirement (*why* it is required) is a good technique to reduce the number of lower-priority requirements. According to requirements consultant Ivy Hooks, doing this can eliminate "up to half" of the requested requirements[4].

The list of questions will change as you learn more, so put the questionnaire under configuration management so that you know exactly what the list of questions was that you asked each person.

Examples of questions that would be asked in the initial survey:

- What are your top needs for the EPMS?
- What are the minimal things it should do?
- Is there anything it should not do?
- If the system could provide more features, what would be most useful?
- If you will be using it, how quickly should it respond to your inputs?
- How often do you think you would interact with it?
- Would you like to be able to customize reports you get?
- What are the key success factors that will tell you the EPMS is successful?

Does this all sound like it will take time? Yes, absolutely it will take time, typically it will take several weeks. But, as stated, earlier, it is absolutely critical to do and to do thoroughly. The time and resources to gather and analyze requirements should be built into the overall project plan, and nothing else should start until this effort is completed.

If you're going to develop your own in-house software tool for portfolio management, your technical staff will develop the more detailed technical requirements that they need. If you're going to purchase a portfolio management tool, you will need to do a search of the available tools and see which one best fits most of your requirements. Note: A caution on selecting a vendor tool—many of them only allow one set of filtering criteria. This makes them relatively useless if our EPMS must prioritize multiple types of projects. This isn't a problem if we develop our own tool. We just build this capability into the tool itself.

Another approach to interviewing stakeholders is not to meet with them individually (there will be too many) but to meet with them in a group setting. This is more useful for lower-level executives and managers where they can see what their peers are saying. If you use this approach, have a prepared set of questions for them.

Another way to gather requirements are to have the users develop working groups. This puts them in the position where they are in charge of defining the requirements. This is best done with a restricted set of more detailed requirements such as user interfaces and security requirements.

You can improve the response rate by making it very easy to do, no more than 10 minutes long, identify who the project sponsor is, ensure it is totally confidential and that answers cannot be traced back to the responder, and clearly identify the benefits of the EPMS to the level of responder. They should appreciate that their input will help design the end result.

3.2.4 A Starting Point

A starting point for the types of functional requirements an EPMS should satisfy might include those shown in Appendix 3.2. Feel free to include other needs that your primary stakeholders can think of. As you compile these, you will see that the stakeholders may not agree with each other. When you notice this, you need to identify the disagreement and involve the stakeholders in resolving it.

Once we have the requirements collected, analyzed, and approved (getting our requirements approved is critical to avoiding future problems), we can used them to start the architecture and design efforts as well as developing the Work Breakdown Structure (WBS) from them.

3.2.5 CareFirst Case

CareFirst Inc.[5] is a not-for-profit health care provider on the east coast of the United States. It has 5,200 employees and provides health care services to nearly 3.4 million members. The following requirements gathering process was crucial to their successful implementation of their PMO.

Inputs

- Project Charter
- Conceptual Architecture Design Document
- Committed Resources

1.0 Requirements Management Process

1.1 Perform "Requirements Management Charter Review Procedure"
1.2 Complete *Requirements Management Engagement Letter Template*
1.3 Perform "Requirements Planning and Scheduling Procedure" and complete *Requirements Management Plan Template*
1.4 Perform "Requirements Kickoff Procedure"
1.5 Perform "Requirements Tool Setup Procedure"

2.0 Requirements Development Process
(Elicitation & Prioritization)

2.1 Perform "Business Process Modeling Procedure"
2.2 Perform "Use Case Procedure"
2.3 Perform "UI Simulation Procedure"
2.4 Perform "Textual Requirements Procedure"
2.5 Perform "PRD Generation Procedure"
2.6 Perform "Requirements Walkthrough Procedure" (optional)

3.0 Requirements Validation Process

2.0 Requirements Development Process
(Elicitation & Prioritization)

3.0 Requirements Validation Process

3.1 Perform "Peer Review Process" on PAL
3.2 Perform "Requirements Validation and Migration Procedure"
3.3 Complete *Fitness for Use Form*
3.4 Perform "Requirements Traceability Procedure"
3.5 Perform "Requirements Project Execution Procedure"
3.6 Perform "Requirements Management Change Control Procedure"
3.7 Perform "Lessons Learned Process on PAL

Outputs

- Requirements Management Engagement Letter
- Kickoff Agenda and Meeting Minutes
- Requirements Management Plan (RMP)
- Business Process Models
- Use Cases
- Prioritized Textual Requirements
- Project Requirements Document (PRD)
- Fitness for Use Form
- Requirements Traceability Matrix (RTM)
- Requirements Management Lessons Learned

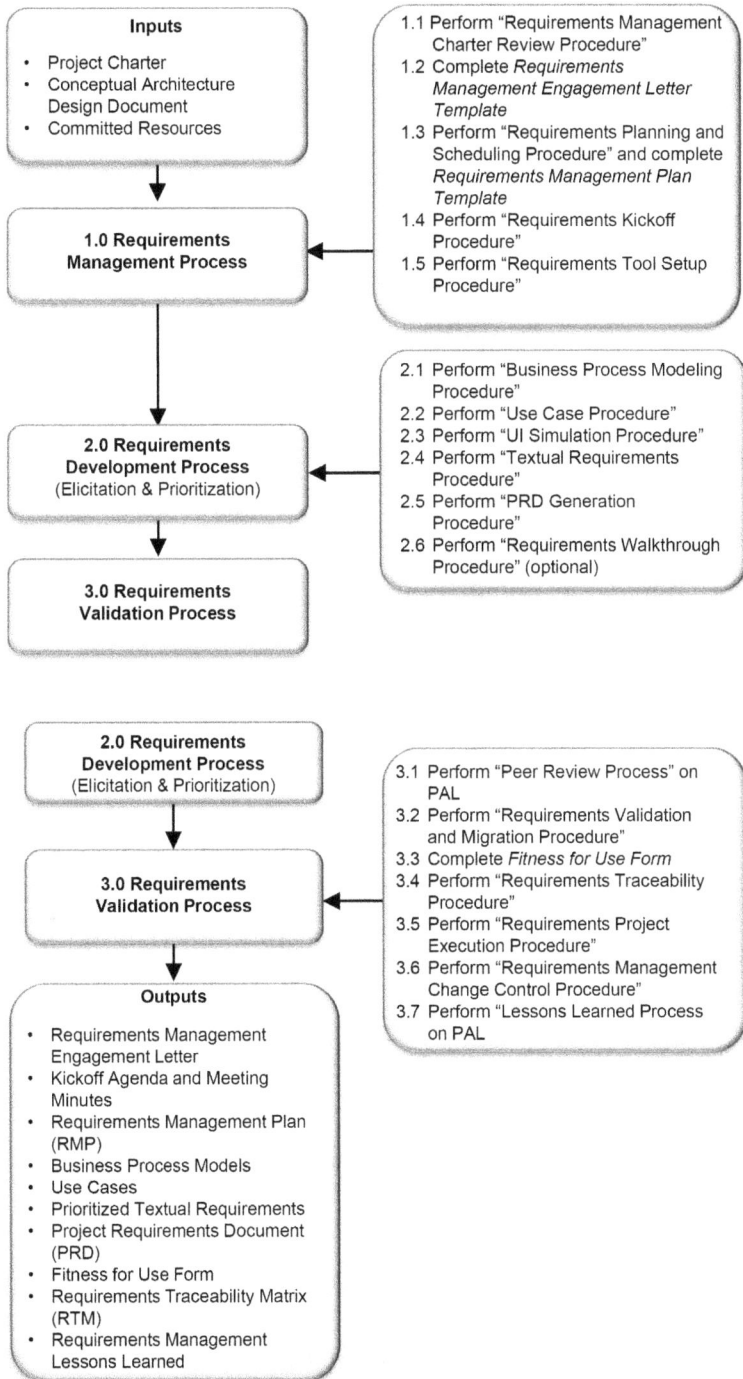

Figure 3.2-1a and b CareFirst requirements process

While this particular approach may not be exactly what your requirements development approach will be, it provides a very useful guideline for how detailed the requirements gathering and management process should be. Keep in mind that everything else from now on is dependent on how well the requirements capture what your primary stakeholders expect. Well mention CareFirst again later.

3.3 Architecture and Design

In this section, we are going to cover five areas:

- Overall architecture
- Detailed filter design
- Scoring
- The processes that make it all work
- Reports

But first, a caution. Many attempts have been made to develop a rational project selection process based on complex filters and calculations such as the Analytic Hierarchic Process (AHP) approach mentioned earlier. Most of these attempts have failed due to their complexity, and the organization goes back to doing things the way they've always been done. The filters themselves are not the problem, the problem is the user interface, and the lack of flexibility in rigid and overly complex filters.

The system you are developing will be used by people who have no knowledge of much of the data needed to efficiently select projects. If I am an accountant in the financial department, how can I possibly know how many people will be required to do the project and how much time it will take (two common questions asked for many commercial products)? A too-complex project request form will cause people to not use it. This is similar to hearing a noise coming from your car engine, and the mechanic asking what the root cause is, how to fix it, what tools he needs, how much it will cost, the benefits of fixing it, and how long it will take.

Keep it simple and easy for people to use and efficient enough that the project selection committee gets what it needs in a timely fashion.

3.3.1 Architecture

The tools are probably the easiest part of the EPMS. There are a lot of good commercially available tools on the market as well as Internet-based services to do portfolio management for you. Which is the "best" tool or approach depends on your requirements. As the tools companies upgrade their tools to compete with each other, the "best" tool changes from year to year.

People's roles and responsibilities in the EPMS are also fairly straightforward. As discussed in other parts of this book, the roles of the stakeholders are easily defined. As usual, with systems such as this one, the specific roles and responsibilities will vary by organization and political influence of the major stakeholders.

Processes are not as easy to define well. In process design, you are trying to think through all the possible things that can happen in the future that the EPMS must be able to handle. For example, how does our system respond when the strategic goals change. How do you design a system that can easily incorporate changes such as this? Being able to handle changes to the basic filters will be important. (The easiest technical answer is that you store the filters in a database and not hard-code them into software.) But, how do you know which changes to make?

Another decision that must be discussed and finalized during design is what happens when projects run late or over budget. Is this the responsibility of the EPMS or of the PMO? If the project is an internal project (such as an infrastructure improvement or a process improvement), the benefits will likely be achieved even if the final result is a little late or costs a little more. Is this acceptable to the steering committee? Will they agree to let the project finish to obtain the benefits?

These types of over-runs are handled differently for projects that are done to increase profits, such as new product development projects or developing a new manufacturing facility. In this case, any delay or cost over-run will probably impact the business justification for the project. Reduced profits or increased costs may cause the project to drop off the selected list because the return on investment is no longer there. In New Product Development, there is a great deal of history to show that the sooner a new product comes to market the greater the market share it will garner, so schedule is highly important, cost much less so.

If the EPMS is to provide the full set of benefits it is capable of, it must include all the project-related work in the enterprise that requires money and people. If it does not include all the project work, then its benefits are lessened, and the projects in the portfolio are more likely to be disrupted by work that was not included. While some authors advocate scoping the EPMS to one department, typically IT, this significantly reduces the benefit of portfolio management because it does not include all the work that supports strategic goals. As we will see later, implementing an EPMS is best done in phases, starting with one department, working out the problems and improving the processes, and then rolling it out to other departments. The IT group, because its organization and mission is typically well defined, is a good place to start.

Other authors suggest limiting the scope of EPMS to the most common type or size of project the organization does. If the normal size project is between 500 and 5,000 man-hours of labor, the EPMS processes should include only those size projects. This suggestion has even more limitations than the previous one. There will be a higher degree of disruption to the portfolio that is caused by both outside projects as well as larger-than-normal projects and smaller-than-normal projects. Under no circumstances should you implement an EPMS that has this limitation. If management wants to impose this restriction, then there are better ways to manage the set of projects than an EPMS.

All that being said, it makes a lot of practical sense to put a lower limit on the size of work that goes through the selection process, so let's not apply the process to small projects. There are just too many of them, and you often cannot plan for them ahead of time. (Really small projects are rarely high priority anyway.) Instead, limit the work in the portfolio to medium- and large-scale projects. Those are the ones that will take the most time, money, and resources. The threshold for a small project will vary by organization. When the U.S. headquarters of Toyota Financial Services installed a PMO, anything under 100 hours of work was not a project, it was just absorbed into daily operational work. Other organizations may choose a lower limit of 250 hours or greater for projects.

Part of the design process is how to handle projects already in work. This can be done in one of two ways. The first is to simply ignore them in terms of priorities. Use their project plans (we assume they have reasonably accurate plans!) to determine resource availability and after that simply monitor their progress to see if the resources will be freed as expected.

The second approach is to perform a separate assessment of them as you would a brand new project. While this has the benefit of seeing how they fit into the overall portfolio, it will tie up resources that could be used to complete the project. If the existing project would normally be approved as part of the EPM selection process, allow it to continue as planned. If it would not have been selected, then someone higher up in management must make the decision to either continue the project or to kill it and free up the resources for higher priority work.

Another item that must be designed into the overall architecture of the EPMS is how to handle regulatory projects. As described earlier, these are projects that are dictated by laws or regulations and must be accomplished. There is no need to create a business case for them because you have no choice except to do them.

One important aspect of regulatory projects is that they often have a well-defined completion date by which they must be completed. If the dictated completion date is within a short period, say six months, then the EPMS must be able to reallocate resources from existing projects and complete the work. The projects that were put on hold to free resources would then be restarted and completed. Of course, every project in the portfolio must be rescheduled due to the disruption created by the regulatory project.

While the executives on the steering committee will tell you what they want to see out of the portfolio management system, a properly designed system has capabilities that they may not be aware of but would be interested in. For example, projects are selected based on their alignment with strategic objectives. But, is it possible to go the other way? To see, for each objective, what projects support it? The answer is yes, if the system is designed that way. For each objective, I can tell you which projects advance that objective. This allows the executives to see which objectives are strongly supported by projects and which are not. It also allows them to select the projects that support objectives that are not currently being supported and to balance out the portfolio against the strategy.

Data Inputs and Storage

For most organizations, the input data will come from requestors typing in the data using the input forms described earlier. The data will be stored in the relational database registry created by the database analysts on the IT project team or within the commercial tool purchased.

If the data already exists in the organization's current approach to selecting projects, it most likely exists in either spreadsheets or small databases. In this case, a conversion program should be developed to extract the data from its existing format, convert it to its new format, and perform whatever data cleaning is necessary.

According to Rajegopal,[6] the list of projects should be kept in a registry that includes all of the characteristics of each project, including the type of project, duration, product being developed, service being supported, ROI, customer, and so on.

If you have poor-quality data, and to be honest most companies do, don't overdesign the precision the calculations are carried out to. When your basic data is only 10 percent accurate, don't design a system that calculates to three decimal places.

3.3.2 Detailed Filter Design

For your development team to create the EPMS software, it is critical for them to understand in great detail what the filters are that we discussed in Step 2.

The output of the EPMS is to provide projects filtered in a way that the most beneficial projects are scored high and less beneficial projects are scored lower. We determine what the score is by asking the right questions, weighting the questions for importance, and rank-ordering the projects based on their scores. During this section, we will develop weighting criteria such that the maximum score a proposed project can get is 1,000. The questions proposed here are generic questions that you can use to think up questions specific to your own situation.

One way to understand quickly how the executive decision makers think is to identify the projects currently in work and ask why those projects were chosen. What made them important enough to schedule? Their answers should help guide you in selecting the filtering criteria.

The questions should be grouped into logical categories such as:

- Strategic fit
- Revenue or profit
- Costs
- Cost savings
- Impacts on market share and growth
- Impacts to internal processes
- Impacts to employees (employee morale and productivity)
- For publicly owned companies impacts to shareholders

Depending on what is important to the organization, we could also ask filtering questions on impacts to the environment or impacts to the neighborhood.

It is important to note that research has shown that selecting projects based on purely financial modeling and criteria fails to select the best projects for the organization. Cooper[7] shows that while financial approaches are the most common, better results are obtained by selecting projects based on their alignment to organizational strategy rather than purely financial criteria. It is important to note that research has shown that selecting projects based on purely financial modeling and criteria fails to select the best projects for the organization. Cooper shows that while financial approaches are the most common, better results are obtained by selecting projects based on their alignment to organizational strategy rather than purely financial criteria. So, when you create weights to the different criteria, give strategic fit a higher weight than ROI or NPV. This will help improve the selection of the R&D-type projects that are more essential to the organization's future than the short-term product development projects.

In order to gain a basic understanding of what the proposed project is, we need some high-level information about it first so that we can more intelligently answer the detailed filtering questions later. These are written descriptions and not score-able questions.

In order to avoid spending time asking for detailed information on a mandatory project we know we have to do regardless of the financial considerations, we will ask those questions first:

- Is this project required for regulatory compliance reasons?
- Is this project required for scheduled maintenance?

A mandatory project that is far out in the future, say one calendar year, 365 days away, can often be scheduled into ,the workload without a major disruption to on-going work, so lets assign that a score of 250 (on our 1,000-point scale). For a project that's due between 180 days and 365 days away, we'll assign a score of 500, and for one that's due in less than 180 days, we'll assign a high score of 750. Those short-term projects are very disruptive and need to be immediately approved.

For the maintenance projects, most of those can be preplanned, as we saw in the last chapter, so we will give them scores lower than mandatory projects but high enough that they will get a final high score. A maintenance project that is more than one year away will be assigned a score of 100, between six months and one year, it will get a score of 250, and if it's due in less than six months, it will get a score of 500.

For the more detailed questions, design the spreadsheet or the database to capture: the question, capture possible answers from 1 to 5, and to allow space for comments. Each answer should be given a range of numbers appropriate to that answer. For example, a general question might be:

What is the estimated payback period for this project?

Table 3.1 Payback period duration estimate example

5	4	3	2	1
< 1 year	1 – 3 years		> 4 years	N/A

Higher scores for each question translate to higher end scores for the project. In this question, a short payback period scores a 5, while a payback period more than four years scores, a 2. Note that we are using payback period here. You can just as easily use ROI, IRR, or one or more of the other financial filters we discussed in the last chapter.

Now let's develop a set of detailed questions that will allow us to score the proposed project. We start by determining how much we expect the project to cost. As we showed in the last chapter, this estimate is going to be a very rough guess, ±75 percent or so. We cannot estimate the costs much closer than this because we haven't done any real analysis of the project.

3.3.3 Processes

Having the filters defined and the scoring process laid out, now how do we actually use the new system? These are business processes that must be carefully designed to be effective and efficient. That nicely explains how the EPMS will work—a set of activities done in the correct sequence that will produce the right output.

What are the major steps that a newly proposed project must go through from initial request to final approval or rejection?

1. Request form opened by the requestor
2. Initial data input by requestor
3. Routed to appropriate departments for additional data
4. Mandatory project?
5. Filtered through financial analysis
6. Meets minimum financial criteria

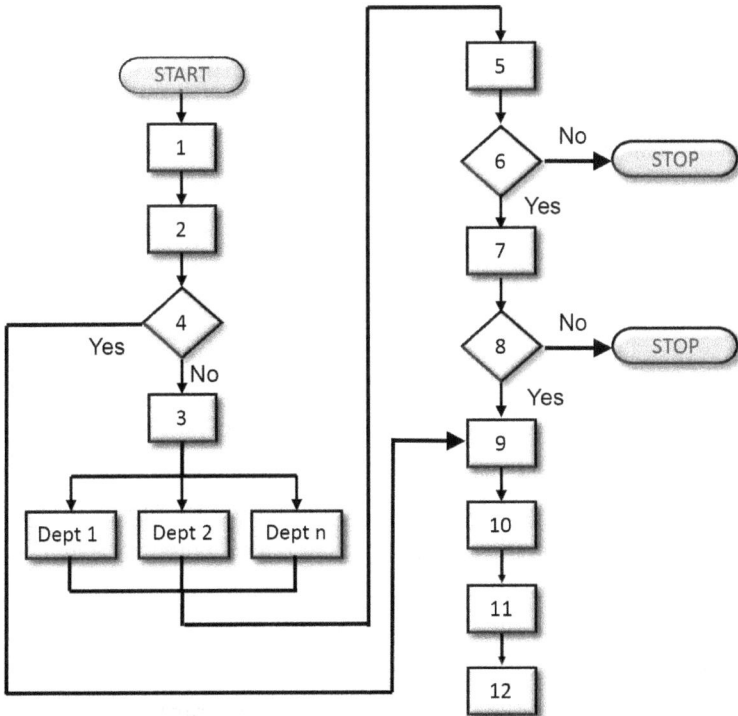

Figure 3.3-1 Process steps

7. Risk assessed
8. Risk is acceptable
9. Project scored
10. Placed in score-order before the steering committee
11. The steering committee approves or rejects
12. If approved, project placed in queue until resources to work on it become available

Let's look first at how people will input requests into the new system. Can they do it from their desks while logged into the internal network? Can they do it through the Internet from anywhere in the world? Can any employee do it, or is it limited to a subset of the employees? This is a crucial decision that must be made by the steering committee or by the project sponsor (who is a *de facto* member of the steering committee).

This illustrates a typical flow for the process. Note that we have made the decision in Step 4 whether the project is mandatory or not. If it is, we skip many of the remaining steps and just score the project. However, it does not have to be in this order. Your organization may wish to gather the financial cost data for the project even if it is mandatory. In this case, we would reorganize the steps to show this.

This is the basic flow of the processes. As in any business process, there are exceptions to the normal flow. One of the EPMS's internal processes is to ensure that projects in work are examined on a regular basis to ensure they still satisfy the original selection criteria. If a project is so late or over budget that it shows up as red on the status reports more than two reporting periods in a row, then it very definitely needs to have the business case rewritten to see if it is still justifiable.

So, what should the steering committee do for projects that are late? If the business case still makes sense, then after the causes of the overruns are determined, they need to find money to continue the project in either its present form or modified. In general, never make a process so rigid and inflexible that you cannot do manual workarounds for exceptions. No one can predict all possible future events, so build in some points where the existing process can.

If a new product project is behind schedule, the primary imperative is to find out why. If there are technology problems that are causing schedule slippage, then one option is to add more people to the project and/or to decrease scope. Adding more people onto the project is rarely beneficial, even though this is the default approach used by many managers. New people coming onto a project almost always decreases productivity of the team because experienced and productive team members must slow down and bring the new people up to speed. Fred Brooks, in his seminal book *The Mythical Man*-Month,[8] showed us many years ago that cost is a factor of people multiplied by time, but progress is not. What can be done with some benefit is to carve out a piece of the late project and outsource it so that the existing team is not disrupted. If this is done as a subproject and given to someone else, the impacts to the current team are lessened.

Another approach is to reduce the scope of the new product. While painful to the marketing executives, meeting schedule is more important than adding more bells and whistles. If adding more features to the product are causing it to fall behind schedule, then the right answer is to not add as many new features. When problems like this occur in any project, the EPMS processes should include an automatic review of the business case to ensure that the project still makes sense.

Another process step that must be included is to reanalyze the entire portfolio when projects are killed. When a project is significantly late or over budget and the decision is made to kill it, the team managing the portfolio should reassess the remaining projects in the portfolio and reprioritize them as needed as well as reassessing the overall risk level of the portfolio.

3.3.4 Reports

Many software programmers enjoy the challenges of developing new software that will help the organization. Developing the output reports? Not so much. Too often, the output reports are a quick addition at the end of the design. But, that's a mistake. The accuracy, believability, and readability of the reports given to management is going to make the EPMS successful or be ignored. If the reports are too detailed, the decision makers won't be able to interpret them. If they're too high level, they're useless. Part of the requirements gather effort is to identify exactly what the final reports generated should look like and what information they need to contain. This was discussed at the end of Step 2.2.

3.4 Scheduling the Project

Law of Project Management
In any large organization, no major project was ever installed on time, within budget, with the same staff that started it. *Yours will not be the first.*

Implementing an EPMS cannot be done quickly. For the EPMS to be successful, the people who are affected by it must be totally committed to working within its framework. They must buy into the idea and the processes. This will require time and multiple meetings with management (be honest—how easy it is to get even four managers together at the same time for a few hours?). Organizational change does not come quickly. In a small organization, you should expect at least a year to get approvals, design the EPMS, implement it, and get buy-in by everyone. IDC[9] published a survey of 13 companies that had deployed an EPMS for at least a year. The average time from the project charter to operations was 37 months. For a large, multinational organization, plan on 2 to 3 years for a successful enterprisewide implementation. For government agencies, where there are multiple groups with different reporting geographies and significantly different priorities, it can take even longer before the EPMS is truly effective. The project phases in a top-level schedule might look something like this:

Note the duration of the project is over two years long the way we are laying it out (assuming 250 working days/year). As in every project,

Outline Number	Name	Duration
1	▼ EPMS Project Schedule	540 d
1.1	▶ Project Initiation	23 d
1.2	▶ Develop Management Plans	33 d
1.3	▼ Project Execution	282 d
1.3.1	▶ Identify EPMS Requirements	116 d
1.3.2	▶ OCM Project Plan	133 d
1.3.3	▶ Detailed Design & Development	176 d
1.4	▶ Testing and Integration	162 d
1.5	▶ Implementation	216 d

Figure 3.4-1 Top-level schedule

there are a lot of uncertainties and assumptions in duration estimates. Yours may be much longer or much shorter than this, depending on your individual circumstances. How do we get to an accurate estimate? That's what this section is about.

3.4.1 WBS

As with all projects, we start the process of developing the schedule by defining the high-level deliverables that need to be done to do the work. This list is called the Work Breakdown Structure, the WBS. The requirements tell us *what* has to be developed, the WBS tells us what the major pieces of the final product are. Then, we define the specific activities to design and produce those pieces. These are the activities that must be completed to successfully deliver the project. The WBS is not a very detailed list, just detailed enough to define the major activities. This is not something you do in your cubicle by yourself. Developing the WBS is a team effort of the major team members. This not only gives you a more accurate WBS it also gives them buy-in to the resulting list of activities. That buy-in makes them more committed to the project work. After all, they're the ones who gave you the activities.

The top-level WBS might look like this:

Table 3.2 Top-level work breakdown structure

1.0	Project management activities		
	1.1	Project initiation	
		1.1.1	Identify primary stakeholders
		1.1.2	Develop project charter
		1.1.3	Obtain charter approval
	1.2	Develop management plans	
		1.2.1	Schedule management plan
		1.2.2	Cost management plan
		1.2.3	Stakeholder management plan
		1.2.4	Communications plan
		1.2.5	Requirements management plan
		1.2.6	Implementation plan
		1.2.7	Quality plan
		1.2.8	Risk plan

(Continued)

Table 3.2 (*Continued*)

		1.2.9	HR management plan
		1.2.10	OCM plan
		1.2.11	Test and integration plan
		1.2.12	Configuration management plan
		1.2.13	Procurement plan
		1.2.14	Management plan approval and baseline
			Go for project execution
	1.3	**Project execution**	
		1.3.1	Identify EPMS requirements
		1.3.2	OCM project plan
		1.3.3	Detailed design and development
	1.4	**Testing and integration**	
		1.4.1	Define test requirements
		1.4.2	Create test data and develop test cases
		1.4.3	Integration testing
		1.4.4	System testing
		1.4.5	Stress testing
	1.5	**Implementation**	
		1.5.1	Management approves pilot project
		1.5.2	Pilot EPMS
		1.5.3	Get management feedback
		1.5.4	Make changes as needed
		1.5.5	Approval to roll out
		1.5.6	Incorporate new proposed projects
		1.5.7	Incorporate existing projects (if approved)
		1.5.8	Begin new project selection process

Notice that this is built around the top-level deliverables on the project. Once you are comfortable that you have captured the major pieces of the EPMS product, the WBS should be communicated to your project sponsor and the steering committee for review, discussion, and approval. Your job is made much easier if they understand what the members of the team will be doing. The WBS is signed by the project sponsor or, even better, by the steering committee. This creates a baseline that cannot be changed without going through the change approval process.

Once the WBS is approved, we can take it down to lower levels of detail in a process called decomposition. To each activity in the WBS, we determine the relationships among the various activities, add resources to them, and determine their duration, and finally, customize the project and resource calendars to determine the overall project schedule. How detailed should the schedule be? Detailed enough to plan what has to go on, but no more detailed than that or else it becomes too burdensome to manage.

Story

In the Fall of 2009 two of our teams spent several months working on a US 10 billion dollar oil refinery in Saudi Arabia. At the program level there were about 3000 activities in the project schedule. Each one of the thirteen contractors had several thousand activities in their schedules for their own portions of the work. And this was at the work package level! The real details were in each work package.

Let's take this highest level now and break it down into the next level of detail:

1. Initiate project
   - 1.1 Develop project charter
   - 1.2 Project charter approval
   - 1.3 Project kickoff meeting

And, as shown in the example in the Appendix, we can decompose the activities until they are detailed enough to allocate resources to and to develop the activity relations and durations.

The WBS in the Appendix that is sufficiently detailed for you to use it as a template and customize it for your own use. Caution: Never blindly follow a template. A template provides thought guidance for you to help think through what you are doing. It's not a cookie cutter to be used without changes.*

---

* After teaching project management to thousands of students worldwide, I have seen that no two students or teams will start with exactly the same WBS for a given project. Your own experience, your organizational culture, the current environment will lead to different WBSs. But, in the end, any reasonable WBS will allow you to create a reasonable schedule. If you've missed an activity in the WBS, it will show up later on.

3.4.2 Estimating

Once we have a good WBS at a reasonable level of detail, we can start the process of developing the schedule. The recommended sequence is to work with your team to determine the sequence of activities. What has to come first, second, third, and so on. What needs to be done sequentially and what can be done in parallel.

A major input to this process is the size of the team and the skills of the project team members you have. The more team members working on the project, the faster the work can be completed, but at a high cost. This is not absolutely true, but it works up to a point. Fewer team members will lower the cost, but the work will take longer. For every project, there is an optimal range of team size that will complete the project efficiently. We'll talk more about resources later.

Once you have the "right" number of people assigned to each activity, the team can estimate the duration for each activity.

This is a major danger point at which projects are either successful or run far beyond their due date. Accurate estimating is one of the most critical parts of scheduling and costing as well as being one of the things we do most poorly. Being trained in estimating provides a significant improvement in the estimates, but no estimate is perfect.

Each activity has uncertainty in its estimates, both cost uncertainties and duration uncertainties. If I can estimate an activity's duration within ±10 percent , I feel confident I can complete the activity as planned. If my critical path has 50 activities on it, and each one has a 10 percent uncertainty in the duration, that can either cause the project to complete extremely early if each activity finishes 10 percent early (causing you to be accused of padding the schedule) or finish extremely late if each activity finishes 10 percent late (causing you to be accused of incompetent scheduling). What will most likely happen is that some activities will finish earlier than planned, and some will finish later than planned. So, on average, you should finish close to the planned schedule if you've done a reasonable job developing the schedule.

Projects are, by definition, unique. This project you're planning has never been done before exactly this way, so you have no history to rely on for the needed activities or their durations. You're trying to predict how long something is going to take when the work itself is weeks or months away. You're trying to predict the future, and nobody is good at that.

We can improve our estimates by using three-point and PERT (the well-known Project Evaluation and Review Technique) estimating techniques, and even better, by using Monte Carlo simulation on the project schedule. But, that kind of detailed schedule analysis is probably not required for an EPMS project.

Even though we don't need to use sophisticated statistical analytical methods for our schedule, there are simple things we can do to improve the accuracy of our scheduling process. One simple thing is to build individual calendars for each team member and put in the days they're not available for project work due to vacation, planned holidays, and other known off days.

Another simple scheduling trick is to not use the default 40 hours per work week that is built into the scheduling software. Why not? Think about what you're scheduling at this phase of the project. You're planning out the work that people will do on the activities weeks or months from now. But, once we're in the middle of the project, we demand that our team members do a lot of things that are not planned activities. Weekly status meetings, change-control board meetings, writing status updates, risk meetings, and many other activities take up time that wasn't planned for at the beginning of the project. On a normal project, these can take up a full eight hours a week.

Think this is way too much? *CIO*[10] magazine published a survey that Intel Corporation did of their own internal knowledge workers. Their research showed that their workers spent about 20 hours/week just on e-mail, and that about one-third of that time, or six hours per week, was wasted. As a result, Intel instituted a "no e-mail Friday" policy.

If you use a standard 40 hours/week, you will force people to put in overtime in order to take into account all these other normal activities. To compensate for this, change the default work week to about 32 hours per week. This is most easily done by changing the default day to 6.5 hours instead of 8. The schedule you put together will be longer than if you used eight hours/day, but it will be more accurate and you will spend less time explaining why your project is late. We want to be as realistic as possible when developing a schedule.

3.4.3 Turning the WBS Into a Schedule

So, now let's start turning these WBS items into a schedule. For the remainder of this section, we'll assume that we have all the resources we need, and that there are no resource limitations or conflicts. In real life, you'll have to deal with these, but for now, let's ignore these constraints.

3.4.3.1 Scheduling the Project Management Itself

The top-level schedule was shown earlier. Now let's break down the initial project management activities and development of the management plans.

The primary activities here are to write the project charter and get it approved, write the various management plans, and hold the kickoff meeting to begin the communications effort. Identifying the stakeholders and the goals of the project are intrinsic to developing the project charter.

The initial project activities generally end with the project kickoff meeting. After that point, the project can be considered to enter the

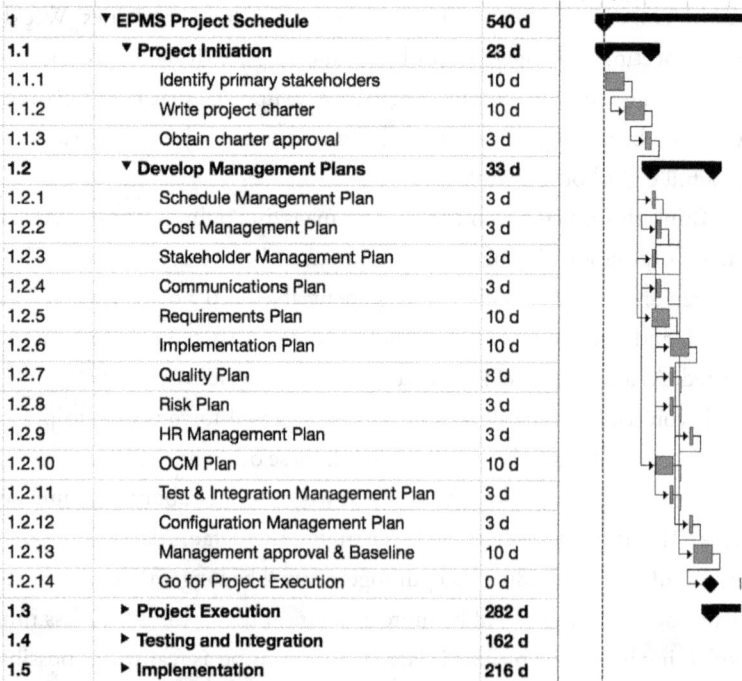

1	▼ EPMS Project Schedule	540 d
1.1	▼ Project Initiation	23 d
1.1.1	Identify primary stakeholders	10 d
1.1.2	Write project charter	10 d
1.1.3	Obtain charter approval	3 d
1.2	▼ Develop Management Plans	33 d
1.2.1	Schedule Management Plan	3 d
1.2.2	Cost Management Plan	3 d
1.2.3	Stakeholder Management Plan	3 d
1.2.4	Communications Plan	3 d
1.2.5	Requirements Plan	10 d
1.2.6	Implementation Plan	10 d
1.2.7	Quality Plan	3 d
1.2.8	Risk Plan	3 d
1.2.9	HR Management Plan	3 d
1.2.10	OCM Plan	10 d
1.2.11	Test & Integration Management Plan	3 d
1.2.12	Configuration Management Plan	3 d
1.2.13	Management approval & Baseline	10 d
1.2.14	Go for Project Execution	0 d
1.3	▶ Project Execution	282 d
1.4	▶ Testing and Integration	162 d
1.5	▶ Implementation	216 d

Figure 3.4-2 Project management planning schedule

execution phase where the planning is substantially completed, and the project team members can begin work.

Note that the management plans are developed in parallel for the most part. The assumption here is that you have reasonable templates to work from, and that all you have to do is fill out the project-specific pieces of the template. If you don't have templates to work from, you should add several more days to each of these. If you don't have enough resources to help, you may need to do these in sequence rather than overlapped. That would require 41 days instead of the 33 shown here.

Note also that we have included what are referred to as "living documents" such as the risk register. These documents generally do not take much time to develop, but are constantly updated as we go through the project. Schedules and budgets are updated weekly, the others are updated as required during the project. Other documents that you will need include a stakeholder register, requirements tracking documents, and others as required.

How much of each person's time should you plan on them for? How much of each step should you allocate to different people? For, planning purposes, as a guideline, look at the chart shown after the RAM to help you think through each step in the process and how much time to allocate (this could be taken into account during the scheduling/costing effort to provide more accurate budget numbers). Note that the numbers do not have to add to 100 percent. During the requirements analysis, 100 percent of the business analysts' time should be devoted to the activity, but only 25 percent of the project manager's time (he/she will be more involved in development schedules, budgets, etc.). Allocations should be made as shown in the Appendix 3.4-3 example.

3.4.3.2 OCM Planning

Once we begin the execution phase of the project, the primary activities are developing the detailed requirements that we need to design the EPMS, start the OCM processes, and do the detailed design and development. Let's take a closer look at the OCM effort. OCM is not a project, it is a program that will not only prepare the organization for the upcoming changes, but may continue after the EPMS has been implemented. At the top level, the activities are:

- Create a sense of need among the stakeholders
- Create a vision of the new processes (in our case, the new EPMS processes)
- Define the impacts of the coming changes to the stakeholders
- Develop the OCM communications plan
- Develop training for the employees affected by the changes
- Now let's look at the next level of detail down for creating the sense of need among the stakeholders. As you can see, this is a very detailed process:

1.3.2	▼ OCM Project Plan	133 d
1.3.2.1	▼ Create sense of need among stakeholder	48 d
1.3.2.1.1	▼ Define problem	12 d
1.3.2.1.1.1	Work with PM to define problem statement	3 d
1.3.2.1.1.2	Develop OCM project charter	3 d
1.3.2.1.1.3	OCM charter approved	5 d
1.3.2.1.1.4	Kickoff meeting with OCM team	1 d
1.3.2.1.2	▼ Define climate for change readiness	21 d
1.3.2.1.2.1	Identify survey/interview participants	3 d
1.3.2.1.2.2	Perform survey and interviews	10 d
1.3.2.1.2.3	Analyze results	5 d
1.3.2.1.2.4	Communicate results	3 d
1.3.2.1.2.5	Change climate assessment complete	0 d
1.3.2.1.3	▼ Finalize OCM strategy	15 d
1.3.2.1.3.1	Create final OCM strategy	5 d
1.3.2.1.3.2	Review with team	5 d
1.3.2.1.3.3	Obtain management approval for OCM approach	5 d

Figure 3.4-3 OCM planning schedule

More details of the rest of the OCM processes are in Appendix 3.4-1.

By developing this level of detail, we can see how the OCM effort evolves and ensures that everything that should be thought of has in fact been identified. For our example, we have come up with an OCM effort duration of 133 days. In reality, OCM is like project communications—it goes on as long as necessary to ensure the stakeholders are satisfied. Don't take the 133 days as a fixed duration. Efforts like OCM are highly dependent on the results they produce. If they need more time, give them more time. The results of the effort are critical, not how long they take. The

OCM effort is not on the critical path once the execution phase begins and should continue as needed to get buy-in for the project.

3.4.3.3 Requirements Planning

Unlike OCM, the effort to identify and develop the detailed requirements for the EPMS can be scheduled much more precisely as shown in Appendix 3.4-2. We can see that we can schedule the specific activities needed, whereas in OCM, the activities are more reactive to how people respond to the project. Note that the project's critical path goes through the requirements. This should always be the case for a project.

Five months to develop requirement (and that assumes you have the staff to gather requirements in parallel)? That seems like a really long time, doesn't it? BUT, it is absolutely critical to get the requirements 100 percent correct. The success of the project depends on the completeness and thoroughness of the requirements. Remember that, for any project, the requirements have to be approved and signed off by the senior decision makers. This takes more time and more coordination meetings than you would think. Be prepared to answer a lot of questions about where the requirements came from, why each one is important, why do they have the priorities they do, and many other detailed questions. By the end of the process, you will likely have memorized the entire set of business requirements.

When identifying the sources of requirements, we have to include sources such as business analysts, executives, existing process documentation, project managers, functional managers, and other stakeholders as discussed earlier.

3.4.3.4 Design and Development

Now that we've defined our requirements and begun the OCM process, let's look at the details of design and development activities in Appendix 3.4-4. If there is a commercial product to be purchased, the schedule there is a little less predictable because of the delays inherent in purchasing anything from an outside vendor. We have the actual purchase shown as only one day, but in reality, it can take weeks to get through the procurement process.

1	▼ EPMS Project Schedule	540 d	
1.1	▶ Project Initiation	23 d	
1.2	▶ Develop Management Plans	33 d	
1.3	▼ Project Execution	282 d	
1.3.1	▼ Identify EPMS Requirements	116 d	
1.3.1.1	Approval to start requirements	0 d	Mar 19, 2020, 5:00 PM
1.3.1.2	▼ Identify sources of requirements	2 d	
1.3.1.2.2	Business analysts	1 d	
1.3.1.2.2	Executives	1 d	
1.3.1.2.3	Existing business processes	2 d	
1.3.1.2.4	Project managers	1 d	
1.3.1.2.5	Functional managers	2 d	
1.3.1.2.6	Other stakeholders	2 d	
1.3.1.3	▼ Develop plan	6 d	
1.3.1.3.1	Identify roles & responsibilities	2 d	
1.3.1.3.2	Identify resources for requirements team	3 d	
1.3.1.3.3	Develop schedule	1 d	
1.3.1.4	▼ Prepare requirements tools	10 d	
1.3.1.4.1	Requirements attributes	1 d	
1.3.1.4.2	Interview questions	5 d	
1.3.1.4.3	Requirements capture sheets	1 d	
1.3.1.4.4	Requirements tracking sheets	1 d	
1.3.1.4.5	Tracking data base	2 d	
1.3.1.5	▼ Gather requirements	83 d	
1.3.1.5.1	Interview stakeholders	21 d	
1.3.1.5.2	Review org documents	21 d	
1.3.1.5.3	Analyze business processes	21 d	
1.3.1.5.4	Analyze & prioritize requirements	10 d	
1.3.1.5.5	Validate requirements	10 d	
1.3.1.6	▼ Document requirements	15 d	
1.3.1.6.1	Business requirements document	5 d	
1.3.1.6.2	System requirements document	5 d	
1.3.1.6.3	Detailed design specifications	5 d	
1.3.1.7	Management Baseline of Requirements Docs	0 d	

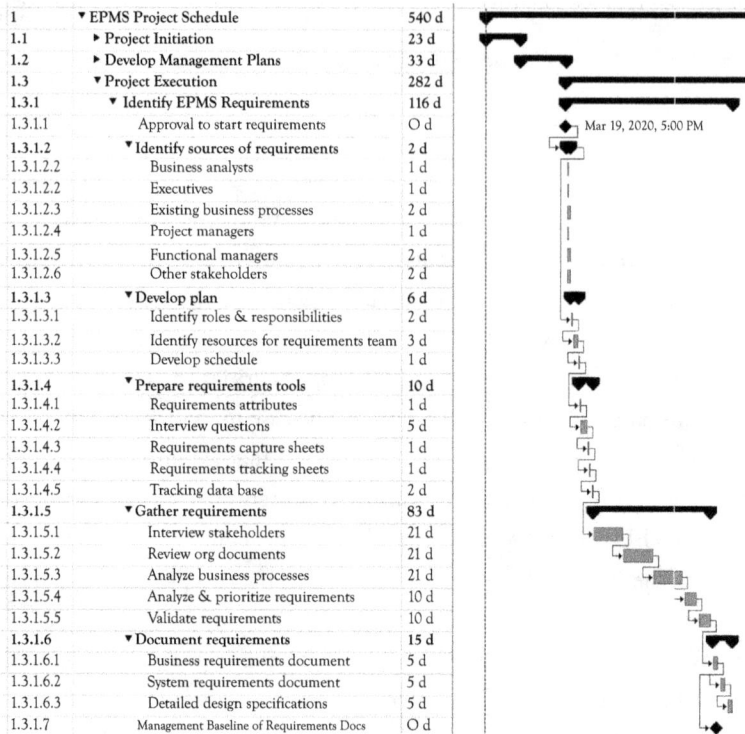

Figure 3.4-4 Detailed requirements development schedule

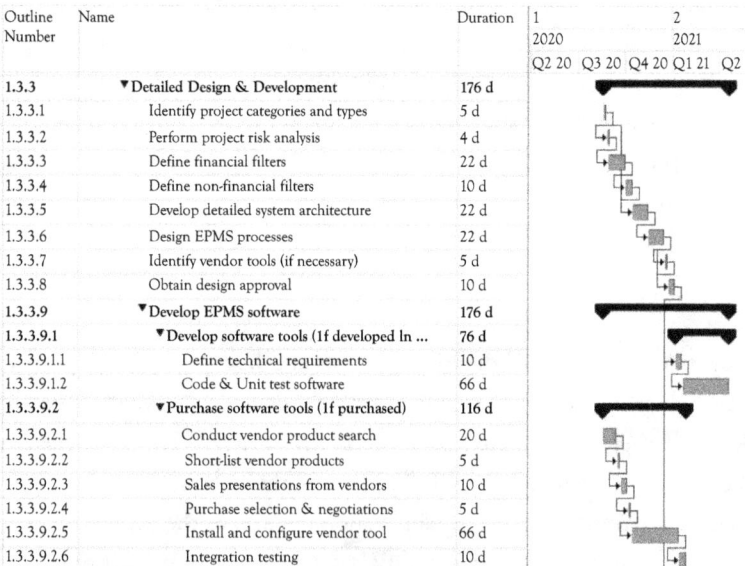

Outline Number	Name	Duration	1 2020		2 2021		
			Q2 20	Q3 20	Q4 20	Q1 21	Q2
1.3.3	▼ Detailed Design & Development	176 d					
1.3.3.1	Identify project categories and types	5 d					
1.3.3.2	Perform project risk analysis	4 d					
1.3.3.3	Define financial filters	22 d					
1.3.3.4	Define non-financial filters	10 d					
1.3.3.5	Develop detailed system architecture	22 d					
1.3.3.6	Design EPMS processes	22 d					
1.3.3.7	Identify vendor tools (if necessary)	5 d					
1.3.3.8	Obtain design approval	10 d					
1.3.3.9	▼ Develop EPMS software	176 d					
1.3.3.9.1	▼ Develop software tools (1f developed ln ...	76 d					
1.3.3.9.1.1	Define technical requirements	10 d					
1.3.3.9.1.2	Code & Unit test software	66 d					
1.3.3.9.2	▼ Purchase software tools (1f purchased)	116 d					
1.3.3.9.2.1	Conduct vendor product search	20 d					
1.3.3.9.2.2	Short-list vendor products	5 d					
1.3.3.9.2.3	Sales presentations from vendors	10 d					
1.3.3.9.2.4	Purchase selection & negotiations	5 d					
1.3.3.9.2.5	Install and configure vendor tool	66 d					
1.3.3.9.2.6	Integration testing	10 d					

Figure 3.4-5 Design and development schedule

These are reasonable steps for the project in a reasonable order. As so many technical consultants like to say: Your mileage may vary. You should feel free to use these schedules as guidelines but to develop your own that will work in your organization.

Somewhere between the design and the implementation steps, you will have to train employees and managers on how to use the EPMS. If your organization has a training department, they can help identify the training requirements, develop training materials, and schedule training sessions for everyone who might interact with the system. The training for employees to enter a new project request should be short because, of course, you've made the input forms simple. The training for managers to understand and interpret what the output of the EPMS is will be longer and more detailed.

3.4.3.5 Testing and Implementation

The final processes in the schedule are testing and implementation as shown here:

1.4	▼ Testing and Integration	162 d
1.4.1	Define test requirements	10 d
1.4.2	Create test data and develop test cases	44 d
1.4.3	Integration testing	10 d
1.4.4	System testing	5 d
1.4.5	Stress testing	3 d

Figure 3.4-6 Test and integration schedule

Isn't the testing phase part of development? Yes and no. It's the experience of this author and many software project managers that because most project managers don't come from a testing background, they tend to short-change testing when it comes to the schedule. It takes more time than you think to develop a strong testing program and the process starts as soon as you've identified the requirements.

The testing should be against the requirements, not against the design, and it should be done by a group independent of the developers. If you test to the design, the design will almost always pass. If you test to the requirements, the design may or may not satisfy the requirements, and this is the place to catch that shortfall. This is why, there is a schedule gap between the first activity "Define test requirements" and the second "Create test data and develop test cases." You can start the testing design early, but you cannot develop test cases or test data until the requirements are complete.

Testing will prove to be the most challenging part of the project to schedule due to the uncertainties of test results. If a module is tested and passes the test, the test results are written up, and the module is set aside for integration testing and the tester moves onto the next module. But, if the module fails the test, the test failure is documented, and the module is returned to the development team for rework. Now the developers have to figure out what went wrong and fix the module. It then goes back for retesting. The time spent in rework by the developers and the retesting is unplanned work. It's not in the schedule. So, a test failure causes schedule pressures on the project.

We can compensate for this uncertainty a little bit by using our historical data (you do have historical data for IT testing, yes?). If history shows that 25 percent of software modules fail testing the first time, we can compensate for it by adding an appropriate amount to each test duration to take into account the rework required. Alternatively, but this is not officially recommended, add supplementary tests into the testing schedule for rework. This is not recommended because experience shows that once management sees these activities, they will demand they be taken out of the schedule. Their logic is that people will do their jobs correctly and so we should not add rework activities that assume failures. Unrealistic, but this is how management thinks.

1.5	▼ Implementation	216 d
1.5.1	Management Approves Pilot Project	5 d
1.5.2	Pilot EPMS	120 d
1.5.3	Get management feedback	22 d
1.5.4	Make changes as needed	44 d
1.5.5	Approval to roll out	10 d
1.5.6	Incorporate new proposed projects	15 d
1.5.7	Incorporate existing projects (if approved)	15 d
1.5.8	Begin new project selection process	0 d

Figure 3.4-7 Implementation schedule

The implementation itself should begin with a pilot project. Test the new EPMS by running one or two existing projects through it and see if they would pass. Discuss the results with the steering committee and get their feedback. If you need to adjust the financial filters, do it now and rerun the pilot project. Keep doing this until the decision makers are happy with the answers and trust what the system is telling them. At that point, you can roll out the EPMS to the organization and start taking requests for projects.

At Toyota Financial Services, we first implemented the EMPS manually. Any employee could send an e-mail suggesting a new project. The information would be taken and input to the system manually at first. Once we had the bugs worked out and the steering committee was comfortable, we automated the process using Lotus Notes. The time needed to identify the details of a proposed project and to get it approved went from months down to two weeks.

3.5—Budgeting the Project

3.5.1 Budgeting Uncertainties

Budgeting any project is more straightforward than developing the schedule in most areas of project management, but it is also less certain and has more variables. If you can develop the schedule to within ±10 percent, you're doing well. But, if the schedule uncertainty is 10 percent, then the budget uncertainty is going to be closer to 20 percent.

Why? The budget has its own uncertainties, and these sit on top of the schedule uncertainties. We know intuitively that the longer an activity goes on, the more it costs. Let's use an artificial example to illustrate how great this uncertainty can be. Let's look at the simplest possible project—a series of activities that are completely sequential as shown here:

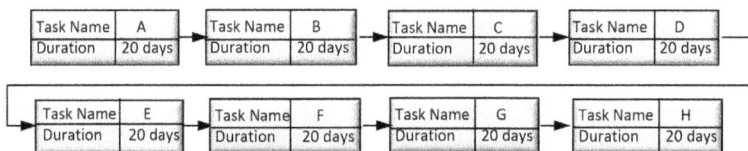

Figure 3.5-1 Sequential activities

For the purposes of this example, we'll state schedule uncertainties for each activity as shown in the following Table 3.3:

Table 3.3 *Duration uncertainties*

Activity	Duration in days	Duration uncertainty
A	20	10%
B	80	25%
C	60	10%
D	40	10%
E	40	10%
F	60	15%
G	100	10%
H	20	10%
I	0	-

Note that we picked a very simple uncertainty, ±10 percent, 15 percent, or 25 percent. A more realistic spread would be something like -10 percent to +20 percent. There is nothing that says the schedule uncertainty needs to be symmetric, but it makes the example easier.

To get the uncertainties in each activity, we will multiply the planned duration by the uncertainty, and then either subtract the uncertainty from the planned duration to get the optimistic duration and the pessimistic duration.

Activities A through E will cost us $1,000 per day. Activities F through H will cost us $1,500 per day. Given these figures, what is the range of dates the project can take and what impact does that have on the project costs? See Table 3.4:

Table 3.4 *Cost and schedule uncertainties*

Activity	Duration	Duration uncertainty	Optimistic duration	Pessimistic duration	Least cost	Highest cost
A	20	10%	18	22	$18,000	$22,000
B	80	25%	60	100	60,000	100,000
C	60	10%	54	66	54,000	66,000
D	40	10%	36	44	36,000	44,000
E	40	10%	36	44	36,000	44,000
F	60	15%	51	69	76,500	103,500
G	100	10%	90	110	135,000	165,000
H	20	10%	18	22	27,000	33,000
I	0	-				
				Project	442,500	577,500

The nominal project cost is $510,000 based on the original predicted durations. But, now look at those bottom row numbers. Just based on the schedule uncertainties, the project can cost anywhere from $442,500 to $577,500. That is a difference of over $150,000. How are you going to explain that to management unless you prepare them in advance for the reality of schedule uncertainties? Remember we said that during the kickoff meeting, you have to ask management what level of uncertainty they're willing to accept? This is why.

Now lets go one step further. As we said earlier, there are budget uncertainties that are independent of schedule uncertainties. For example, when you identify the team members and add their cost to the project activities, what cost do you use? For contractors, the costs are defined in the contract and known. But, for employees, the situation is different. In most countries, you're not allowed to know their actually salaries. That's a violation of their privacy. So, you go to the HR department and get the average salary for the job grade of each required skill set you've identified.

If the team member assigned to the project has been there for years and has a salary higher than average, the activities she works on are going to be more expensive than planned, and your budget is going to look bad because that team member cost more than you expected. You could not have predicted this.

If the team member assigned is new to the company and relatively inexperienced, their salary is going to be below average, and your budget is going to look good. You could not have predicted this either. Other sources of cost uncertainty include the future cost of purchased materials and contractual changes.

So, there are impacts to your budget that were unpredictable. Let's take these into account and extend our example to take into account these uncertainties. As before, we will use reasonable budget uncertainties for each activity, say ±10 percent. But, this time, the budget uncertainties will be added on top of the schedule uncertainties.

Why use 10 percent for uncertainty? Because it is a relatively common level of uncertainty in many projects. Using the same cost numbers as before, we can multiply the optimistic and pessimistic durations by the cost uncertainties and subtract or add the uncertainties to get the optimistic and pessimistic cost numbers. In Table 3.5, these are labeled "Budget Most Optimistic" and "Budget Most Pessimistic."

Table 3.5 Total project cost variation

Activity	Duration	Duration uncertainty	Cost uncertainty	Budget most optimistic	Budget most pessimistic
A	20	10%	10%	$16,200	$24,200
B	80	25%	10%	54,000	110,000
C	60	10%	10%	48,600	72,600
D	40	10%	10%	32,400	48,400
E	40	10%	10%	32,400	48,400
F	60	15%	20%	61,200	124,200
G	100	10%	25%	101,250	206,250
H	20	10%	10%	24,300	36,300
I	0	-	-		
			Potential project total costs	$370,350	$670,350

Look at those bottom-line costs! Wow! That's a range of $300,000 between the absolute best the project can do and the absolute worst. And, this analysis didn't even do a thorough risk assessment, we just looked at the normal uncertainties in the schedule and costs.

Obviously, this example was developed to show extremes. The average project should come in somewhere relatively close to the planned. Just as in schedules, some activity costs will come in above planned and some below. So, the average of many activities will be closer to planned than to the extremes (assuming you did a reasonable job in estimating your costs).

3.5.2 Costing the Project

When you develop your budget, what costs do you put in? Certainly, the salaries of each team member (constrained by the uncertainty mentioned previously) and the contract costs of any contractors used. For a pure software project, the costs are almost exclusively salaries of team members. For other types of projects, such as construction, there are a multitude of other costs associated with the work.

Part of the project's budget is contingency funds for risks. If a risk happens, it will have cost and schedule impacts. There are methods to develop a detailed risk budget, but for a project such as this, the amount of time required is probably not worth the benefits. A simpler approach is to take an industry average for similar projects. In this case, because there are risks both from staff resistance to the EMPS as well as software risks, take 25 percent of the final planned cost and ask for that as contingency funds in addition to the planned budget. If you have multiple risks on your project (and you do), at least some of them will happen. You just don't know which ones. So, protect yourself by asking for contingency money at the beginning.

Some of your personnel resources will not be counted against the cost of the project. For example, you will need to interview the executives while gathering requirements and meeting with them to status the project and to get feedback. Their costs are typically not accounted for on the project but are covered in overhead. If you meet with functional managers and project managers, their time is also not typically charged against the project.

If you are planning on buying a software tool as a portfolio management tool, the cost of the tool will count against the project as will the cost of the IT department's implementation of the tool, the configuration of the tool, and the testing to ensure the tool does not interfere with other existing software.

Before you even begin, management will ask you how much, roughly, this EPMS implementation will cost. They need to know that so that they can decide if they want to pay for it or not. At this stage, before the project is approved, the cost is going to be very inexact. A figure that is ±50 percent is often good enough.

More detailed costing can only be developed after we have a detailed schedule. We'll estimate the resources needed and their hourly salaries to arrive at a cost for the project. Let's start with the OCM activities as an example. In Table 3.6, we show the salaries we have assigned the resources:

Table 3.6 Project salaries

Resource	Cost
Project manager	$0/hr
OCM lead	$75/hr
Communications lead	$50/hr
Lead business analyst	$30/hr
Business analyst 1	$25/hr
Business analyst 2	$25/hr
Trainer	$50/hr

Not that the project manager has a zero cost associated. This is because that salary has already been allocated to the general project management activity. If we put in an hourly salary here, that would give us double booking of that salary and result in an inaccurate final cost.

We allocate the resources against the most detailed activities in the schedule to come up with the total number of hours the resource worked and the costs for each resource. Remember a statement we made at the beginning of this section: The numbers are only accurate to within 10 to 20 percent. So, take the scheduling tool's cost numbers carefully and add 20 percent management reserve.

As an example: how much does it cost to perform the activity "Create a Sense of Need Among Stakeholders?"

Note 1: For some resources that work throughout the project, such as the project manager and project administrative assistant, it is easier to enter their costs on a daily rate for the duration of the project instead of trying to attach their costs to specific activities. They are working on the project even if they are not tied to a schedule activity. If the schedule is 381 days long and the project manager makes $100/hour or $800/day, the cost for the project manager is $304,800. Similarly, if the project admin assistant makes $25/hour, their cost to the project will be $76,200. You enter these as fixed costs at the top level of the project rather than as activity-driven costs.

Note 2: If you work in a matrix organization, then you assign resources to the individual activities and determine their costs. When they are not

1.3.2.1	▼ Create sense of need among stakeholder	48 d	$51,120.00
1.3.2.1.1	▼ Define problem	10 d	$8,400.00
1.3.2.1.1.1	Work with PM to define problem statement	1 d	$840.00
1.3.2.1.1.2	Develop OCM project charter	3 d	$2,520.00
1.3.2.1.1.3	OCM charter approved	5 d	$3,000.00
1.3.2.1.1.4	Kickoff meeting with OCM team	1 d	$2,040.00
1.3.2.1.2	▼ Define climate for change readiness	23 d	$28,520.00
1.3.2.1.2.1	Identify survey/interview participants	5 d	$6,200.00
1.3.2.1.2.2	Perform survey and interviews	10 d	$12,400.00
1.3.2.1.2.3	Analyze results	5 d	$6,200.00
1.3.2.1.2.4	Communicate results	3 d	$3,720.00
1.3.2.1.2.5	Change climate assessment complete	0 d	$0.00
1.3.2.1.3	▼ Finalize OCM strategy	15 d	$14,200.00
1.3.2.1.3.1	Create final OCM strategy	5 d	$6,200.00
1.3.2.1.3.2	Review with team	5 d	$5,000.00
1.3.2.1.3.3	Obtain management approval for OCM approach	5 d	$3,000.00

Figure 3.5-2 Cost for creating a sense of need

needed on the project, you return them to their home shop and no longer count their cost against the project. If you have a dedicated team for the duration of the project (common in projectized organizations), you simply multiply their salaries times how long the project is just as in the previous note. For the purposes of this example, we'll assume that we only pay for the work team members do on the project, except for the project manager and the admin assistant.

The entire OCM effort will cost:

1.3.2	▼ OCM Project Plan	224 d	$160,160.00
1.3.2.1	▶ Create sense of need among stakeholder	48 d	$51,120.00
1.3.2.2	▼ Create vision for new EPMS	8 d	$7,920.00
1.3.2.2.1	Team creates vision statement	3 d	$4,920.00
1.3.2.2.2	Obtain management approval	5 d	$3,000.00
1.3.2.3	▼ Define change impacts	54 d	$23,280.00
1.3.2.3.1	Define impacted stakeholders	2 d	$2,480.00
1.3.2.3.2	Identify impacts of changes to stakeholders	5 d	$6,200.00
1.3.2.3.3	Complete job impacts assessment	3 d	$3,720.00
1.3.2.3.4	Complete change impacts assessment	2 d	$2,480.00
1.3.2.3.5	Management approval of change impact assessment	10 d	$8,400.00
1.3.2.4	▼ Communications plan	114 d	$53,160.00
1.3.2.4.1	Identify major communications messages	2 d	$2,000.00
1.3.2.4.2	Identify key concerns and issues	5 d	$6,200.00
1.3.2.4.3	Identify key messages for each audience	3 d	$2,520.00
1.3.2.4.4	Identify appropriate comm media for each stakeholder category	1 d	$1,000.00
1.3.2.4.5	Identify timing of each message	1 d	$640.00
1.3.2.4.6	Write communications plan	2 d	$800.00
1.3.2.4.7	Begin communications efforts	100 d	$40,000.00
1.3.2.5	▼ Develop Training	51 d	$24,680.00
1.3.2.5.1	Review change impacts to determine training requirements	3 d	$3,000.00
1.3.2.5.2	Identify trainers	1 d	$400.00
1.3.2.5.3	Identify training participants	2 d	$2,480.00
1.3.2.5.4	Develop training plan and schedule	5 d	$2,000.00
1.3.2.5.5	Create training materials	20 d	$8,000.00
1.3.2.5.6	Determine training facility requirements	2 d	$800.00
1.3.2.5.7	Perform training	20 d	$8,000.00

Figure 3.5-3 OCM costs

If you're wondering where some of the odd numbers, such as $31,039.95 under communications come from, it's because communications is not a 40 hour/week effort. So, we allocated only 25 percent of the communications lead time to the activity. The odd numbers are constraints in the software's calculation for the effort. Remembering that these are only estimates, instead of showing $31,039.95 for communications activities, round it up to $32,000 or so. It's just as accurate.

Similarly, we can identify the detailed costs for gathering the requirements, making the same assumptions as before. The costs for 116 days of work to determine and lock down the business requirements are in the range of $130,000. Expensive? Sure, but much cheaper than NOT developing solid requirements and spending the rest of the project adapting to continuously changing requirements during the execution phase.

Doing the same thing for the rest of the project gives us a project cost as shown. We end up with a cost of $1,700,000+ for the project ±10 percent:

For the project manager, we gave them an hourly salary of $100 and the project admin an hourly salary of $40 and then just multiplied that hourly salary times the number of hours in the project's duration.

This sounds like a lot of money, and management will push hard on justifying spending almost $2 million on a new system. But refer back to Section 1.3. The research done by IDC shows a return on investment of $5.57 for each dollar spent on an EPMS. So, you can tell management that this investment will return almost $9,000,000 by doing this project. That's a lot of savings and benefits.

Note that we have deliberately ignored some costs. We're assuming that your organization has a Quality Assurance/Quality Control group already in existence, so the cost of managing the quality of the EPMS will come under their purview and not be charged against the project budget.

3.6 Quality Expectations

This is where we start getting into the fuzzier aspects of project management. There are no calculations here, and the only filters are the mental expectations of management and of the users. If you can identify and satisfy those expectations, you will have produced a high-quality EPMS.

What does quality mean to you? When you go to buy a car, or a television set, or a new software application, how do you judge it? What tells you it's a quality product? How would you judge the quality of an EPMS? More importantly, how will the users and the decision makers judge the quality of the EPMS you will be delivering to them? As U.S. Supreme Court justice Potter Stewart said in 1964 about obscenity,

"I can't define it, but I'll know it when I see it" (rephrased). Quality is unfortunately treated much the same way.

ISO 8402 defines quality as "Quality is the totality of characteristics of an entity that bears on its ability to satisfy stated or implied needs." I'm not sure I understand what that really means. It's hard enough to satisfy stated needs, it's virtually impossible to satisfy unstated, implied needs.

The Project Management Institute (PMI) defines quality as "The degree to which a set of inherent characteristics fulfills requirements." That's somewhat better.

But, probably, the most useful definition of quality comes from Juran "Quality is fitness for use." If the product does what I expect it to do, it's a quality product. A Proton (a Malaysian-made car with a reputation for unreliability) can be a quality product just as a BMW or an Audi can if it meets my expectations regardless of whether I have low expectations or high ones. An article published in *Air Transport Magazine* in 2013 showed that people who fly discount airlines are generally satisfied with their flights because they did not expect anything other than to arrive safely and close to on-time (that explains a lot about Southwest Airlines).

What does quality mean for an enterprise portfolio management system? Ultimately, that is a question that you will have to ask your users and your executives, but in general, we can state the following, very-high-level quality objectives:

1. The EPMS selects the projects that most strongly support strategic goals, just as the executive management team would
2. At an acceptable level of risk
3. Presents the proposed projects to us in a way that allows management to make intelligent decisions
4. Removes the biases in project selection
5. Within a reasonable response time
6. Provides a historical record of projects
7. Easy to use
8. Cheap to maintain, preferably free
9. Allows the selected projects to be scheduled based on their priority and the availability of resources

The first three are tied to the functional requirements. Those are what the decision makers want out of the EPMS. The next six are tied to nonfunctional requirements.

If it satisfies management's expectations, both stated and unstated expectations, it is a quality product. Unfortunately, management may not come out and tell you that it should be easy to use and cheap to maintain, those are often part of the unstated expectations that will make it hard for you to decide if you have satisfied them or not.

The best approach is to identify the quality expectations as requirements, if possible. For example, the prior statement "provides a historical record of projects" can be entered into the development as a requirement that must be satisfied. For other expectations, this becomes more of an interpretation than a requirement. "Easy to use" means different things to different people and is virtually impossible to quantify.

Of course, much of the technology depends on the requirements you pulled out of the users. If they're too busy to spend time to determine and communicate what their expectations are, the system will not satisfy them, and they'll decide that it is "poor quality." This is where requirements and quality intersect. It's a poor-quality system if it doesn't satisfy my requirements.

There are three major categories of quality requirements for an EPMS.

- The user interface
- The processing software itself
- The output reports

User Interface

The first category is the user interface. It should be easy to use (intuitively obvious). The users, upper management, don't care what happens behind the screens, they care about (a) does it do what they want and (b) is it easy to use. Everything else is just technology to them, and they trust the techies to do a good job with that. This is the area where the techies in your company, or vendors you hire, should shine.

Alan Cooper[11] recommends having members of the development team identify typical *personae* (in today's Internet environment, we would call them avatars) of the expected users and interact with the software from the perspective of that user. This allows the developers to look at the interface from the perspective of the normal, untrained, busy user.

Behind-the-Screen Quality

The second major category is the "behind-the-screen" technology. If the system takes two hours to generate a report, or keeps crashing, or doesn't present accurate data, it's a poor-quality system, no matter how easy it is to use. This is the second area where the techies in your company, or vendors you hire, should shine. This part of the project depends entirely on them and your ability to manage the development. And, of course, on whether you gathered the technical requirements thoroughly.

The Output

The output is the final deliverable from the EPMS. This is the list of rank-ordered projects that is produced for management by the system. It is a "quality product" only if management agrees that this is a reasonable selection of projects and they would have picked the same projects.

Project Management Quality

Separate from the quality of the final product, a third major category is the quality of the development effort. If you keep bugging the management to get their requirements out of them, they will just find you irritating. If you fall seriously behind schedule, or far over budget, you're not doing a quality job managing the project.

Is the project well managed? Is the project manager following the established processes in our organization? Or, if we do not have established processes, is the project manager following industry best practices? While project managers have a lot of discretion in how to best manage their projects most effectively, it is best to either follow the organizations established processes or get a deviation from them approved by management.

Project managers need to be optimistic about their projects. If you do not truly believe you can complete this effort successfully, you will never convince anyone else of it. But, that optimism can sometimes cause you to be less than objective about problems. You may downplay risks as being less serious than they are. That small schedule slip may portend something serious slowly happening.

Highly experienced project managers have learned that it can be very helpful to get someone objective to occasionally look at the project and give them guidance. This is what project auditors are trained to do. They cannot tell you if you have the right technical solution or the best design, but they can give you feedback on how well the project is being managed and where you might want to make changes.

Project managers in some industries, such as the financial industry or in government projects, are well familiar with auditors and can expect to be audited randomly or regularly if the project is seriously behind or over budget. Scared of auditors? Then, call them project reviewers and see how they can help you.

Because an EPMS is a complex socio-technical system, we can expect that we probably got most of it right if we followed the processes in this book but that we'll need to make changes later on. As people use it, they will come up with ideas for improving it and making it more useful to them. You should plan on doing a user survey in three months or in six months to get feedback on whether it met their expectations or not, and how to improve it now that they have used it for a while. Even while you're developing this first project, you should consider the possibilities of a follow-on project in a few months to make adjustments to the initial delivery.

3.7 Risk

Law of Project Management
A little risk management saves a lot of fan cleaning.

We talked about risk analysis in the previous chapter as it applies to identifying projects to review within the EPMS; now let's discuss risk more specifically about the risks involved in developing and implementing the EPMS itself.

Every project has risk associated with it, and this one has more risk than your normal IT project. As we discussed in Chapter 1, when you make changes to how people work, there will be resistance. And, resistance creates risk—lack of cooperation, risk of schedule delays, risk of continuous change requests, refusal to use the system that's delivered, and so on. Unless you have identified these risks in advance and are prepared to deal with them, the project will suffer. If you want to make the project successful, you will spend time identifying those things that can keep that from happening.

Let's look back at the Risk Breakdown Structure we developed in Step 2.4 and make it more specific to this effort. This divided risks into four generic categories:

- Technical
- External
- Organizational
- Project-related

Shown as a mind map, the typical risks (you may well have others!) we would concentrate on are:

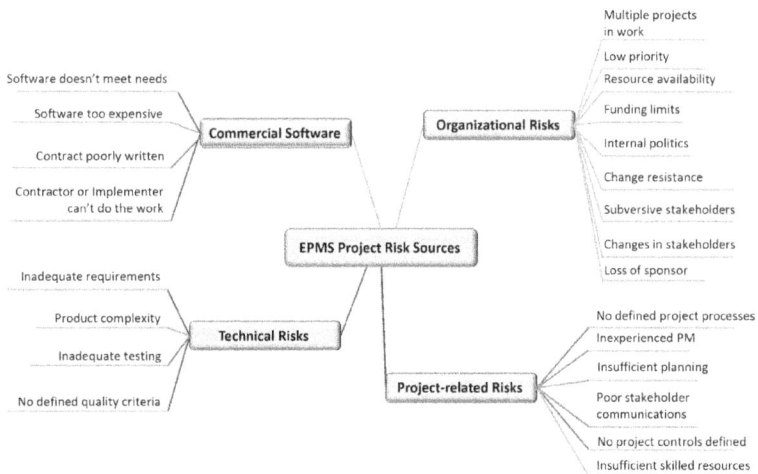

Figure 3.7-1 Mind map of risks

Think also about the risk question templates we discussed earlier. This approach is a reasonable one to take for our EPMS project also.

Let's look at very common risks in developing a major infrastructure project such as an EPMS.

3.7.1 Organizational Risks

Multiple Projects

Common situation: We live in an environment where there is not just one project being done, but multiple ones. After all, isn't that why we're developing a portfolio management system?

Risk impact: This multiproject environment creates risks for us. We're competing with all the other projects for resources, for management time, for priority, and for budget. A common risk in this environment is created by multiple projects using the same resources. If one project runs late and ties up resources that I need, that creates schedule problems for me.

Mitigation approach: Ensure you are aware of other ongoing projects that are using your planned resources and any schedule issues they may be having. It's best to have a bi-weekly or monthly status review of all projects in work.

Low Priority

Common situation: The most common situation is when our project conflicts with other projects or with ongoing operational work.

Risk impact: W will be out-prioritized, and the EPMS work will slow down.

Mitigation approach: Hopefully, this will never come up. Your EPMS project should be the #1 priority from the start; otherwise, you shouldn't be doing it. If your priority changes, there needs to be a serious discussion with the steering committee to see if their priorities are changing.

Resource Availability

Common situation: This is tied to not having enough of the right skilled resources that is mentioned in project-related risks. This is a result of not having the resources available when you need them.

Risk impact: The resources you need for the project will not be available when needed. This could be a lead developer, a critical business analyst, or even a manager who doesn't have the time to communicate what she needs from the EPMS. A significant impact on schedule is usually the result.

Mitigation approach: The project manager should never assume that the resources will be available when needed. This is something you need to monitor constantly to ensure there won't be any problems as you get closer to needing specific resources.

Hint: If a manager is too often not available to meet with your team, this may be an indication that they are not fully supportive of the EPMS project and will cause further problems in the future. Always be on the lookout for this behavior.

Funding Limitations

Common situation: You have been given approval for the project, but with the caveat that you reduce the budget by 10 percent because "we can't afford to do it for this cost."

This is often just a manager trying to show how decisive a manager he or she is. They have probably not done any analysis to lead them to this conclusion, it is just their normal reaction to any budget given them.

Risk impact: You will be forced to do the project with less-than-required funding. But, a reduction in cost will reduce the scope of work. (There is a famous Dilbert cartoon where Dilbert's pointed-haired boss tells him to reduce the budget by 10 percent. When Dilbert objects, the boss says that anything can be cut by 10 percent without an impact. To which Dilbert responds and says *"Cool. I'm cutting back to 36 hours a week."*)

Mitigation approach: As in other risks, you cannot prevent a manager from telling you to cut back by a percentage, but you can prepare an impact analysis showing what cannot be done if the budget is reduced and present it at the next status meeting to the steering committee.

Politics

Common situation: This is probably the most common risk among organizations large enough to develop an enterprisewide portfolio management system. At the upper levels of most large organizations, there is always political maneuvering taking place.

Risk impact: This can be a major risk because any change in the organization can have a significant impact on the project, to the point where it is canceled outright if a new manager is one who doesn't support the EPMS.

Mitigation approach: There is unfortunately very little you can do to mitigate this risk. The best approach is to keep good communications with upper managers so that you hear about things changing as early as possible. This is one of those risks that project managers worry the most about—the risks they don't see coming and have no control over.

Change Resistance

Common situation: The people who will use the system don't want to change how they're working right now.

Risk impact: The organization will spend a lot of money and effort and will abandon the final result without using it. Think this can't happen to your project? In fact, it is very common with complex projects such as ERP implementations. Many organizations have spent millions of dollars on implementing ERP or CRM (client relationship management) systems and then abandoned them after employees wouldn't use them.

Mitigation approach: We discussed this extensively in the section on OCM. You have to approach this very carefully and thoroughly. You won't eliminate all resistance, but by communicating effectively, you can minimize the resistance and the impacts.

Subversive Stakeholders

Common situation: Stakeholders who, in their opinion, will be negatively affected by the success of an EPMS implementation will resist the implementation, either overtly or covertly.

Risk impact: Delay or cancelation of the project.

Mitigation approach: This comes down to keeping close communications with your stakeholders—all of them. And not just the direct stakeholders, also the people who may influence them. If you have good relationships with your primary stakeholders and open communications, they can tell you if they are hearing anything that might slow the project down.

Change of Stakeholders

Common situation: People get promoted or moved around the organization.

Risk impact: If you lose a strongly supportive stakeholder, he or she might get replaced with someone who is not as supportive.

Mitigation approach: Pay attention to changes in the organization. When there is a change, identify what the impact might be on your project.

3.7.2 Project-Related Risks

Poor Project Processes

Common situation: You are working in an organization that doesn't have well-developed, standardized project management approaches. Each project manager does things their own way, and there's no consistency in how projects are managed or project status is reported.

Risk impact: Research done by Serge Schiltz[12] among others shows clearly that organizations that have immature project management processes are significantly more likely to over-run project cost and schedule estimates than more mature organizations.

Mitigation approach: By yourself, you're probably not going to change the corporate culture and implement strong, standardized project management processes across the organization. The best mitigation approach is to very clearly define the processes you're going to use on the EPMS project and ensure that everyone involved is trained in the processes and understands them.

Inexperienced Project Manager

Common situation: This is a hard risk to admit to that we don't have the skills to do this project.

Risk impact: That the EPMS project will be poorly planned and managed, leading to not just delays and cost overruns but the loss of credibility. A failure here will make it much harder to start up the project again.

Mitigation approach: If you are a normal project manager, you're probably very good at managing the normal IT or business process project (which is why you were asked to do this). But, ask yourself if you have all the requisite political and OCM skills needed to navigate the project past the resisters and doubters.

244 SUCCESSFULLY ACHIEVING STRATEGY

Research by the corporate executive board[13] shows that 41 percent of the top performing project managers have both IT and business experience versus 24 percent of the bottom performers who have both sets of experiences. Being able to understand both sides is really important to success as is the ability to communicate effectively to both the techies and the suits. You need both of these groups to understand and to fully buy-into the project.

Inadequate Planning

Common situation: Not having a well-developed project plan, either through lack of experience or being under severe time pressure to *"show progress, don't just spend time planning."*

Risk impact: Poor planning leading to late deliveries, cost over-runs, and loss of confidence in the project and in the project manager.

Mitigation approach: This is one area where you have the ability to significantly mitigate the risk. Plan out the planning process itself. Identify the steps, determine what resources you have to plan the project, and the relationships and durations of the activities. Too many projects have taken longer than planned because the planning process itself was not well defined. As military pilots like to say: *"Plan to fly, then fly the plan."*

Poor Stakeholder Communications

Common situation: People keep calling you or e-mailing you for status updates. Management says they're not sure what's going on with the project. Subversive stakeholders are able to criticize the project when there's no evidence to counteract the criticisms.

Risk impact: There is a significant risk of losing control of the project, losing its priority, and having the project put on hold until management is more comfortable with it.

Mitigation approach: There is a reason that PMI says that 50 percent of a project manager's time is spent in communications—there are a lot of problems that are created when you do not communicate effectively. You are in full control (or you should be) of project communications. A clear, thorough, and distributed communications management plan is critical.

According to Dr. Lynda Bourne,[14] *"Depending on the type of project, between 50% and 90% of the risks in the risk register are associated with stakeholders."* And, for projects with heavy software involvement such as an EPMS, the number is closer to 90 percent.

The more effectively you communicate, the fewer the risks you will have to deal with. Build a project website on the organization's intranet. Keep it fully updated with status, accomplishments, and risks and continually point people to it for project information.

Insufficient Skilled Resources

Common situation: Not having the right skilled resources to develop and to implement the EPMS. This is related to the availability of the resources you do have.

Risk impact: That the work will not get done in accordance with the plan. The project will be late and potentially canceled if management does not see progress.

Mitigation approach: The project plan needs to be fully integrated among schedule, scope, and cost. The only way to fully integrated all of these areas is by developing the details of the resources needed to perform the work. During the schedule development effort, identify every resource you need by skill set so you can easily recognize whether you have the requisite skills in-house or need to go outside the organization to get them.

The Association for the Advancement of Cost Engineering International (AACEI)[†] strongly recommends not developing a schedule without having the resources fully identified and loaded. Research done by the company Independent Project Analysis[15] shows a significant improvement in project performance when cost, schedule, and scope are fully integrated.

No Control Mechanisms

Common situation: This is the area of project governance. Who is ensuring that any project in the organization, including yours, is being well managed and in accordance with either approved PM standards or recognized best practices?

[†] AACE International 32R-04

Risk impact: While lack of control mechanisms won't cause you any specific problems, they will prevent early identification of problems that you might be running into.

Story

In the construction industry the poster child for lack of oversight is the Sydney Opera House in Sydney, Australia. Originally planned at a five year construction schedule and for a cost of $7,000,000 Australian dollars (in 1957 dollars) it was finally completed over 10 years late and for a cost of $102,000,000 Australian dollars, a 1400% cost overrun. While there were a number of problems that lead to this, lack of governance by the New South Wales government is often mentioned as a contributing factor.

A more modern horror story is the Scottish Parliament building at Holyrood. Originally estimated at 25-35 million pounds, it ended up at 450 million pounds. The overrun was largely blamed on poor oversight and governance.

Mitigation approach: If there are no established control mechanisms in place in your organization, you should have a discussion with the steering committee on performing that role. This has two advantages: it provides some objective oversight for your project and it makes them feel more involved (making management feel more involved is always beneficial to a project manager).

3.7.3 Technical Risks

Inadequate Requirements

Common situation: This is one of the major killers of projects—not thoroughly understanding the full set of detailed requirements. Either through not appreciating that your success largely depends on understanding what management wants, not having the resources who understand how to do this, or being under serious schedule pressure to get it done quickly.

Risk impact: This can be potentially a major risk for the project, depending on just how many of the requirements are missing or poorly phrased.

Most of your really important requirements are business requirements, not purely technical ones. In the worst case, the project will be in such poor shape, it will be canceled.

Mitigation approach: Plan heavy commitment from your business analysts early in the project. Defining the business requirements is a core part of their work on the project.

Don't shortcut this part of the project. Spend the time to identify the stakeholders who need to be involved, get their input, and thoroughly analyze the requirements (look for contradictions between stakeholders, missing requirements, and so on). For something as complex as an EPMS, you should easily plan to spend several weeks on the requirements depending on the resources available and the availability of the stakeholders.

Dirty Data

Common situation: What do I mean by dirty data? For any data-driven effort, such as an EPMS, to be successful, the set of data to be entered into the system must be complete (you need all the data), the data must be accurate, and the data must be current. If there are inaccuracies in the data (missing data, duplicated data, data errors), the data is considered dirty and should not be used. As database analysts (DBAs) like to say: *GIGO* (garbage in, garbage out). If one of your selection filters has been programmed with bad data, the impact on project selections can be severe.

Risk impact: While dirty data will not impact the implementation of the EPMS, it could have a significant impact on the output. Bad data will lead to bad recommendations on which projects to select.

Mitigation approach: The majority of the organization's existing data is often scattered in multiple databases around the organization as well as in individual spreadsheets. There is rarely any quality process for ensuring the data is complete and accurate. Part of the implementation effort will be to identify where all the data exists, clean it up, and transfer it to the new EPMS.

Inadequate Testing

Common situation: When you look at the typical software development schedule, testing and integration are the latest activities on the schedule. This makes perfect sense. But, it means that when the development runs late, the common thing to cut to save schedule over-run is testing. Why? Because testing is almost always on the critical path and cutting testing looks like it might save time.

Risk impact: Cutting testing can be extremely dangerous because you may implement software that has significant bugs in it, resulting in significant cost and schedule impacts due to rework.

Mitigation approach: The only approach to mitigating this is to keep on top of the schedule progress so that if you start falling behind you can recover more easily by crashing the schedule. Never cut testing/integration work.

No Defined Quality Criteria

Common situation: In the press of planning the project and getting the work started, the quality requirements are never developed or not developing in enough detail to be useful.

Risk impact: The implemented system will be not meet expectations and will not be used as designed.

Mitigation approach: Usually, the quality expectations are gradually understood as you go through the requirements gathering process and analyze the nonfunctional requirements. Some of the quality criteria can be quantified, such as query response time and system uptime. But, some of the criteria, such as usability and user-friendliness, are difficult to quantify ahead of time.

The best approach to mitigate the nonquantifiable criteria is to regularly show the steering committee and a user group what they're getting and to get their feedback as to whether it meets their expectations or not. Communications again! Are you noticing how many areas of the project are improved with good communications?

3.7.4 Risks in Commercial Software

Software does not Meet Needs

Common situation: You bought portfolio management software that does not meet your needs. This occurs when the software's capabilities are mis-represented by the vendor's sales people or when there was pressure to purchase a particular package.

Risk impact: The software will not perform as expected, and the money and resources will have been wasted.

Mitigation approach: Carefully identify your specific requirements and select software that meets most of your needs (you probably won't find software that meets 100 percent of your unique needs) and works in your technology environment.

Don't trust what the vendors' sales staff are telling you. Filter the possible software packages down to just a few, then check their user groups to see what people are saying about the software. When you call the vendors in for a best and final presentation, make sure they bring a technical rep who is familiar with the software and prepare a set of detailed questions to ask during the presentation. Finally, video-tape the presentation so that you have a record of what was said (there are two well-known software companies whose salespeople will walk out of a presentation if they know they will be video-taped. Ask around for who they are).

Software too Expensive

Common situation: You've found commercial software you want, but the purchasing and licensing costs are well above your budget.

Risk impact: Running over budget.

Mitigation approach: Instead of purchasing the package outright, investigate working with the vendor to use the software on the vendor's site as a software-as-a-service (SaaS) option or as a cloud-based service.

Contract Poorly Written

Common situation: The contracting person wrote a bad contract.

Risk impact: You find that major parts of the work needed was not included and will cost considerably more.

Mitigation approach: Get involved with the contracting process and ensure that everything needed to purchase, configure, and implement the package was included.

Contractor/implementer cannot do the work

Common situation: The contractor/implementer/consultant who was hired sends in a crew of highly inexperienced staff that are being trained on your project.

Risk impact: The work doesn't get done on time, within budget, or to poor quality. (This is a surprisingly common problem even with the large, international consulting firms. In their negotiations, they promise you their best available staff, and send you their new hires.)

Mitigation approach: Don't be afraid to push back and refuse to accept the staff they give you. Your contract should include a clause that gives you approval power over any resumes they offer and veto power over any staff they send.

3.8 Organizing the Project

How you organize the various stakeholders in the project can make the project easy to manage, or extremely difficult. As the project manager, you need to create an organization that supports decision making both for you, for the project sponsor, and for the people who report to you. There are multiple books on organizational theory, but supporting the decision process is really what effective organization is about.

There are two primary parts to creating an effective project organization: the organization chart, which shows reporting relationships, and well-defined roles and responsibilities. The Responsibility Assignment Matrix (RAM) in its various formats and associated role descriptions for each team member are developed during the early planning portion of the project.

3.8.1 *Stakeholders During Planning, Design, and Implementation*

The project manager should look at the existing resources available within their organization to see what can be utilized on the project. If your organization has a quality assurance department, they should be brought into the project to develop the definitions of quality for the EPMS and monitor it during development. Groups involved in security, privacy, and regulatory compliance should also be involved in the effort as required.

The stakeholders most heavily involved during the planning/design/implementation effort are:

- Project manager
- Project sponsor
- Steering/governance committee
- PMO manager (if you have a PMO)
- Chief financial officer
- CIO, technical leads, test leads
- Business analyst
- Portfolio manager
- Business unit managers
- OCM lead
- Procurement (if a commercial tool will be purchased)

Other stakeholders will be involved in the requirements and design effort, such as quality assurance support, but as inputs to the development rather than as leaders.

Project Sponsor

The project sponsor is the highest level executive who has direct responsibility for the success or failure of the EPMS. This person is the project's champion at the executive level. He or she ensures the project gets the priority it needs and appropriate funding and resources. When there is political disagreement at top management levels about the EPMS, the project sponsor leads the resolution efforts. She may also chair the Change Control Board (CCB) for the EPMS project.

Project Manager

The project manager (PM) is the day-to-day lead for the project. The PM heads up the planning effort, ensures the requirements are fully defined, monitors the OCM efforts as well as the design work to ensure schedules and budgets are met. The PM has the core responsibility to make the project successful, regardless of the obstacles that will arise during the effort. The PM sits on the CCB for the project and ensures that quality requirements are satisfied as well as keeping the project on schedule and within budget. Publications by PMI as well as any major textbook in project management can provide much more detail on the roles and responsibilities of the PM.

Steering/Governance Committee

This is the high-level committee that will provide the ultimate approval and guidance for the EPMS project. The project sponsor is a member of this committee as are senior managers of the business units involved in the portfolio selection process. A significant part of the project manager's time will be spent working with this committee and keeping them updated on the status.

Portfolio Manager

This is the person who will manage the EPMS after it is implemented in the organization. They work closely with the BA to ensure it meets the business needs and in developing the operational processes. They work closely with the technical leads to ensure they understand the underlying architecture and design of the EPMS. They also work closely with both the project sponsor and the PM during the development effort. If the organization has a PMO, most likely, the portfolio manager reports to the PMO.

The portfolio manager may be supported by a portfolio administrator who ensures that during the operational phase of the system that regular status reports are performed, risks are monitored, and other administrative tasks are completed to ensure the system is operating as expected. More about the portfolio manager at the end of this section.

PMO Manager

If there is a PMO within your organization, it is most common for the portfolio management process and tools to be managed within the PMO. The PMO manager and staff should be heavily involved in the development of the EPMS so that it fits most effectively within their organization.

Chief Financial Officer

The CFO or his/her lead staff will get involved in determining the financial filtering criteria to select projects.

CIO and Technical Leads

The CIO is always involved in any project which requires IT resources. They will delegate most of the technical decision making to the technical leads but may be heavily involved in setting priorities and in scheduling of resources and IT activities.

The technical leads (architecture, software, database, and hardware if needed) will be the main decision makers for technical design/development decisions needed to satisfy the requirements. They will be heavily involved in the schedule development and are participants in the CCB as required.

Business Analyst

The business analyst (BA) should be the lead person on developing the business requirements. All of the more detailed technical and operational requirements are derived from the business requirements, so this is a key area for the project. The BA might work together with a process analyst to help develop the operational processes for the EPMS. The BA attends the CCB to identify any impacts to the business requirements or processes resulting from change requests.

Business Unit Managers

These are the heads, or their representatives, of the different business units whose projects will be part of the overall portfolio. They will have an input to the project selection criteria and the EPMS output reports. Their primary interest will be to ensure that projects that are important to them are properly selected. These criteria will need to be balanced out so that the selection process emphasizes projects that provide the greatest benefit to the overall organization, not to individual business units.

OCM Lead

Because the EPMS will create a major change in the organization, the OCM effort will be a significant amount of work to understand the organization's readiness for the change and to prepare the organization for the new EPMS system. The lead on this effort works closely with the project manager to ensure the organization will be ready once the system is in operations.

Procurement

If the EPMS approach is to procure a commercial product instead of developing one internally, the procurement lead works with the PM, with the BA, and with the technical leads to identify the specific requirements the tool must satisfy and to ensure it is compatible with the existing IT infrastructure.

3.8.2 Responsibility Assignment Matrix

No project should begin without a clear understanding of roles and responsibilities by each participant. This is usually communicated using some form of a RAM along with an organization chart showing the reporting relationships.

One common form of RAM is called a RACI matrix, where each deliverable is listed with who participates in that deliverable and their level of involvement. RACI stands for Responsible, Accountable, Consulted, and Informed.

A more detailed RAM is a "SPIRAL" format, where each deliverable is allocated to the major participants in the project according to whether they:

S—Have sign-off authority
P—Participate in developing the deliverable
I—Provide an input to the deliverable
R—Review the final deliverable for acceptability

A—Are accountable to making sure the work gets done

L—Leads the effort for that deliverable.

Appendix 3.8 has one example of how the responsibility allocations might look. Depending on your organization's approach, your RAM might be different.

In an effort as significant as implementing an EPMS there are going to be multiple stakeholders, many of them at a decision making level. The primary stakeholders during the development effort should have their roles and responsibilities clearly defined and communicated so they understand exactly how they and everyone else fits into the effort. Initial R&Rs should be communicated during the project kickoff meeting, with more detailed R&Rs defined during the planning effort. During the actual operations of the EPMS, the stakeholders will be different, as we'll see later.

Critical stakeholders are going to be the executive level. We're developing an EPMS to select projects that will be most beneficial to the organization based on criteria they select. When done properly, the timeline for selecting strategically important projects will go from a month-long process to a relatively short one because much of the criteria have been automated.

3.8.3 Organization Chart

How should you organize the reporting relationships? The academic answer is to determine the work that needs to be done and the best way to accomplish it.

For business process/IT type projects, the general org chart should look similar to the following, depending on your organization's normal project approaches:

As the saying goes, your mileage may vary. It depends on how your organization normally does projects. There is an assumption here: the EPMS system will reside in the PMO, and the portfolio lead will be different than the implementation project manager.

Portfolio Manager Redux

Once the EPMS is in place, the most important person in effective operations is the portfolio manager. This is the person who makes the whole system of processes and software run smoothly to provide the inputs

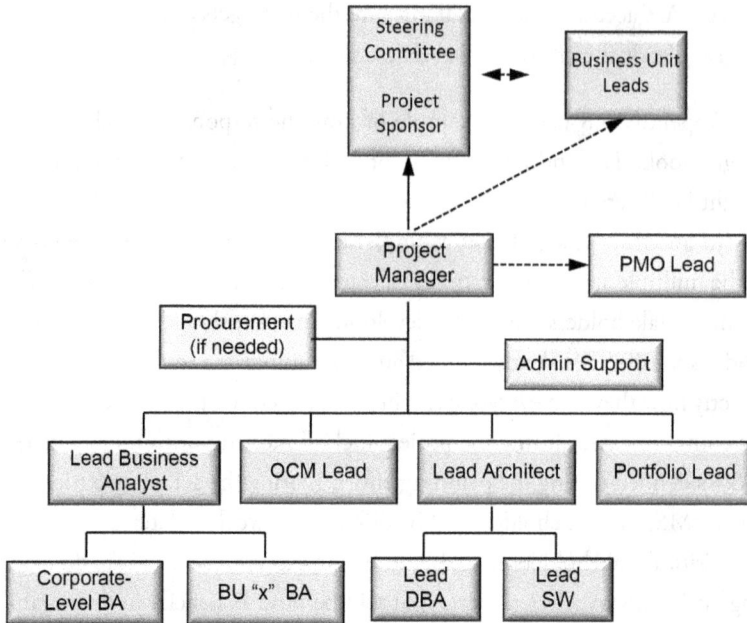

Figure 3.8-1 Typical organization chart for IT projects

upper management needs to make decisions on which projects to put their money into.

The specific roles and responsibilities of the portfolio manager will vary with each organization, from a lowly reporting status to having a significant input to the decision process. In a paper[16] published in 2012, academic researchers Aileen Koh and Lynn Crawford from the Bond University in Australia report on the roles of the portfolio manager in a small number of Australian entities.

In one energy distribution company, the portfolio manager reports to a portfolio review board (PRB), which is chaired by the CEO and includes the CFO, CIO, and other senior executives. In the preproject stage, this person is responsible for identifying, categorizing, prioritizing, and evaluating the benefits (using NPV and ROI) of all project business cases for the PRB to select and approve. The quarterly performance of the portfolio is reported to the PRB. After the EPMS was implemented, the IT department alone was able to save 30 percent of their IT project investment budget.

By contrast, in another organization, a financial and insurance company, they report that the head of the portfolio management practice is managed by the head of the strategic IT department. The enterprise PMO is a small organization of only a few people and provides more project management services than true portfolio management processes. So, the roles and responsibilities can vary considerably depending on the needs of the organization.

3.9 Implementing the EPMS

Most articles on implementing portfolio management systems are focused on off-the-shelf software. They describe how to prepare the organization through OCM and make certain that everyone involved is fully aligned with the new system.

Good news! By this point in the book, you have already done the majority of that work—defining management expectations, designing the software and the processes, preparing both management and employees for the EPMS. The only thing left at this point is to "go live."

At this point, you should have almost everything you need to implement the new portfolio management system checked off, as shown in Table 3.9-1:

So, what's missing? The detailed strategy for "Go Live" and approval to do so.

Table 3.9-1 Check-off list for project start

1	A high-level project sponsor and a steering committee	√
2	Detailed requirements and expectations from major stakeholders	√
3	An OCM approach to prepare everyone	√
4	A good understanding of the processes to implement	√
5	A good design	√
6	Detailed project filtering criteria	√
7	Selected tools (if you're buying tools)	√
8	A detailed schedule	√
9	An approved budget	√
10	Defined quality criteria	√
11	A good understanding of the specific risks and a risk management process	√
12	Committed resources, organization chart, and a RAM	√
13	A detailed implementation approach and plan	
14	Approval to go ahead and implement	

3.9.1 It's All About the Data

If your team developed the new EPM system, they identified the most efficient database architecture for all the data required. If you purchased an off-the-shelf system, the database is already part of the package, and it may, or may not, fulfill your organizations infrastructure.

As we discussed in the section on risk, the data in your organization is probably spread around in multiple databases, MS Access files, and Excel spreadsheets in multiple different formats and quality. Getting all of this data into the new database is often a major source of problems implementing a new system. All of the project data needed for the EPMS:

- Must be identified, no matter where it is in the organization
- The source of the data defined so that it can be fed into the EPMS
- The quality of the data determined
- The data extracted from existing formats, cleaned up, reformatted, and fed into the EPMS database

The success of the project selection process depends on whether the system has all of the data it needs and the quality of the data. So, this step is critical in the implementation.

Story (Church op cit)[5]

CareFirst is a health care provider on the East Coast of the United States. They have over 3 million members spread through several states and 5,200 employees. When they first developed their EPMS they looked at where the data existed and found the needed data in multiple locations and in multiple formats:

When the processes that provided the data were determined, they found the following process interfaces:

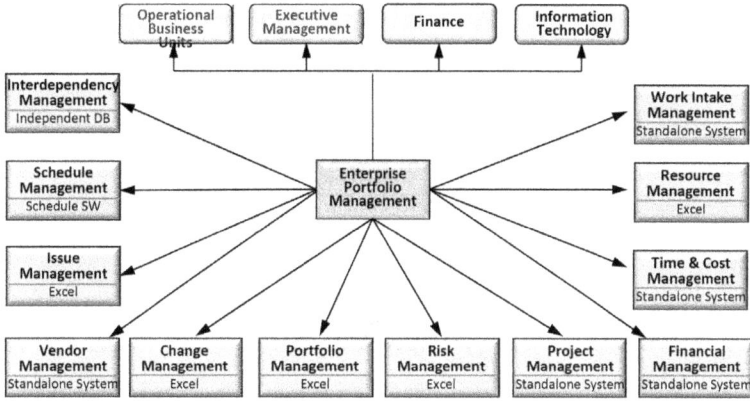

Figure 3.9-1 CareFirst existing data locations

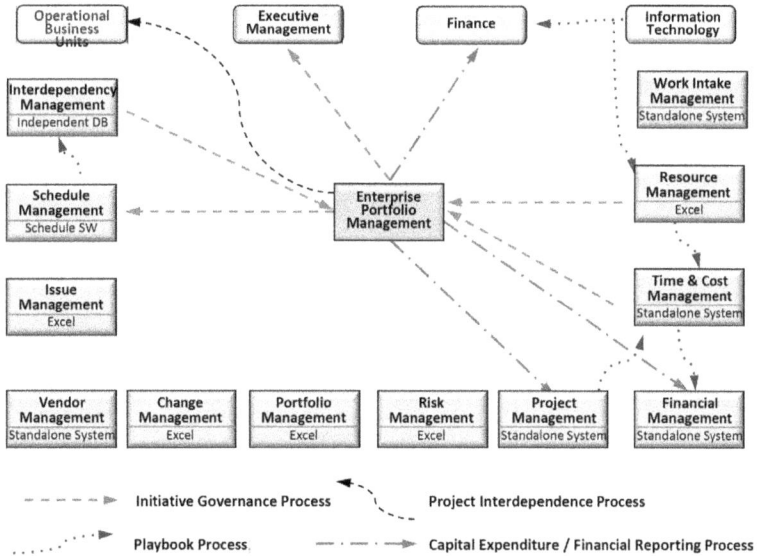

Figure 3.9-2 CareFirst existing process interfaces

Combining the data with the processes results in the following complex set of interfaces:

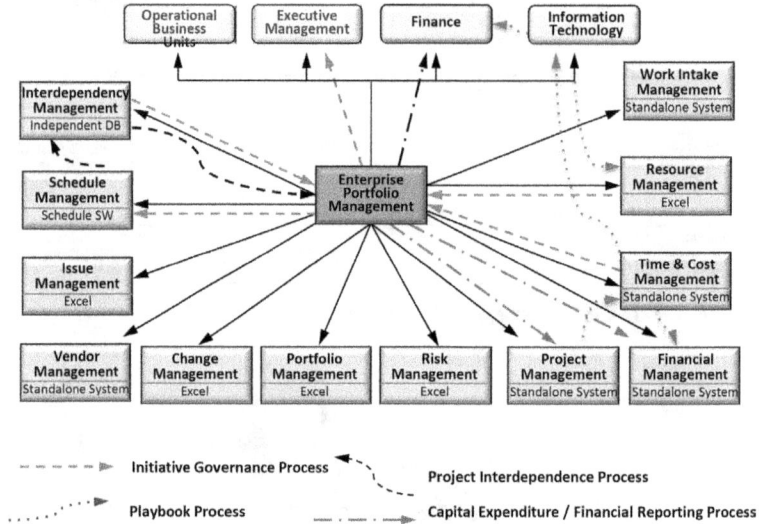

Figure 3.9-3 Complexity of CareFirst data/process interactions

One of their primary goals was to simplify the entire process. After completing the new EPM design the data flow looks like this:

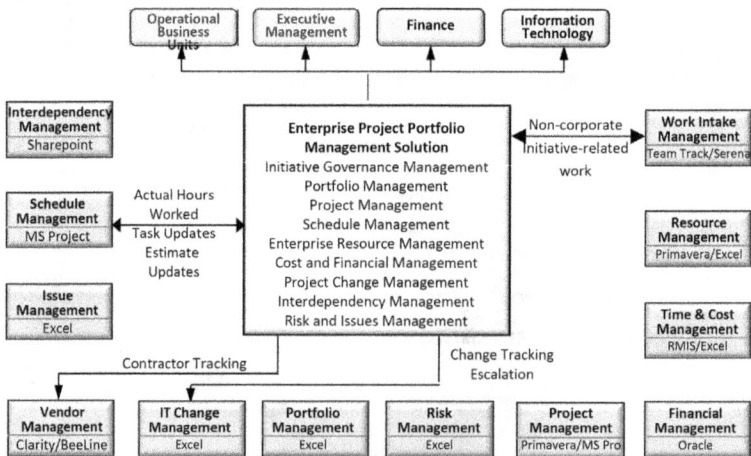

Figure 3.9-4 CareFirst redesigned data flow

*Much simpler and much more efficient. The total cost for their Enter-
prise PMO was $3.2 million and was done in three phases. The new
system reduced the time and cost of meeting requirements for new
projects by 20%, resulting in a $29,000,000 savings.*

In order to gain valuable analysis from all of the data in the EMPS,
it is essential that the data structure, the taxonomy, is well defined. This
structure is the framework for the data that ensures the data is comparable
across different projects and different types of projects.

Métier,[17] which develops enterprise-level portfolio management and
optimization software packages, published a white paper titled *Implementing Project Portfolio Management*, which says: *When well defined this way
the data can be used in multiple types of analysis, reducing the time required
to produce metrics and results. For example, you might want to classify your
projects by organizational departments. Without a standard taxonomy, you
would only be able to analyze projects that are classified within an individual
department, or compare the set of projects between departments.*

Frequently, within organizations, there are similar types of projects
being conducted in different departments. For example, you may have a
"customer satisfaction" project type that occurs in several departments.
Using a multidimensional taxonomy, you could analyze the performance
and impact of "customer satisfaction" projects across the organization,
examine which department performs best on these types of projects,
identify duplicative work, or define processes from one department that
could be standardized for all "customer satisfaction" efforts. In order
to develop the optimal structure for your data, you should take into
consideration:

- Organizational structure
- Organizational mission and goals
- Enterprise architecture, or existing support systems
- Services provided, clients served, types of clients and services
- Reporting requirements (create categories that ease report
  generation)

3.9.2 Approaches to "Go Live"

There are three possible approaches to putting the system into production and use.

3.9.2.1 Implement All at Once

This approach, sometimes called the "Big Bang" approach, implements the process, the software, and the filters all at the same time. This approach is strongly discouraged. It has a huge failure rate and can cause the entire effort to be discarded. In 2007, the Los Angeles Unified School District (LAUSD), one of the largest school districts in the United States with over 90,000 employees, hired Deloitte and Touche to completely replace their computer system. They used the big bang approach by deleting the old system before they installed the new system only to find out the new system didn't work. The problems and lawsuits were massive and dragged on for years.

3.9.2.2 Implement as a Pilot Project

In this approach, the steering committee selects a subset of the organization, such as a divisional IT department, and implements the EMPS only in that organization. If the system also ranks these projects highly, then you can be sure the filters are working. If the system does not rank these projects high, then the filters should be adjusted. From a scheduling standpoint, piloting in one part of the organization should be done for 3 to 6 months to ensure enough data is captured.

Alternatively, the pilot could consist of a few high priority projects and a few low priority projects. If the EPMS identifies and ranks those projects properly, then the filters are working as expected. This approach should only take a few weeks.

These two pilot approaches will tell you whether the filters reasonably reflect what the organization wants to prioritize or whether the filters need to be adjusted.

3.9.2.3 Implement on New Projects Only

Here we ignore the existing projects completely and only input new project requests to the EPMS. As the steering committee meets, they can review the list of proposed projects and agree with the list (in which case the filters are fine) or make changes to the list (in which case, the filters need to be adjusted). This approach may follow the pilot approach mentioned previously. This is a good approach if there is an already-existing queue of projects waiting to be started.

The downside to this is that as long as existing projects have not completed, the portfolio will not reflect the full set of projects in work. Only when all existing projects are done, will all projects be in the portfolio. However, this is a temporary situation and allows people time to adjust to the project requesting process.

3.9.3 Implementation Steps

1. Obtain approval to go live.
2. Ensure any training has been successfully completed. (We did not discuss training here because it is so unique to your organization that only very generic comments could be made.)
3. Move software and database from development system into production.
4. Provide log-ons and passwords to everyone who has access.
   a. Ensure each individual's log-on has the proper access for their level of security and privacy.
5. Identify which part of the organization that the pilot will be done in.
6. Identify projects that are being proposed (you might have already done this) and input them into the system.
7. Present the results to management and incorporate any changes requested.
8. Ramp up capacity by either of the following:
   a. Add existing projects to the system, or
   b. Incorporate projects from another part of the organization outside the pilot group

3.9.4 Improving the EPMS

The incremental approach to fully integrating an EPMS is the best approach, as was already mentioned. Start with a pilot project and build on that. Use the results of the pilot project to advertise the success of

Nonexistent	Informal	Developing	Managed	Optimized
Level is defined by nothingness-no evidence of portfolio management activity, no governance, no processes and no effort to identify strategic priorities	Level is defined by beginnings – new governance, new requirements, new processes and structures, and leadership begins strategic planning	Level is defined by uncertainty – governance is tested and challenged, processes are developing, documentation is developed, leadership identifies strategic priorities	Level is defined by certainty – governance is established, processes are managed and dcoumentation is in place, investments are aligned with strategic priorities, performance baseline is established	Level is defined by successes – governance is effective, processes are refined, documents are complete and accessible, program achieves strategic objectives, performance measures provide insight for decisions

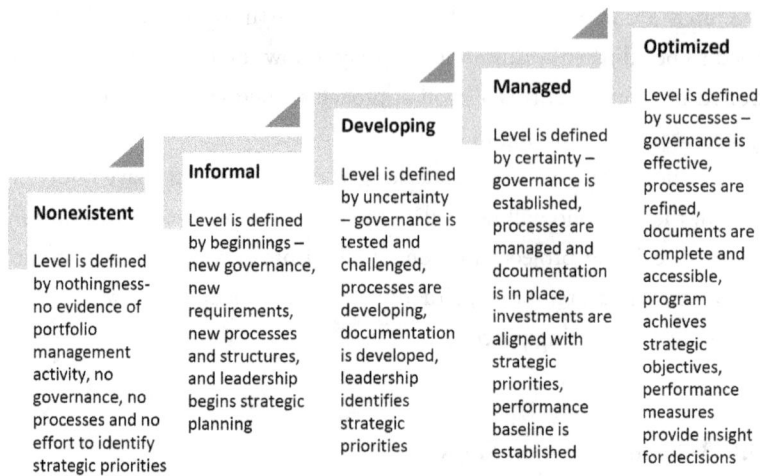

Figure 3.9-5 Growth in maturity levels of an EPMS

the EPMS in identifying and prioritizing the most strategically beneficial projects. This incremental approach is the most effective way to implement the EPMS. Recall in Section 1.4, we discussed the Mayo Clinic's incremental approach.

Many organizations that implement a portfolio management system start off with no recognized or standardized approach to identifying beneficial projects. As the following graphic shows,[18] organizations evolve from a nonexistent system to a fully mature one. By the time you have developed and implemented the EPMS as designed, your organization will be at the "Managed" level with a high degree of maturity. Then it is a matter of additional effort to optimize the new processes.

Step 3 Summary

In Step 1, we prepared the organization for the coming EPMS that would significantly change how projects were selected. In Step 2, we discussed in detail how to design the EPMS to make it as effective as possible, selecting the optimal projects for the organization without any managerial bias. In Step 3, we laid out the details of the project that would be necessary to implement the EPMS.

Project success is frequently determined by how well the project is initialized by the project manager and the project team. Getting the right people involved in developing the project charter and attending the kick-off meeting gets everyone pointed in the right direction, so no one can come along later and state that they weren't involved early.

Projects live or die depending on how thoroughly the requirements are captured and used to define the scope of work required. Stakeholders are critical in this process, and we discussed how to identify the different types of stakeholders and get them involved. We expended on the work in Step 2 with additional details for the design of the filters.

We then moved into the details of developing the schedule and budget. Both of these begin by identifying the primary parts of the final product and of the project process itself to identify "what" needs to be done. This is the WBS. From the WBS, we can identify the details of the work, the "how" to do it in order to create accurate schedules and budgets. We provided detailed examples of these schedules and budgets that can be used as templates for your own implementations. The more detailed and accurate the schedule, the less likely you are to run into significant problems during the project. For some organizations, internal projects are not subject to detailed budget management. Once senior management has decided to authorize a project, they will continue with the project even if it experiences large cost over-runs. (The project manager may get yelled at, but the project is likely to continue because management is reluctant to waste the time and money already spent.)

We spent a significant amount of time on the project's risks. Each organization has their own unique risks, but these risks can be categorized into general buckets such as technical risks, personnel risks, poor project processes, and so on.

We moved into organizing the project to increase success—who needs to be involved, who reports to who, who has decision authority, and so on.

We closed Step 3 with a short section on implementing the final EPMS. The process of doing this is so unique to each organization that we could only provide a high-level overview of how to do the actual implementation.

Appendices

Appendix 1.7

Appendix 1.7 Stakeholder Support Planning Template

Stakeholder name	Their project role	Ability to influence project 1–5	Impact to them if project is successful -5 to +5	Their level of interest 1–5	Their expectations of the project	Specific issues they may have with the project	Their current status	Our desired support from them	Action plan and com- munications

Current status options: strong advocate, generally supportive, neutral, generally critical, subversive

Appendix 2.1

Project XXXX
Business Requirements Document

Project #_____

<Project Manager Name>
Project Manager

<Business Consultant Name>
Project Business Consultant

Document Version X.X

<Date>

Document Information

Revision History

		Business Requirements Document	
Version	Date	Author(s)	Revision Notes
		\<Project Manager\>	

Business Requirements Document Approval

The signatures below acknowledge agreement with, and support of the Business Requirements Document for <Name of Project>.

Role	Signature	Date
Project Sponsor	_____ _____ <Name> <Title>	_____
Project Manager	_____ _____ <Name>	_____
Business Analyst	_____ _____ <Name>	_____
Information Security Officer	_____ _____ <Name>	_____
Network Operations	_____ _____ <Name>	_____
Manager, Development	_____ _____ <Name>	_____
Manager, I&T	_____ _____ <Name>	_____
PMO	_____ _____ <Name>	_____
Other Business Unit Signatures (As Required)		
<BU>	_____ _____ <Name> <Title>	_____

Table of Contents

Appendices:
Completed and Signed Project Request Form
Approved Project Change Requests against BRD

<Instructions: The gray text is explanatory to assist the project manager and the business analyst in filling out the requirements document. Please remove it when you customize the document for your project.

The intention of the Requirements Document is to build on the information gathered when the Project Request Form was filled out. It will contain sufficiently detailed information that the technical team members can create a technical architecture and design that exactly satisfies what the customer was asking for.

The Business Analyst begins the process by gathering the business requirements from the customers. The Project Manager completes the process by turning the business requirements into a set of functional requirements that can be used to develop the technical solution. Those are documented in the System Requirements Document (SRD).>

1.0   Project Overview

<This section is intended to provide a high-level overview of the project and of the product being implemented.>

1.1   Project Background

<The history of how this project was requested. The reasons that led up to its being asked for. What is the purpose of this project?>

1.2   Project Objectives

<3–5 specific objectives this project will accomplish. Objectives can be taken from the project charter document.>

1.3   Project Scope

<A description of what is included in the scope of this project. Stating clearly what is in scope and what is not in scope for this project can ensure that there are no *holes* where stakeholders expected the project to produce something that the project manager was not aware of.>

1.4   Out-of-Scope Items

<Statements about what is not in scope for this project. This paragraph sets the boundary conditions for the project and manages the customer's expectations about what will be included and what will not be included. It also tells the technical personnel what will not be done as part of this project.>

1.5   Project Justification

<Any ROI or benefit/cost analysis that has been done.>

1.6   Assumptions Made

<Assumptions that were made in developing the business and functional requirements.>

1.7   Known Risks and Issues

<Any risks and issues that are known at this time.>

1.8   Impacts to Other Projects

<Impacts to, or interfaces with, other projects to the extent known at this time.>

1.9   Organizations Impacted

<This section identifies the organizations that are impacted by either this project or by the product implemented by the project.>

1.10   Technical Environment

<This section describes at a high level the technical environment that the product will be implemented in. The project manager will requires input from the technical personnel to complete this section.>

2.0   Roles and Responsibilities

<This section describes what the roles and responsibilities of the various project stakeholders are in relationship to the requirements. It should include:

- Who will gather the requirements
- Who will manage them and ensure that all requirements have test cases

- Who will be on the Change Control Board that manages and approves changes
- Who is allowed to request changes to requirements, etc.
- And so on>

3.0   Business Needs and Requirements

<The goal of virtually all efforts is to satisfy a business need. The need could be for the company to increase revenue or to save costs, or the need could be for corporate or for the information technology (IT) department itself to improve efficiency or to implement a required system upgrade. These are all requirements that the business has.

Accurately capturing these business needs is one of the most critical steps in the early stages of a project. Without a clear and thorough understand of why we are doing this project, there is a high probability that an ineffective or a wrong solution will be implemented, wasting costs and resources. There are few efforts more critical to project success than accurately capturing business needs.>

4.0   Functional Requirements

<Once the business needs are thoroughly understood, they are turned into descriptions of what the product will do and how well it will do it. This section takes the business requirements and turns them into descriptions of the product's functionality.>

5.0   Performance Requirements

<This section documents the performance requirements that the product should have.>

6.0   Business Process Requirements

<Virtually, all projects that implement products into company will create changes to either business processes or to technical processes. This section captures those process changes that have been identified at this point. A more detail process gap analysis is done later during the project.>

7.0   Security and Privacy Requirements

<Because many of the products that are implemented by projects involve processing information, information security requirements are documented here. The Project Manager should document security requirements as the process for security certification begins with requirements.>

8.0   Procurement Requirements

<If there are products or service procured from outside the organization they are documented here.>

9.0   Requirements Management Process

<Describe in general how the requirements will be tracked and managed during this project. For example, requirements will be tracked in a requirements management system, no requirements will be changed without an approved change request, and so on.>

Appendices:

A.   Completed and Signed Project Request Form

<Attach a copy of the Project Request Form to this document after the PRF has been signed and approved.>

B.   Project Change Requests

<Attach all copies of any change requests that have been approved by the Change Control Board against this BRD.>

Appendix 2.2

Project Request Form

Request #: YYYY-NNNN
Requested By:
Department:
Contact Information #:
Request Date: 2/1/2011
Required Delivery date:
Approval Date:

Mandatory

> Is this request required for regulatory compliance reasons?   Y   N
> Is this a system upgrade required for ongoing maintenance?   Y   N

Strategic Alignment

Which of the Strategic Framework areas does this request apply? (CHECK ALL THAT APPLY)

- Strategic Goal 1
- Strategic Goal 2
- Strategic Goal 3
- ...

What is the primary reason for performing this initiative?

- Revenue generation
- Cost savings
- New business opportunity/competitive advantage
- Internal process improvement
- Production expansion
- Process improvement
- Other _____

Please describe the current situation or the problem needing solution.

What are the benefits obtained by approving this project?
What is the impact of not approving this project?

Are other alternatives available?

Project cost estimates-related questions:

Initial investment	Rating				
1. What is the estimated initial investment for technology infra-structure (HW and SW)	☐ 5	☐ 4	☐ 3	☐ 2	☐ 1
2. What is the estimated technology consulting costs required for this?	☐ 5	☐ 4	☐ 3	☐ 2	☐ 1
3. What is the estimated upfront technology vendor expense?	☐ 5	☐ 4	☐ 3	☐ 2	☐ 1
4. What is the estimated training expense required to support this initiative?	☐ 5	☐ 4	☐ 3	☐ 2	☐ 1
5. Estimated upfront facilities invest-ment that will occur as a result of this initiative.	☐ 5	☐ 4	☐ 3	☐ 2	☐ 1
6. What is the estimated upfront non-IT cost of this project?	☐ 5	☐ 4	☐ 3	☐ 2	☐ 1
7. What is the estimated cost of non-IT consultants or contractors for this effort?	☐ 5	☐ 4	☐ 3	☐ 2	☐ 1
	$0 or N/A	< 1M	1–2M	3–5M	> 5M

Where the answers get scored a "5" if the cost is zero or simply not applicable. They get scored a "4" if the cost is less than $1M, a "3" if the cost is between $1M and $2M, a "2" if the cost is between $3M and $5M, and a 1 if the cost is greater than $5M. These numbers should be modified into numbers that are appropriate for your organization and for the types of projects being proposed.

Financial annual revenues, annual costs, annual cost savings, and market share

Annual revenues	Rating				
1. If applicable, please estimate the annual gross revenue that will be generated from this new product.	□ 5	□ 4	□ 3	□ 2	□ 1
2. If applicable, please estimate the annual direct product expenses that will be generated from this new product.	□ 5	□ 4	□ 3	□ 2	□ 1
3. If applicable, please estimate the annual gross revenue that will be generated from this enhancement to an existing product	□ 5	□ 4	□ 3	□ 2	□ 1
4. If applicable, please estimate the annual direct product expenses that will be generated from this enhancement to an existing product	□ 5	□ 4	□ 3	□ 2	□ 1
	> 5M	3–5M	1–2M	< 1M	$0 or N/A

Annual cost savings	Rating				
1. What is the estimated annual consultant/contractor/vendor/technology savings?	□ 5	□ 4	□ 3	□ 2	□ 1
2. What is the estimated annual operating expense savings?	□ 5	□ 4	□ 3	□ 2	□ 1
3. What is the estimated improvement in productivity?	□ 5	□ 4	□ 3	□ 2	□ 1
4. What is the estimated improvement in process efficiencies?	□ 5	□ 4	□ 3	□ 2	□ 1
5. What is the estimated annual technology cost savings?	□ 5	□ 4	□ 3	□ 2	□ 1
	> 5M	3–5M	1–2M	< 1M	$0 or N/A
6. What is the estimated headcount savings (FTE) expected annually?	□ 5	□ 4	□ 3	□ 2	□ 1
	> 20	11–19	5–10	1–4	0 or NA

Annual expense impact	Rating				
1. What is the estimated annual business vendor expense?	☐ 5	☐ 4	☐ 3	☐ 2	☐ 1
2. What is the annual estimated technology maintenance expense?	☐ 5	☐ 4	☐ 3	☐ 2	☐ 1
3. What is the estimated annual operating expense?	☐ 5	☐ 4	☐ 3	☐ 2	☐ 1
4. Estimated annual increase in either credit or residual value losses that will occur as a result of this initiative.	☐ 5	☐ 4	☐ 3	☐ 2	☐ 1
	$0 or N/A	< 1M	1–2M	3–5M	> 5M
5. What is the estimated net new headcount (FTE) required on an annual basis?	☐ 5	☐ 4	☐ 3	☐ 2	☐ 1
	0 or NA	1–4	5–10	11–19	> 20

Market share	Rating				
1. How much will this project improve our market share in our main product lines?	☐ 5	☐ 4	☐ 3	☐ 2	☐ 1
2. How much will this project improve our market share in our lower-margin product lines?	☐ 5	☐ 4	☐ 3	☐ 2	☐ 1
3. How much will this project improve our market share in our main geographic markets?	☐ 5	☐ 4	☐ 3	☐ 2	☐ 1
4. How much will this project improve our market share in our developing markets?	☐ 5	☐ 4	☐ 3	☐ 2	☐ 1
	>10%	5–9%	1–4%	< 1%	N/A

Impacts to internal processes, customer relationships, and employees

The answers here are too difficult to judge on a numerical basis, so they are high impact, moderate impact, low impact, or no impact

Internal processes	Rating				
1. To what degree does this project help us to show measurable efficiency gains?	☐5	☐4	☐3	☐2	☐1
2. To what degree will this project utilize our relationship with other divisions and business partners to serve our customers better?	☐5	☐4	☐3	☐2	☐1
3. To what extent does this project improve the process for meeting a client need?	☐5	☐4	☐3	☐2	☐1
4. To what extent does this project improve the process for meeting a customer need?	☐5	☐4	☐3	☐2	☐1
5. To what degree does this project provide an innovative process to meet distributor needs?	☐5	☐4	☐3	☐2	☐1
6. To what degree will this project contribute to building an IT infrastructure to meet our strategic objectives of improving internal process and maximizing customer relationships?	☐5	☐4	☐3	☐2	☐1
	High	Moderate		Low	No

Customer relationships	Rating				
1. To what degree does this project involve the enhancement/improvements to current projects and services to meet customer needs	☐5	☐4	☐3	☐2	☐1
2. To what degree does this project involve the development of new products and services to competitively meet customer needs?	☐5	☐4	☐3	☐2	☐1
3. To what degree does this project foster retailer loyalty by bringing value (e.g., convenience, speed, improved customer services, etc.)	☐5	☐4	☐3	☐2	☐1

4. To what degree does this project foster customer loyalty (satisfaction and retention) by bringing value to the customer?	□ 5	□ 4	□ 3	□ 2	□ 1
5. To what degree does this project improve customer acquisition by bringing value to the retailer and/or customer?	□ 5	□ 4	□ 3	□ 2	□ 1
	High	Moderate		Low	None

Employees and organization	Rating				
1. To what degree will this project create a shift in the corporate culture toward higher performance?	□ 5	□ 4	□ 3	□ 2	□ 1
2. To what degree will this project improve communications within the organization?	□ 5	□ 4	□ 3	□ 2	□ 1
3. To what degree will this project enhance the skills and competencies of our employees?	□ 5	□ 4	□ 3	□ 2	□ 1
4. To what degree will this project improve productivity within the organization?	□ 5	□ 4	□ 3	□ 2	□ 1
	High	Moderate		Low	None

Now we have enough information to provide estimates on how important this project is to the organization. But, our questions regarding the project cost were very rough and high level. Let us estimate the costs a little better by sending the request form to the different departments and asking them to estimate how much they expect to spend on the project. We can make this easier for them by breaking the project down into more detailed phases and ask them to estimate their costs for each phase.

Phase	IT estimate	Manufac-turing estimate	Dept 1 estimate	Dept 2 estimate	Dept 3 estimate
Requirements analysis					
Planning					
Design					
Development					
OCM					
Testing					
Implementation					
Training					

Based on the feedback obtained, we can develop very rough cost estimates for the project.

Appendix 2.4

Project Name: _____   Date: _____

Project Manager (s): _____   Project Total Risk Score*: 0

Project profile item		Risk score		Risk weight		Project risk score
SIZE						
1. Total system and programming man-hours for the system						
a. 100 to 3,000		Low—1				
b. 3,000 to 15,000		Med—2		5		
c. 15,000 to 30,000		Med—3				
d. Over 30,000		High—4				
2. System development duration estimate in calendar time						
a. 12 months or less		High—3				
b. 13 to 24 months		Med—2		4		
c. Over 24 months		Low—1				
3. The work will be performed by:						
a. Mostly by on-site personnel		Low—1				
b. Significant portions by on-site personnel		Med—2		2		
c. Mostly by off-site personnel		High—3				
4. Number of departments (other than IT) involved with the system:						
a. One		Low—1				
b. Two		Med—2		4		
c. Three or more		High—3				
5. Approximate number of end users						
a. Up to 20		Low—1				
b. 20–50		Med—2		1		
c. Over 50		High—3				

Project profile item	Risk score	Risk weight	Project risk score
6. Number of different geographic locations in which the system will operate		2	
a. One	Low—1		
b. Two or three	Med—2		
c. More than three	High—3		
7. Number of existing information processing systems the new system will interface with		3	
a. None	Low—1		
b. One	Low—1		
c. Two	Med—2		
d. More than two	High—3		
STRUCTURE			
8. The system description		5	
a. Totally new system	High—3		
b. Replacement of an existing manual system	Med—2		
c. Replacement of an existing automated system	Low—1		
9. If a replacement system is proposed, the percent of existing functions that will be replaced on a one-to-one basis		4	
a. 0–24	High—3		
b. 25–50	Med—2		
c. 50–100	Low—1		
d. Unknown	High—3		
10. The severity of procedural changes needed for the proposed system		5	
a. Low—1	Low—1		
b. Medium—2	Med—2		
c. High—3	High—3		
d. Unknown	High—3		

Project profile item	Risk score	Risk weight	Project risk score
11. The user organization changes needed to meet the new system requirements			
a. No	0		
b. Minimal	Low—1	5	
c. Somewhat	Med—2		
d. Major	High—3		
e. Unknown	High—3		
12. The general attitude of the users			
a. Poor—anti-information	High—3		
b. Fair—some reluctance	Med—2	5	
c. Good—understands value of IT solution	Low—1		
13. Upper-level user management commitment to the system			
a. Somewhat reluctant to unknown	High—3	5	
b. Adequate	Med—2		
c. Extremely enthusiastic	Low—1		
14. Established joint IT/user team			
a. None	High—3		
b. Part-time user representative appointed	Med—2	5	
c. Full-time user representative appointed	Low—1		
TECHNOLOGY			
15. Special non-standard hardware (for us) required			
a. None	0		
b. Servers	High—3		
c. Peripherals	High—3	5	
d. Clients	High—3		
e. Routers	High—3		
g. Unknown	High—3		

Project profile item	Risk score	Risk weight	Project risk score
16. Number of vendors that are involved in the system hardware		2	
a. One	Low—1		
b. Two	Med—2		
c. Three or more	High—3		
d. Unknown	High—3		
17. The system software is new to the IT project team		5	
a. No	0		
b. Programming language	High—3		
c. Database	High—3		
d. Data communications	High—3		
e. Other—specify (Unknown)	High—3		
18. The user knowledge in IT systems		5	
a. First exposure	High—3		
b. Previous exposure but limited knowledge	Med—2		
c. High degree of capability	Low—1		
19. The user representative knowledge in the proposed application area		5	
a. Limited	High—3		
b. Understands concept but no experience	Med—2		
c. Has been involved in similar implementation efforts	Low—1		
20. The IT team knowledge in the proposed application area		5	
a. Limited	High—3		
b. Understands concept but no experience	Med—2		
c. Has been involved in similar implementation efforts	Low—1		

Project profile item		Risk score		Risk weight		Project risk score
INTERNAL/EXTERNAL RISKS						
21. Categories of risks involved						
a. Internal		Low—1				
b. Combination of internal and external		High—3		5		
c. External		High—3				
TOTAL PROJECT RISK SCORE						

*High risk is greater than 166; medium risk is between 140 and 166; low risk is less than 140.

Appendix 3.2

Typical Top-Level Requirements

Functional Requirements:

1. Develop a filtering system that supports the strategic goals. The filters should include financial filters to identify the projects with the greatest financial benefits.
2. Select projects that most strongly support those goals and are most profitable.
3. Identify the risks for each project.
4. Identify the resources needed for each project.
5. Minimize the impacts of each project on existing work.
6. Give management the flexibility to select projects that are close in benefits.
7. Communicate project status on an ongoing basis.
8. Make the filters responsive to changes in strategy.
9. Identify conflicts among projects.
10. Identify similar projects and remove duplicate projects.
11. Provide portfolio-level metrics.
12. Allow decision-makers to kill projects as required and reassign the resources to other projects.
13. The system should show me which projects support each strategic objective.
14. Archive historical data for completed projects.

Performance Requirements

1. Within two weeks of a new project being requested have it analyzed through the portfolio process.
2. Present the Steering Committee a rank-ordered list of projects on a quarterly basis.

Implementation Requirements

1. Develop the portfolio management organization and processes.
2. Train employees and management in the processes.
3. Integrate the processes into the organization.
4. Provide documentation on the processes.
5. Identify and implement tools as necessary to support the EPMS.
6. Integrate existing projects into the tools.

These are just examples of questions that might be asked. Consider assigning weights to them to assist in prioritizing the final requirements.

Appendix 3.4-1

Details of OCM Plan

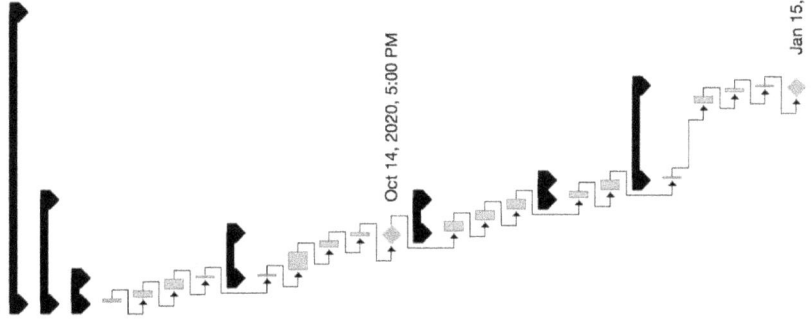

ID	Task Name	Duration
1.3.2	OCM Project Plan	133 d
1.3.2.1	Create sense of need among stakeholder	48 d
1.3.2.1.1	Define problem	12 d
1.3.2.1.1.1	Work with PM to define problem statement	3 d
1.3.2.1.1.2	Develop OCM project charter	3 d
1.3.2.1.1.3	OCM charter approved	5 d
1.3.2.1.1.4	Kickoff meeting with OCM team	1 d
1.3.2.1.2	Define climate for change readiness	21 d
1.3.2.1.2.1	Identify survey/interview participants	3 d
1.3.2.1.2.2	Perform survey and interviews	10 d
1.3.2.1.2.3	Analyze results	5 d
1.3.2.1.2.4	Communicate results	3 d
1.3.2.1.2.5	Change climate assessment complete	0 d
1.3.2.1.3	Finalize OCM strategy	15 d
1.3.2.1.3.1	Create final OCM strategy	5 d
1.3.2.1.3.2	Review with team	5 d
1.3.2.1.3.3	Obtain management approval for OCM approach	5 d
1.3.2.2	Create vision for new EPMS	8 d
1.3.2.2.1	Team creates vision statement	3 d
1.3.2.2.2	Obtain management approval	5 d
1.3.2.3	Define change impacts	44 d
1.3.2.3.1	Define impacted stakeholders	2 d
1.3.2.3.2	Identify impacts of changes to stakeholders	5 d
1.3.2.3.3	Complete job impacts assessment	3 d
1.3.2.3.4	Complete change impacts assessment	2 d
1.3.2.3.5	Management approval of change impact assessment	0 d

Appendix 3.4-2

Requirements Schedule

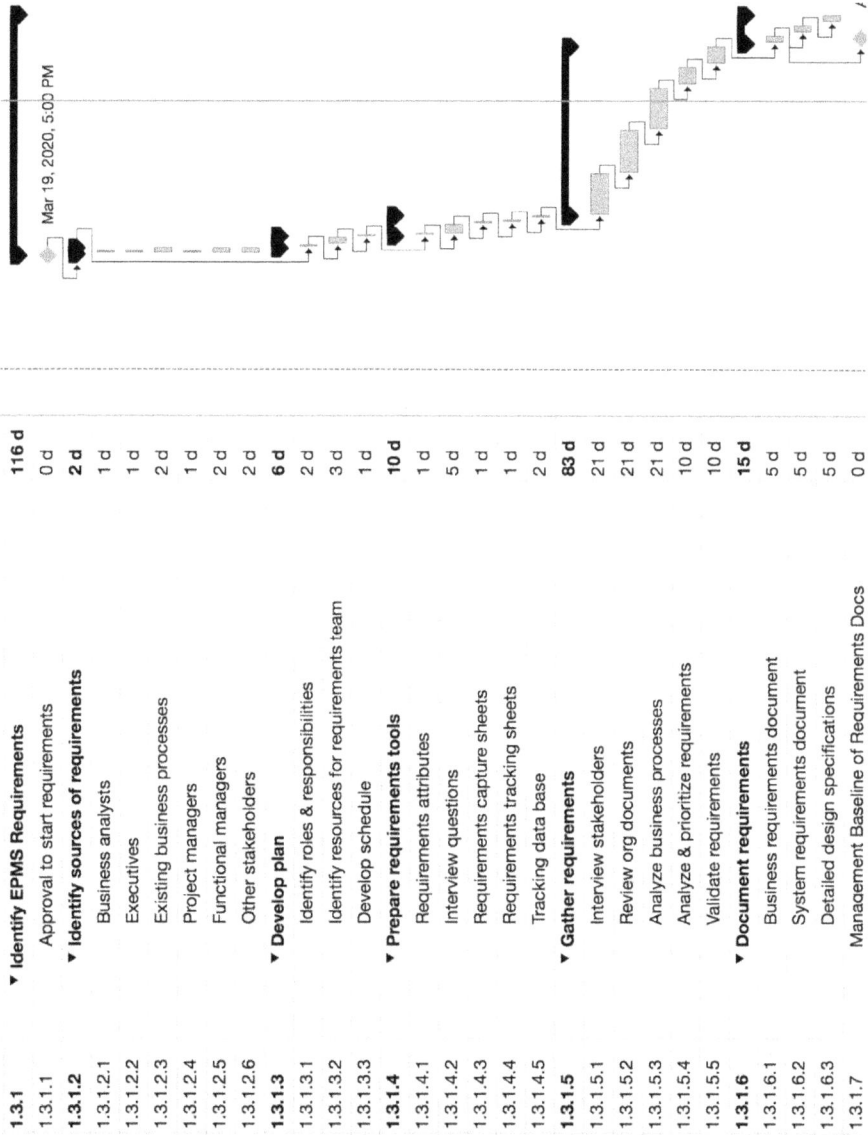

Mar 19, 2020, 5:00 PM

ID	Task Name	Duration
1.3.1	▼ Identify EPMS Requirements	116 d
1.3.1.1	Approval to start requirements	0 d
1.3.1.2	▼ Identify sources of requirements	2 d
1.3.1.2.1	Business analysts	1 d
1.3.1.2.2	Executives	1 d
1.3.1.2.3	Existing business processes	2 d
1.3.1.2.4	Project managers	1 d
1.3.1.2.5	Functional managers	2 d
1.3.1.2.6	Other stakeholders	2 d
1.3.1.3	▼ Develop plan	6 d
1.3.1.3.1	Identify roles & responsibilities	2 d
1.3.1.3.2	Identify resources for requirements team	3 d
1.3.1.3.3	Develop schedule	1 d
1.3.1.4	▼ Prepare requirements tools	10 d
1.3.1.4.1	Requirements attributes	1 d
1.3.1.4.2	Interview questions	5 d
1.3.1.4.3	Requirements capture sheets	1 d
1.3.1.4.4	Requirements tracking sheets	1 d
1.3.1.4.5	Tracking data base	2 d
1.3.1.5	▼ Gather requirements	83 d
1.3.1.5.1	Interview stakeholders	21 d
1.3.1.5.2	Review org documents	21 d
1.3.1.5.3	Analyze business processes	21 d
1.3.1.5.4	Analyze & prioritize requirements	10 d
1.3.1.5.5	Validate requirements	10 d
1.3.1.6	▼ Document requirements	15 d
1.3.1.6.1	Business requirements document	5 d
1.3.1.6.2	System requirements document	5 d
1.3.1.6.3	Detailed design specifications	5 d
1.3.1.7	Management Baseline of Requirements Docs	0 d

Appendix 3.4-3

Resource Utilization

Deliverables	Project manager	CIO/tech leads	Business analyst(s)	OCM lead	Portfolio manager	Finance	BU leads	Project sponsor	Steering committee
Step 2—designing the EPMS									
2.1 Find the real needs	25%		100%		50%		25%	A/R	A/R
2.2 Design considerations	10%	50%	55%	10%	25%		25%	A/R	A/R
2.3 Doing financial calculations	5%	5%	15%	25%		50%	25%	10%	A/R
2.4 Risks	5%	5%	10%	5%		5%	5%	5%	
Step 3—plan and implement									
3.1 Creating the project plan	60%	25%	25%	10%	10%			A/R	
3.2 Scope	35%	75%	100%	20%			5%	A/R	
3.3 Architecture/design	20%	100%	100%		25%				
3.4 Schedule	50%	25%	25%	10%				A/R	
3.5 Budget	25%	25%		10%		50%		A/R	
3.6 Quality	5%	20%	20%		10%		10%	A/R	
3.7 Risk	10%	20%	20%	20%				A/R	
3.8 Organizing	25%	5%	5%					A/R	
3.9 Implementation	25%	50%	100%	50%	25%		25%	A/R	A/R

Appendix 3.4-4

Design & Development Schedule

Outline Number	Name	Duration
1.3.3	▼ Detailed Design & Development	176 d
1.3.3.1	Identify project categories and types	5 d
1.3.3.2	Perform project risk analysis	4 d
1.3.3.3	Define financial filters	22 d
1.3.3.4	Define non-financial filters	10 d
1.3.3.5	Develop detailed system architecture	22 d
1.3.3.6	Design EPMS processes	22 d
1.3.3.7	Identify vendor tools (if necessary)	5 d
1.3.3.8	Obtain design approval	10 d
1.3.3.9	▼ Develop EPMS software	176 d
1.3.3.9.1	▼ Develop software tools (if developed in…	76 d
1.3.3.9.1.1	Define technical requirements	10 d
1.3.3.9.1.2	Code & Unit test software	66 d
1.3.3.9.2	▼ Purchase software tools (if purchased)	116 d
1.3.3.9.2.1	Conduct vendor product search	20 d
1.3.3.9.2.2	Short-list vendor products	5 d
1.3.3.9.2.3	Sales presentations from vendors	10 d
1.3.3.9.2.4	Purchase selection & negotiations	5 d
1.3.3.9.2.5	Install and configure vendor tool	66 d
1.3.3.9.2.6	Integration testing	10 d

Appendix 3.8

RAM

Deliverables	Project manager	OCM lead	Business analysts	CIO/ tech leads	DBA	BU managers	Portfolio manager	PMO lead	QA	CFO	Project sponsor	Steering committee
Project management deliverables												
Project charter	SPA					SI	SI	SI			SAI	SAI
Scope management plan	SPA	I	PI				PI	PI			S	S
Schedule management plan	SPA		I			I	I	PI			S	S
Budget management plan	SPA									I	S	
Organizational change management	SA	P									S	S
Interface management plan	SA			PI							S	
Risk and issues management plan	SPA		I	PI		P	P	P	RI		SAI	S
Communications management plan	SPA	P	P	I		I	I	I			S	
Resource management plan	SPA			I	I			PI			S	
Quality management plan	SRA			I	I				AP		S	
Procurement management plan	SRA			PI		I	I				S	

	C1	C2	C3	C4	C5	C6	C7	C8	C9	C10	C11	C12
Configuration management plan	SA			P	I						S	S
Planning and analysis												
Business requirements specs	SPA										SRAI	SR
Technical requirements specs	SPA										SA	S
Detailed WBS and OBS	SPA										S	
Baseline schedule	SPA	P	P		I			PI	PI		SR	SR
Baseline budget	SA	P	P		I	I		I	I	AP	SR	SR
Business process analysis	SA	AP			I	I		I	I		SR	SR
COTS review (if required)	SA		SA	I							SI	
Phase review/lessons learned	A	I	I	I	I	I	I	I	I	I	I	I
Design												
Software architecture	SRA	I	SPA	P	R	R		R	R		S	S
Database architecture	SA	PA	SA			PI		SPI	PI		SRA	
New processes	SRA	I		SPI		PI	PI	SPA	SR	R	SRA	SR
Filtering metrics	SRA	P	I		SPA	SPA	SR	SR	R		SRAI	SR
Phase review/lessons learned	A	I	I	I	I	I	I	I	I	I	I	I

Deliverables	Project manager	OCM lead	Business analysts	CIO/tech leads	DBA	BU managers	Portfolio manager	PMO lead	QA	CFO	Project sponsor	Steering committee
Development												
Software development	SA		I	SAI	I				R		R	
Database development	SA			SAI	SA						R	
New processes	SA	I	SAI	I		IR	IR	IR			SRA	SRA
Integration plan	SA	I	I	SPA		IR	R	R	R		S	
Phase review/ lessons learned	A	I	I	I	I	I	I	I	I	I	I	I
Testing and documentation												
Test plan and log	R		I	SPA	I							
Test results	R			A								
Implementation plan	SPRA	PR	PRA	IR		IR	IR	IR			SRA	R
Fully tested product	SA		A	A		A	A	A	A		SA	SA
Phase review/ lessons learned	A	I	I	I	I	I	I	I	I	I	I	I

Implementation											
Go live	SPRA	I	P	P	P	P	P	P		SA	SA
Activated new business processes	SPRA	I	PA	PA	PA	R	R	P		SA	SA
End of project review/lessons learned	A	I	I	I	I	I	I	I	I	I	I
Post-implementation											
Project completion report	A	I	I	I	I	I	I	I	I	SAI	SAI
Stakeholder satisfaction report	A									R	R

ROLE DEFINITION KEY

P = PARTICIPANT — Does the work

A = ACCOUNTABLE — Owns the work; responsible for getting it done

R = REVIEW REQUIRED — Who does the sign-off person expect to review the deliverable

I = INPUT REQUIRED — Must provide input into the work in progress

S = SIGNOFF — Accepts or rejects the deliverable; final step

Notes

Preface

1. Svejvig and Schlichter (2020).
2. Martinsuo (2020).
3. EIU (November 2015).
4. Mauboussin (2012).
5. Success in Disruptive Times (2018).
6. Lavallo et al. (March-April 2020).
7. McKinsey (2020).
8. The Impact of PMOs on Strategy Implementation, PMI Pulse of the Profession (2013).

Step 1: Prepare the Organization

1. PMI PoP (2012).
2. Parth (2017).
3. Benko and McFarlan (2003).
4. Bivins and Bible (May 2015).
5. McFarlan (1981)
6. Payne (1995).
7. Forrester (2011).
8. Cooper et al. (2001).
9. Buffet and Clark (2006).
10. Maniak et al. (September-October 2014).
11. Davies et al. (2012).
12. Forrester (November 2013).
13. Santosus (September 15, 2003).
14. Clark and Wheelwright (1993).
15. Bannister and Remenyi (2009).
16. Goldratt (1998).
17. Gilliland and Landis (1992).
18. PMBOK Guide® (n.d).

19. PMI Thought Leadership Series Report 2015– Delivering on Strategy, the Power of Project Portfolio Management, Project Management Institute.
20. Abdollahyan (May 2012).
21. Perry & Hatcher (September 2008).
22. TechRepublic (2012).
23. Flyvbjerg (2009).
24. Elegbede (October 2017).
25. Lassa (March 2009).
26. Hubbard (2014).
27. Waxer (2005).
28. Lancaster (January 17, 1995).
29. Schiemann (1992).
30. Kahneman (2012).
31. Hammer and Champy (1993).
32. Collins (2001).
33. Economist Intelligence Unit (July 2013).
34. IBM (1998).
35. Cooper et al. (2003).
36. Rizzuto (July 28, 2005).
37. Light and Hayward (2005).
38. META Group (2002).
39. Robbins (August 4, 2008).
40. Petit and Hobbs (2012).
41. Stronach (2012).
42. Cooper et al. (January-February 2004).

Step 2: Designing the Enterprise-Level Portfolio Management System

1. Abdollahyan (2012).
2. Stang and Handler (2012).
3. Maniak et al. (August/September 2014).
4. Prieto (2013).
5. Blichfeldt and Eskerod (2008).
6. Kendall and Rollins (2003).

7. Hahn (2017).

8. Sonta-Draczkowska and Mrozewski (2020).

9. Taylor (October 21, 2008).

10. Cooper et al. (2001).

11. Wood (2006).

12. Foti (April 16, 2007).

13. Liss (2001).

14. Emerson (2009).

15. Cooper et al. (2004).

16. Panorama (2009).

17. Courtney (2001).

18. Charan (2009).

19. Royce (August 25–28, 1970).

20. Morris (2005).

21. Flyvbjerg and Buhl (2002).

22. Flyvbjerg and Buhl (2004).

23. Kutsch and Hall (2009).

24. Teller and Kock (2013).

25. Leifer et al. (2000).

26. PMBOK Guide® (2016).

27. Dewan, Shi, and Gurbaxani (2007).

28. eQuest (2005).

29. Hoffman (2006).

30. McDonough and Spital (2003).

Step 3: Planning and Implementing the EPMS

1. CPB – Project Portfolio Management Maturity: A Benchmark of Current Business Practices, a Center for Business Practices Research Report Available at www.cbponline.com

2. McGaughy (August 18, 2004).

3. Harrington (1991).

4. Hooks and Farry (2001).

5. Church (November 14, 2012).

6. Rajegopal et al. (2007).

7. Cooper et al. (2001).

8. Brooks (1974).

9. IDC (2008).

10. CIO (July 1, 2007; p. 13).

11. Cooper (2004).

12. Schiltz (2003).

13. CEB (2007).

14. Bourne (September 2015).

15. McFadden (November 9, 2004).

16. Koh and Crawford (December 2012).

17. Optimize Your Business: Balance Risk and Reward with Métier's Portfolio Optimizer Technology, 2013, published by Métier.

18. Hostetter and Norris (July 2017).

References

Abdollahyan, F. 2012. *Management of Value as PPM Strategy*, presented at the PMI EMEA Congress in Marseille, France.

Abdollahyan, F. May 2012. *Management of Value as PPM Strategy*. Presented at the PMI EMEA Congress in Marseille, France.

Bannister, F., and D. Remenyi. 2009. "Multitasking: the Uncertain Impact of Technology on Knowledge Workers and Managers." *The Electronic Journal Information Systems Evaluation* 12, no. 1, pp. 1–12, Available online at www.ejise.com

Benko, C., and F.W. McFarlan. 2003. *Connecting the Dots*. Boston: Harvard Business School Press.

Bivins, S., and M.J. Bible. May 2015. "Portfolio Decisions to Maximize Strategic Benefits." *PM World Journal* 4, no. 5, www.pmworldjournal.net (accessed February 2016).

Blichfeldt, B.S., and P. Eskerod. 2008. "Project Portfolio Management – There's More to it than What Management Enacts." *IJPM* 26, no. 4, pp. 357–365.

Bourne. September 2015. "Series on Effective Stakeholder Engagement: Stakeholders and Risk." *PM World Journal* 4, no. 9. www.pmworldjournal.net

Brooks, F. 1974. *The Mythical Man-Month*. Addison Wesley Longman Publishing Co.

Buffet, M., and D. Clark. 2006. *The Tao of Warren Buffett*. New York, NY: Scriber.

CEB. 2007. *Attributes of a High Performing Project Manager*. Corporate Executive Board.

Charan, R. 2009. *Leadership in the Era of Economic Uncertainty*. McGraw-Hill.

Church. C. November 14, 2012. PMI PMO Symposium.

CIO, July 1, 2007. p. 13.

Clark, K.B., and S.C. Wheelwright. 1993. *Managing New Product and Process Development* New York, NY: Free Press.

Collins, J. 2001. *Good to Great*. New York, NY: HarperCollins.

Cooper, A. 2004. *The Inmates are Running The Asylum*. Sams - Pearson Education.

Cooper, R.G., S.J. Edgett, and E.J. Kleinschmidt. 2001. "New Product Development: Results of an Industry Practices Study." *R&D Management Magazine* 31, no. 4. Results of a research study done jointly by Stage-Gate Inc. and The Product Development Institute Inc.

Cooper, R.G., S.J. Edgett, and E.J. Kleinschmidt. 2001. "New Product Development: Results of an Industry Practices Study." *R&D Management Magazine* 31, no. 4. Jointly by Stage-Gate Inc. and The Product Development Institute Inc.

Cooper, R.G., S.J. Edgett, and E.J. Kleinschmidt. 2001. *Portfolio Management for New Products*, 2nd ed. Cambridge, MA: Perseus. See also Petit, Y., and Hobbs. 2012. *Project Portfolios in Dynamic Environments: Organizing for Uncertainty*. Project Management Institute.

Cooper, R.G., S.J. Edgett, and E.J. Kleinschmidt. 2003. "Results from an APQC Study (American Productivity & Quality Center)." *Best Practices in Product Innovation: What Distinguishes Top Performers*. Product Development Institute. www.prod-dev.com

Cooper, R.G., S.J. Edgett, and E.J. Kleinschmidt. 2004. "Benchmarking Best NPD Practices." *Research-Technology Management* 47, no. 1, pp. 50–60, 43–55.

Cooper, R.G., S.J. Edgett, and E.J. Kleinschmidt. January-February 2004. "Benchmarking Best NPD Practices." *Research-Technology Management* 47, no. 1, pp. 31–43; RTM47, 3, May-June 2004, 50–60; and: RTM, 47, 6, January-February 2005, 43–55.

Courtney. 2001. "20/20 Foresight: Crafting Strategy in an Uncertain World." *McKinsey Quarterly*, http://mckinseyquarterly.com/article_print. aspx?L2=21&L3=37&ar=2256

CPB – Project Portfolio Management Maturity: A Benchmark of Current Business Practices, a Center for Business Practices Research Report Available at www.cbponline.com

Davies, R., T. Koller, and M. Goedhart. 2012. From *Avoiding a Risk Premium that Unnecessarily Kills Your Project*. Copyright © 2012 McKinsey & Company.

Dewan, S., C. Shi, and V. Gurbaxani. 2007. *Investigating the Risk–Return Relationship of Information Technology Investment: Firm-Level Empirical Analysis*. University of California at Irvine. http://informs.org/article. php?id=1340&p=1|

Economist Intelligence Unit. July 2013. *Why Good Strategies Fail: Lessons from the C-Suite*.

EIU. November 2015. *Implementing the Project Portfolio, A Vital C-Suite Focus*. Written by the Economist Intelligence Unit and published by PMI.

Elegbede, W. October 2017. *From the Ground Up: Building PMO Alignment with Mayo Clinic's EPMO*. presented by Mayo Clinic Project Manager at the PMI NA Congress.

Emerson. 2009. *Energy Logic: Reducing Data Center Energy Consumption by Creating Savings that Cascade Across Systems*.

eQuest 2005. "eQuest Consulting 2005 Survey." Available from http:// equestconsulting.com.au/EQuest_Consulting_EPM_Survey_2005.pdf

Flyvbjerg, B. 2009. "Survival of the Unfittest." *Oxford Review of Economic Policy* 25, no. 3, pp. 344–367.

Flyvbjerg, H., and Buhl. 2002. "Underestimating Costs in Public Works Projects." *Journal American Planning Association* 68, no. 3, pp. 279–295.

Flyvbjerg, H., and Buhl. 2004. "How (In)accurate are Demand Forecasts in Public Works Projects." *Journal American Planning Association* 71, no. 2, pp. 131–146

Forrester. 2011. *Want Faster (and Better) Delivery Practices? Teach Your PMO and Project Managers to Really Work Together.* Forrester Research.

Forrester. November 2013. *Strategic PMOs Play a Vital Role in Driving Business Outcomes.* Forrester Consulting.

Foti, R. April 16, 2007. "Priority Decisions." *PM Network*, pp. 24–29.

Gilliland, S., and R. Landis. 1992. "Quality and Quantity Goals in a Complex Decision Task: Strategies and Outcomes." *Journal of Applied Psychology* 77, no. 5, pp. 672–681.

Goldratt, E. 1998. *Project Management the TOC Way.* Croton-on-Hudson, NY: North River Press.

Hahn, D. 2017. "Methods and Magic to Strategic Planning." PMI Annual North American Convention in Chicago, US.

Hammer, M., and J. Champy. 1993. *Re-Engineering the Corporation.* Reed Business Information.

Harrington, H.J. 1991. *Business Process Improvement.* New York: NY, McGraw-Hill.

Hoffman, 2006. "Weighting Project Risks." Available from http://computerworld.com.au/php/id;1562391188

Hooks and Farry. 2001. *Customer-Centered Products: Creating Successful Products Through Smart Requirements Management.* New York. NY: AMACOM.

Hostetter, S., and S. Norris. July 2017. "Ranking Portfolio Management Maturity." *PM World Journal* 4, no. 7. www.pmworldjournal.net

Hubbard, D.W. 2014. *How to Measure Anything – Finding the Value of Intangibles in Business*, 2nd ed. Hoboken, N.J: John Wiley & Sons.

IBM. 1998. Fundamentals of Change Management, IBM Executive Training.

IDC. 2008. *How Project and Portfolio Management Solutions Are Delivering Value to Organizations.* IDC White Paper by Randy Perry and Eric Hatcher.

Kahneman, D. 2012. *Thinking, Fast and Slow.* New York, NY: Farrar, Straus and Giroux.

Kendall, G.I., and S.C. Rollins. 2003. *Advanced Project Portfolio Management and the PMO: Multiplying ROI at Warp Speed.* Boca Raton, FL: J. Ross publisher.

Koh, A., and L. Crawford. December 2012. "Portfolio Management: The Australian Experience." *Project Management Journal* 42, no. 6, pp. 33–42. Published by PMI.

Kutsch, E., and M. Hall. 2009. "The Rational Choice of not Applying Project Risk Management in Information Technology Projects." *Project Management Journal* 40, no. 3, pp. 72–81.

Lancaster, H. January 17, 1995. "Reengineering Authors Reconsider Reengineering." Interview with Michael Hammer and James Champy. *The Wall Street Journal.*

Lassa, T. March, 2009. *GM's Survival Strategy: Divisions, Nameplates to Disappear.* Motor Trend Magazine.

Lavallo, D., T. Koller, R. Uhlanger, and D. Kaneman, D. March-April 2020. *Your Company Is Too Risk-Averse, Harvard Business Review.* Published by Harvard Business School.

Leifer, R., C.M. McDermott, G.C. O'Connor, L.S. Peters, M.P. Rice, and R.W. Veryzer. 2000. *Radical Innovation: How Mature Companies can Outsmart Upstarts.* Boston, MA: Harvard Business School Press.

Light, R., and Hayward. 2005. According to Gartner, Inc.'s Field Research Among More than 200 Commercial Firms in Various Enterprises, There is a Connection between IT Investment Planning and the Relative Profit Performance of a Company.

Liss, D. 2001. "Calculate Your ROI, Make Two Envelopes..." Available at http://gantthead.com/Gantthead/articles/articlesPrint/l, 1685,96418,00.html

Maniak, R., C. Midler, S. Lenfle, and M. Le Pellec-Dairon. August/September 2014. "Value Management for Exploration Projects." *Project Management Journal* 45, no. 4, pp. 55–66. Published by the Project Management Institute.

Maniak, R., C. Midler, S. Lenfle, and M. Le Pellec-Dairon. September-October 2014. "Value Management for Exploration Projects." *Project Management Journal* 45, no. 4, pp. 55–66.

Martinsuo, M. 2020. "The Management of Values in Project Business: Adjusting Beliefs to Transform Project Practices and Outcomes." *Project Management Journal* 51, no. 4, pp. 389–399.

Mauboussin. 2012. https://realclearmarkets.com/blog/MauboussinOnStrategy ShareRepurchaseFromAllAngles_MIPX014745.pdf (accessed January 2013).

McDonough, E.F., and F.C. Spital. 2003. "Managing Project Portfolios." *Research-Technology Management* 46, no. 3, pp. 40–46.

McFadden. November 9, 2004. *Best Schedules Practices.* Independent Project Analysis, Inc. at NWCCC.

McFarlan, F.W. 1981. "Portfolio Approach to Information Systems." *Harvard Business Review* 59, no. 5, pp. 142–150.

McGaughy. C. August 18, 2004. "Gartner Shines the Light on PPM." http://gantthead.com/article.cfm?ID=219526

McKinsey. 2020. "Why You've Got to Put Your Portfolio on the Move." https://mckinsey.com/ (accessed July, 2020).

META Group. 2002. "IT Investment Management: Portfolio Management Lessons Learned." A META Group White Paper (www.metagroup.com).

Morris, P.W.G. 2005. *Managing the Front-End: How project managers shape business strategy and manage project definition. PMI®.* Global Congress Proceedings – Edinburgh, Scotland.

Optimize Your Business: Balance Risk and Reward with Métier's Portfolio Optimizer Technology, 2013, published by Métier.

Panorama. 2009. "Panorama Consulting Group 2009 Publication." *Where's the ROI?*

Parth. 2017. *Project Portfolio Management Strategies for Effective Organizational Operations*, ed. Romano, L. IGI Global Publisher.

Payne, J.H. 1995. "Management of Multiple Simultaneous Projects." *International Journal of Project Management* 13, no. 3, 163–168.

Perry & Hatcher. September 2008. "How Project and Portfolio Management Solutions are Delivering Value to Organizations." IDC.

Petit, Y., and B. Hobbs. 2012. *Project Portfolios in Dynamic Environments*, p. 10. Project Management Institute.

PMBOK Guide®. 2016. *Guide to the Project Management Body of Knowledge*, 6th ed. Newtown Square, PA: Project Management Institute.

PMBOK Guide®. n.d. *Guide to the Project Management Body of Knowledge.* 6th ed. Published by the Project Management Institute.

PMI PoP. 2012. *Pulse of the Profession: Project Portfolio Management.* Published by PMI, Newtown Square, PA: PMI.

PMI Thought Leadership Series Report 2015– Delivering on Strategy, the Power of Project Portfolio Management, Project Management Institute.

Prieto, B. 2013. *Project Selection in Large Engineering Construction Programs. PM 4. World Journal* 2, no. 12, www.pmworldjournal.net

Rajegopal, S., P. McGuin, and J. Waller. 2007. *Project Portfolio Management: Leading the Corporate Vision.* New York, NY: Palgrave Macmillan.

Rizzuto, J. July 28, 2005. "Trading Places." Projects@Work, Available at http:// projectsatwork.com/article.cfm?ID=226042

Robbins, G. August 4, 2008. "Closing the Gap between Project Management and Governance." http://pmboulevard.com/Default.aspx?page=View%20 Content&cid=2672&parent=92

Royce. August 25–28, 1970. "Managing the Development of Large Software Systems: Concepts and Techniques." Presented at the Western Electronic Show and Convention (WesCon), Los Angeles, CA.

Santosus, M. September 15, 2003. "Why More Is Less" *CIO Magazine.*

Schiemann, W. 1992. "Why Change Fails." *Across the Board.*

Schiltz, S.J. 2003. *A Practical Method for Assessing the Financial Benefit of Project Management.* City University. Available at http://project-management.ch/ pages/DocumentsSoireesDebat/costofbadpm_schiltz_v11.pdf

Sonta-Draczkowska, E., and M. Mrozewski. 2020. "Exploring the Role of Project Management in Product Development in New Technology-Based Firms." *Project Management Journal* 51, pp. 294–311.

Stang, D., and R. Handler. 2012. "MarketScope for IT Project and Portfolio Management." *Software NY Times*, http://nytimes.com/2012/09/23/technology/data-centers-waste-vast-amounts-of-energy-belying-industry-image.html?pagewanted=allApplications

Stronach, M. 2012. "Committing to the Value of PPM." http://project management.com/articles/275534/Committing-to-the-Value-of-PPM (accessed November 4, 2012).

Success in Disruptive Times. 2018. *PMI 2018 Pulse of the Profession.* Newtown Square, PA: PMI.

Svejvig, P., and B.R. Schlichter. 2020. "The Long Road to Benefits Management: Toward an Integrative Management Model." *Project Management Journal* 51, pp. 312–327.

Taylor, P. October 21, 2008. "Does IT work?: IT-Related Productivity Gains in Decline." *The Financial Times*, Available at http://ft.com/cms/s/0/85bd0b50-9efc-11dd-98bd-000077b07658,dwp_uuid=4dce8136-4a24-11da-b8b1-0000779e2340.html?nclick_check=1

TechRepublic. 2012. "Rejected: 74% of Organizations Have no Plans to Deploy Windows 8." November 3, 2012 at http://techrepublic.com/blog/window-on-windows/rejected-74-of-organizations-have-no-plans-to-deploy-windows-8/6828

Teller, J., and A. Kock. 2013. "An Empirical Investigation on How Portfolio Risk Management Influences Project Portfolio Success." *IJPM* 31, pp. 817–829.

The Impact of PMOs on Strategy Implementation, PMI Pulse of the Profession. 2013. Newtown Square, PA: PMI.

Waxer, C. 2005. *How Lowes Grows.* CIO Magazine.

Wood, M.R. 2006. "PPM: Concepts, Tools and Approaches." November 13, 2006, http://gantthead.com/article.cfm?ID=233833

About the Author

Frank Parth, MS, MSSM, MBA, PMP, is the Founder of Project Auditors LLC, a past member of PMI's Board of Directors and of the PMI Educational Foundation Board. He has coauthored or contributed chapters to multiple books in project management, has published numerous papers in project management and systems engineering, and has given speeches at multiple conferences around the world.

He had his first career in the aerospace industry, ending as the assistant technical director in the Integration Offices of a USAF satellite program. In 1993, Mr. Parth began consulting in program management and systems engineering while teaching in the Graduate School of the University of Southern California. He headed up systems engineering at TRW Information Systems during a major infrastructure upgrade and created Program Management Offices (PMOs) for several Fortune 1000 companies. He has consulted to clients in multiple industry sectors, including telecom, construction, high tech, chemical processing, utilities, government, aerospace, health care, and financial services.

Mr. Parth taught project management and systems engineering at the University of California, Irvine, beginning in 1994 and was core to the creation of UCI's Project Management Certificate Program and in developing the Business Analyst and the Systems Analyst Certificate Programs. He has taught courses at the University of Southern California, the Claremont Graduate School, and at the American University of Sharjah in the UAE. In 2003, UCI recognized him with an Outstanding Service Award. In 2009, he received PMI's Distinguished Contribution Award as well as Mensa International's Distinguished Contribution Award. In 2019, PMI awarded him its highest award—the Eric Jennett International Award for Project Management Excellence.

Index

www.ingramcontent.com/pod-product-compliance
Lightning Source LLC
Chambersburg PA
CBHW061127220326
41599CB00024B/4198